BEFORE AND AFTER *CORROBOREE*:
THE MUSIC OF JOHN ANTILL

Before and After *Corroboree*: The Music of John Antill

DAVID SYMONS
The University of Western Australia

LONDON AND NEW YORK

First published 2015 by Ashgate Publishing

Published 2016 by Routledge
2 Park Square, Milton Park, Abingdon, Oxon OX14 4RN
711 Third Avenue, New York, NY 10017, USA

Routledge is an imprint of the Taylor & Francis Group, an informa business

Copyright © David Symons 2015

Bach musicological font developed by © Yo Tomita

All rights reserved. No part of this book may be reprinted or reproduced or utilised in any form or by any electronic, mechanical, or other means, now known or hereafter invented, including photocopying and recording, or in any information storage or retrieval system, without permission in writing from the publishers.

Notice:

Product or corporate names may be trademarks or registered trademarks, and are used only for identification and explanation without intent to infringe.

David Symons has asserted his right under the Copyright, Designs and Patents Act, 1988, to be identified as the author/editor of this work.

British Library Cataloguing in Publication Data
A catalogue record for this book is available from the British Library

Library of Congress Cataloging-in-Publication Data
Symons, David (David J.)
 Before and after Corroboree : the music of John Antill / by David Symons.
    pages cm
 Includes bibliographical references and index.
 ISBN 978–1–4724–3536–1 (hardcover : alk. paper)
 1. Antill, John – Criticism and interpretation. 2. Music – Australia – 20th century – History and criticism.
 I. Title.
 ML410.A639S96 2016
 780.92–dc23   2015022695

ISBN 9781472435361 (hbk)

Contents

List of Music Examples   *vii*

Introduction: A Creative Career in Two Stages Defined by an Australian Music Icon   1

1   Before *Corroboree*   9

2   *Corroboree* – The Turning Point   43

Interlude: Antill After *Corroboree*: An Overview   75

3   After *Corroboree* (1) – Theatre Works   79

4   After *Corroboree* (2) – Orchestral Works   127

5   After *Corroboree* (3) – Choral and Vocal Works   165

Epilogue: John Antill as a 'One Work Composer'?   189

Appendix 1: List of Original Compositions by John Antill   193

Appendix 2: *Corroboree*: Antill's Original Choreographic Outline   199

Appendix 3: Select Bibliography   201

Index   *203*

List of Music Examples

1.1	*Princess Dorothea*, opening	16
1.2	'Blue Eyed Mary', bb. 5–14	20
1.3	'The Lost Joy', bb. 1–6	21
1.4a	'A Deep Pool' (No. 1 of *Nature Studies*), beginning of middle section	22
1.4b	'To a Waterfall' (No. 2 of *Nature Studies*), bb. 1–10	23
1.5	*Endymion*, orchestral prelude, bb. 1–20(2)	25
1.6	*Endymion*, opening of Diana's arioso	26
1.7	*Endymion*, opening of Ensemble of the Fates	27
1.8	*Endymion*, final scene (chorus)	28
1.9	*Here's Luck*, No. 4, bb. 1–16	31
1.10	*Here's Luck*, No. 5, bb. 1–9(2)	32
1.11	*The Glittering Mask*, Act II, 'Corroboree', bb. 1–7	33
1.12	'My Sister The Rain', bb. 1–12	37
1.13	*Capriccio*, opening	39
1.14	*Capriccio*, second section	40
1.15	*The Circus Comes to Town*, opening	41
2.1	*Corroboree*, 'Welcome Ceremony', bb. 66–68	54
2.2	*Corroboree*, 'Welcome Ceremony', bb. 196–202(1)	55
2.3	*Corroboree*, 'Dance to the Evening Star', bb. 2–5(2)	56
2.4	*Corroboree*, 'A Rain Dance', bb. 98–105	57
2.5	*Corroboree*, 'Spirit of the Wind', bb. 1–12	58
2.6	*Corroboree*, 'Spirit of the Wind', bb. 83–90(1)	59
2.7	*Corroboree*, 'Homage to the Rising Sun', bb. 1–11	60
2.8	*Corroboree*, 'The Morning Star Dance', bb. 1–13(2)	62
2.9	*Corroboree*, 'Procession of Totems', bb. 230–237	63
2.10	*Corroboree*, ' Procession of Totems', bb. 275–284(2)	64
2.11	*Corroboree*, 'Closing Fire Ceremony', bb. 464–467	65
2.12	*Corroboree*, conclusion of 'Closing Fire Ceremony'	66
3.1	*The Unknown Land*, I, b. 1	85
3.2	*The Unknown Land*, I, bb. 47–55	85
3.3	*The Unknown Land*, I, bb. 2–3	86
3.4	*The Unknown Land*, II, bb. 1–8	87
3.5	*The Unknown Land*, II, bb. 27–33	88
3.6	*The Unknown Land*, IV, bb. 1–9	89

3.7	*The Unknown Land*, IV, bb. 29–35(1)	89
3.8	*Wakooka*, No. 1, bb. 1–5(1)	92
3.9	*Wakooka*, No. 15, bb. 25–32	93
3.10	*Wakooka*, No. 10, bb. 13–20	94
3.11	*Wakooka*, No. 11, bb. 3–7(1)	95
3.12	*G'Day Digger*, bb. 1–8	97
3.13	*G'Day Digger*, bb. 25–30	97
3.14	*Burragorang Dreamtime*, Rehearsal Letter C	101
3.15	*Burragorang Dreamtime*, Rehearsal Letter J+	102
3.16	*Black Opal*, Introduction, bb. 21–28	105
3.17	*Black Opal*, Scene 1, Rehearsal Letter F	106
3.18	*Black Opal*, Scene 1, Rehearsal Letter AA	107
3.19	*Black Opal*, Scene 2, Rehearsal Letter M	108
3.20	*The Music Critic*, bb. 37–46	115
3.21	*The Music Critic*, bb. 232–237(2)	116
3.22	*The Music Critic*, bb. 558–561	117
3.23	*The First Christmas*, bb. 14–21	120
3.24	*The First Christmas*, bb. 24–30	122
3.25	*The First Christmas*, bb. 326–330(1)	123
3.26	*The First Christmas*, bb. 369(4)–379	124
3.27	*The First Christmas*, bb. 233–239(1)	125
4.1	*A Sentimental Suite*, Theme (Prelude), bb. 1–12	133
4.2	*A Sentimental Suite*, Scene 5, bb. 605–612	133
4.3	*A Sentimental Suite*, Scene 6, bb. 838–841	134
4.4	*A Sentimental Suite*, Scene 3, bb. 428–433	134
4.5	*A Sentimental Suite*, Scene 3, bb. 460–465	135
4.6	*An Outback Overture*, bb. 1–6	138
4.7	*An Outback Overture*, bb. 152–159	139
4.8	*Overture for a Momentous Occasion*, bb. 32–36	141
4.9	*Overture for a Momentous Occasion*, bb. 68–75	142
4.10	*Overture for a Momentous Occasion*, bb. 156–159	143
4.11	*Overture for a Momentous Occasion*, bb. 182–189	144
4.12	*Symphony on a City*, I, bb. 1–7	148
4.13	*Symphony on a City*, I, bb. 73–78	148
4.14	*Symphony on a City*, I, bb. 113–115	150
4.15	*Symphony on a City*, II, bb. 13–18(2)	150
4.16	*Symphony on a City*, III, bb. 1–8	151
4.17	*Symphony on a City*, III, bb. 12–15	152
4.18	*Symphony on a City*, III, bb. 65–68	153
4.19	*Concerto for Harmonica and Orchestra*, I, bb. 1–4(1)	155
4.20	*Concerto for Harmonica and Orchestra*, I, bb. 19–23	156
4.21	*Concerto for Harmonica and Orchestra*, II, bb. 1–5(1)	156
4.22	*Concerto for Harmonica and Orchestra*, III, bb. 1–8	157

List of Music Examples

4.23	*Paean to the Spirit of Man*, bb. 1–10	159
4.24	*Paean to the Spirit of Man*, bb. 36–44	160
4.25	*Paean to the Spirit of Man*, bb. 120–124	161
5.1	*The Song of Hagar*, Introduction, bb. 1–8	169
5.2	*The Song of Hagar*, No. 1, bb. 1–8	170
5.3	*The Song of Hagar*, No. 9, bb. 667–673	171
5.4	*Festival Te Deum*, bb. 1–8(1)	173
5.5	*Festival Te Deum*, bb. 36(6)–42	174
5.6	*Cantate Domino*, bb. 1–8	176
5.7	*Five Songs of Happiness*, No. 1, bb. 1–10(2)	178
5.8	*Five Songs of Happiness*, No. 2, bb. 23–26	179
5.9	*Five Songs of Happiness*, No. 3, bb. 7–11	180
5.10	*Five Australian Lyrics*, No. 1, bb. 1–5	183
5.11	*Five Australian Lyrics*, No. 2, bb. 17–22(2)	184
5.12	*Five Australian Lyrics*, No. 3, bb. 44–55	185
5.13	*Five Australian Lyrics*, No. 5, bb. 1–10	186

Corroboree Suite by John Antill © Copyright Boosey and Hawkes Music Publishers Ltd. Print rights for Australia and New Zealand administered by Hal Leonard Australia Pty Ltd ABN 13 085 333 713 www.halleonard.com.au. Used by permission. All rights reserved. Unauthorised reproduction is illegal.

Five Australian Lyrics by John Antill © Copyright Boosey and Hawkes Music Publishers Ltd. Print rights for Australia and New Zealand administered by Hal Leonard Australia Pty Ltd ABN 13 085 333 713 www.halleonard.com.au. Used by permission. All rights reserved. Unauthorised reproduction is illegal.

Introduction
A Creative Career in Two Stages Defined by an Australian Music Icon

On Sunday afternoon, 18 August 1946, there occurred a musical event which must rank as one of the most noteworthy in the history of Australian art music. This was the première of music from the ballet *Corroboree* by the hitherto little-known composer John Antill. Initially inspired by a memory of the sounds and rhythms of Aboriginal music which Antill had heard as a boy more than 30 years previously in a performance by an Aboriginal group at La Perouse, south of Sydney, the music of *Corroboree* was performed at a concert in the Sydney Town Hall by the Sydney Symphony Orchestra conducted by its soon-to-be-appointed chief conductor, Eugene Goossens. Goossens, who had been on a tour of Australia under the auspices of the (then) Australian Broadcasting Commission (ABC), had made it known that he wished to find contemporary Australian music to perform while on tour. Apparently some 40 or so scores were submitted to him for examination.[1] However, the extremely reticent Antill did not put his score, on which he had been working for about eight years, forward for consideration. Nevertheless the conductor John Farnsworth-Hall, who had heard Antill rehearse the *Corroboree* music at an ABC workshop/symposium under Farnsworth-Hall's direction some two years previously, alerted Goossens as to its existence. Goossens asked to see Antill's work and after examining his 45-minute score, enthusiastically embraced it, and conducted a suite of extracts from it at a concert less than a fortnight following his initial perusal of Antill's music.[2] The performance received a tremendous ovation and Goossens subsequently gave performances to equally enthusiastic audiences both in London and in Cincinnati (where Goossens was at that time chief conductor). Goossens is reported to have said after the Sydney première, 'John Antill's Corroboree is, in my opinion, the most significant work from the pen of a contemporary Australian composer I have been privileged to examine'.[3]

---

[1] Jennifer Hill, 'Clive Douglas and the ABC: Not a Favourite Aunt' in Nicholas Brown et al. (eds) *One Hand on the Manuscript: Music in Australian Cultural History 1930–1960* (Canberra: Humanities Research Centre, Australian National University, 1995), p. 240.

[2] Details of the première of *Corroboree* are documented in Beth Dean and Victor Carell, *Gentle Genius: A Life of John Antill* (Sydney: Akron Press, 1987), p. 90. For further discussion of the respective roles of Goossens and Antill in creating the suites from the full ballet score, see Chapter 2.

[3] *ABC Weekly*, 21 September 1946; quoted in Ibid.

Thus, overnight, John Antill became a national celebrity, and for many years *Corroboree* remained the best-known work of an Australian-born and resident composer. Its colourful and dissonant idiom, reminiscent of the early twentieth-century 'primitivist' styles of Stravinsky, Bartók and others, was a striking departure from the predominantly conservative styles of all but a handful of Australian composers at this time. It also attained an iconic status as a symbol of Australian nationalism in music perhaps not equalled nor yet eclipsed until the advent of Peter Sculthorpe's *Sun Music 1* some 20 years later.[4] Furthermore, *Corroboree* not only marked Antill's 'coming out' as a composer (at the relatively late age of 42), but also marked a shift of emphasis in his work which was thereafter to be dominated by compositions of overtly Australian subject matter or reference. As will be seen in subsequent chapters, Antill took on the mantle of an Australian 'nationalist' both in his works and in his pronouncements on the nature of Australian music in general. This orientation was (as will also be seen) one shared by a significant group of Australian artists, writers and composers during the 1940s and 1950s. Antill's own background, however, might seem to have made him a less than likely member of such a group.

John Henry Antill was born in Sydney on 8 April 1904. His family was of solidly middle class stock and closely connected with the Anglican Church. The young Antill was initially educated at Sydney's St Andrew's Cathedral Choir School where he was steeped in the music of the English choral tradition from an early age. Indeed Antill acknowledged the Cathedral and its music as a 'most important influence on his musical career'.[5] This influence was to remain in later years as Antill continued to be closely connected with the music of the Cathedral throughout his life. He left the Cathedral School in 1917 (as did all scholars at the age of 14, coinciding with the expected period of voice breaking) and completed his secondary education at another Sydney Anglican school, Trinity Grammar School. Following his secondary schooling, he was apprenticed for five years as a draughtsman at the New South Wales (NSW) Government Railways, where his father was also employed. He completed his apprenticeship successfully in 1925 and – having now learnt a 'useful trade' at his father's insistence – was free to pursue his first love of music with the acquiescence and financial support of his family.[6] After a year and a half of private lessons with St Andrew's organist and choirmaster Fred Mewton, Antill enrolled at the (then) New South Wales Conservatorium of Music for full-time study late in 1926, where his principal teachers were

---

[4] James Murdoch, *Australia's Contemporary Composers* (Melbourne: Macmillan, 1972), pp 11–12. Murdoch claims that 'contemporary Australian music dates from Corroboree'.

[5] Dean and Carell, *Gentle Genius*, p. 15.

[6] Diary of 1925, Papers of John Antill (1904–1986), MS 437, S4/1, Australian Manuscript Collection, National Library of Australia, Canberra. Subsequent references to this collection will be noted as 'AP' followed by the series/folio package (or folder) number of the source.

Gerald Walenn (violin) and – most significantly – Alfred Hill (composition and theoretical subjects). Hill became Antill's chief composition mentor; moreover, under his guidance, Antill also developed as a true 'Kapellmeister', gaining wide experience as an orchestral performer on violin, clarinet and bass clarinet in the Conservatorium (later ABC) orchestra under the direction of Hill or the Conservatorium's Director, William Arundel Orchard. He completed his studies at the Conservatorium by the end of the 1920s, but continued to play in the orchestra into the early 1930s, during which time he also gained valuable experience with the J.C. Williamson Opera Company, variously as an orchestral player, a member of the chorus and as a rehearsal conductor. In addition to this, Antill had been conducting numerous small vocal ensembles for radio broadcasts since the earliest days of radio in Australia in the 1920s, and this activity continued, following his initially casual employment from 1932 with the fledgling Australian Broadcasting Commission. From 1936 Antill became a salaried staff member of the ABC, undertaking a number of roles from conducting to music production, composing, arranging and editing music for broadcast performances. He was later (1949) appointed the Commission's Federal Music Editor,[7] an extremely demanding full-time post which he held until his retirement in 1969. During his period as Federal Music Editor he also remained active as a conductor, mainly of his own works. He died in Sydney on 29 December 1986, following a relatively uneventful retirement during which his considerable status as a major composer was recognised through periodical concerts of his music, including special tributes and concerts to mark his 70th, 75th and 80th birthdays. Further recognition included the award of the OBE and CMG in the 1971 and 1981 Queen's Birthday Honours Lists respectively,[8] the conferring of the first Honorary Doctorate of Creative Arts by the University of Wollongong in 1985, and a gold plaque in his honour presented by the Australasian Performing Right Association (APRA) in the same year.[9]

Antill's life has been chronicled in detail in a biography by Beth Dean and Victor Carell, published in 1987 and titled *Gentle Genius: A Life of John Antill*.[10] Dean (1918–2012) and Carell (1916–2001) were two prominent (husband and wife) ballet dancers and choreographers who were closely associated with the composer from the time of the 1954 ballet production of *Corroboree*, for which they provided the scenario and choreography (see Chapter 2). A biography of Antill had been previously commissioned by the Australia Council Music Board from Austin Goldberg, a close friend of the composer's later years. However Goldberg died on 23 May 1986, having undertaken considerable research for, but having written only preliminary drafts of the intended volume. Dean and Carell completed the biography, their account of Antill's life and compositional activity being drawn from Goldberg's research notes and drafts as well as their own research, based on

---

[7] Murdoch, *Australia's Contemporary Composers*, p. 10.
[8] Dean and Carell, *Gentle Genius*, pp. 168 and 181.
[9] Ibid., p. 190.
[10] See footnote 2.

personal interviews with the composer as well as the perusal of memorabilia then accessible to the authors.[11]

Prior to the appearance of Dean and Carell's biography – and despite much media coverage of Antill, mainly arising from performances of *Corroboree* – the composer's life and work had been treated at any length only in two fairly short book chapters – by Patricia Brown[12] and James Murdoch[13] – while brief critical comments on his music were made in larger surveys of Australian music by Roger Covell[14] and Andrew McCredie.[15] To date, there have also been short encyclopaedia entries in the 1980 and 2001 editions of *The New Grove Dictionary of Music and Musicians*[16] and (more recently) *The Oxford Companion to Australian Music.*[17] Such relatively minor scholarly attention, however, has, until recently, been typical of that accorded to most of Australia's resident composers of what is often identified as the 'post-colonial period' – that is, the period from Federation (1901) to around 1960.

During Antill's lifetime, primary sources in the public domain pertaining to the composer's life and work were scant, and therefore not conducive to the fullest account of his career and achievements. After his death, however, the bulk of his surviving manuscript scores and other memorabilia were deposited by the composer's family in the Australian Manuscript Collection at the National Library of Australia in Canberra (NLA). These resources include not only a comprehensive collection of extant manuscript scores but also a voluminous amount of memorabilia, comprising diaries, correspondence, newspaper clippings, handwritten or typed notes and texts of talks etc., and work lists compiled at various stages of the composer's career.[18] This invaluable and comprehensive collection has enabled the most accurate picture so far to emerge of both the chronological and stylistic evolution of Antill's extensive creative output; and has already been the primary (though not of course exclusive) source for two articles by the present

---

[11] Beth Dean and Victor Carell, research notes and working papers 1904–1985, MLMSS 7804, State Library of NSW.

[12] Patricia Brown, 'John Antill' in Frank Callaway and David Tunley (eds), *Australian Composition in the Twentieth Century* (Melbourne: Oxford University Press, 1978), pp. 44–51.

[13] Murdoch, *Australia's Contemporary Composers*, pp. 11–15.

[14] Roger Covell, *Australia's Music: Themes of a New Society* (Melbourne: Sun Books, 1967), pp. 154–7.

[15] Andrew McCredie, *Musical Composition in Australia* (Canberra: Australian Government Printing Office, 1969), pp. 10–11.

[16] Elizabeth Wood, 'Antill, John (Henry)' in Stanley Sadie (ed.) *The New Grove Dictionary of Music and Musicians* (London: Macmillan, 1980), Vol. 1, p. 470; Patricia Brown, 'Antill, John (Henry)' in Stanley Sadie and John Tyrrell (eds), *The New Grove Dictionary of Music and Musicians*, second edition (London: Macmillan, 2001), Vol. 1, p. 734.

[17] Pauline Petrus, 'Antill, John Henry' in Warren Bebbington (ed.) *The Oxford Companion to Australian Music* (Melbourne: Oxford University Press, 1997), pp. 25–6.

[18] See footnote 6 for full citation of this collection.

author.[19] This book represents a major expansion of the material covered in these publications and is intended to provide the most detailed study to date of the work of one of the foremost composers of Australia's post-colonial period.

The two 'stages' of Antill's career referred to in the title of this Introduction were sharply defined as a direct result of the enormous fame of *Corroboree*. During the first of these 'stages' – the period prior to the appearance of this work – Antill was a little-known composer whose only performed works comprised some very small-scale pieces and arrangements for the vocal ensembles that he conducted, and perhaps a few solo songs and other pieces performed at the Conservatorium during his student years there. From his earliest years, however, Antill's greatest creative impetus had been for the medium of stage music – initially opera. As Chapter 1 will show, Antill's pre-*Corroboree* output is dominated by a significant group of both complete and (more often) incomplete operatic scores. One of these, the Keats-inspired 'lyric masque' *Endymion* (1930), achieved performances in Sydney and Melbourne in 1953. The remainder of Antill's early operatic projects, however, were either destroyed, abandoned incomplete or else put aside when completed with no prospect or expectation that they would ever be performed. Indeed, *Corroboree*, on which he laboured from about 1936 until 1944, might well have suffered the same fate save for the opportunity afforded by the 'workshopping' of extracts under Farnsworth-Hall and the conductor's subsequent recommendation that Goossens examine the work.

With the advent of *Corroboree* Antill's situation as a composer altered radically and this event inaugurated a new, second 'stage' of his career. As an 'instant celebrity' composer he now became the recipient of numerous commissions, from the ABC and various other individuals and organisations. Not surprisingly perhaps, these were for works in the 'public' domain of further ballet scores, as well as for various 'occasional' pieces for public events. As Roger Covell has observed, he 'seemed to be at times a kind of composer-laureate for state occasions'.[20] Ironically the pressures of the commissions, arising directly from the huge success of *Corroboree*, were predominantly for works of modest dimensions or limited performing resources. These, together with his increasingly busy workload at the ABC, acted as a deterrent to the production of more ambitious compositions requiring extended planning and gestation and which might have extended his now very considerable reputation as a major composer. Indeed, the 'occasional' nature of many of Antill's works after *Corroboree* has led to some negative criticisms, such as that of Covell that Antill's post-*Corroboree* compositions are the 'diligent makeweights of an extremely competent musician'.[21] However this

---

[19] David Symons, 'Before *Corroboree*: Toward a Clearer Perspective of the Early Music of John Antill', *Musicology Australia*, Vol. 30 (2008), pp. 29–48; David Symons, '*Corroboree* and After: John Antill as a "One-work" Composer?', *Musicology Australia*, Vol. 34/1 (2012), pp. 53–80.
[20] Covell, *Australia's Music*, p. 155.
[21] Ibid., p. 154.

comment somewhat overstates the situation in that Antill's output after *Corroboree* nevertheless includes a relatively small, but significant number of compositions of a substance comparable to his magnum opus. This issue will be explored in detail in later chapters of this book.

The following study of Antill's music, then, will show clearly the 'two-stage' development of the composer's creative output. It is not intended as a further study of the composer's life, but will draw upon existing available sources for essential biographical background where appropriate – most notably Dean and Carell's biography mentioned earlier. Their book provides a detailed and useful chronological perspective of Antill's life, its most significant shortcoming being some inaccuracies in the dating of some of Antill's early works. The most striking of these is the consistent dating of *Endymion* (mentioned above) – by Dean and Carell as well as in all post-1950s worklists – from around the year 1920 instead of from 1929–1930, the actual date of composition as revealed by the manuscript scores and Antill's diary entries referring to the composition of the work. These inaccuracies came to light in the author's examination of the Antill Papers and were discussed at length in the article on Antill's early works.[22] This issue will be examined again in Chapter 1 of this book.

The treatment of Antill's music will be essentially one of descriptive analysis, its aim being to show the range of the composer's creative style and achievement. Although an overall perspective of his total output will be offered, and a comprehensive catalogue of his surviving original works provided in Appendix 1, the treatment of his music in the text will be selective, examining in detail only those works which are of greater substance, including (but not limited to) those which have reached public performances and/or recordings.

Acknowledgements

As stated earlier, the research leading to the writing of the author's previous articles and the present book has relied centrally upon the comprehensive resources contained in the Antill Papers in the NLA. Primary acknowledgement is therefore due to the staff of the Australian Manuscript Collection at the NLA together with the composer's daughter, Mrs Jill Antill-Rose, who graciously gave permission for materials from the Antill Papers to be accessed and copied. Thanks are also due to Meredith Lawn of the State Library of New South Wales for providing materials from the papers of Beth Dean and Victor Carell held in its Manuscript Collection. Special thanks must go to successive librarians of the Wigmore Music Library, The University of Western Australia – Jenny Wildy and Linda Papa – for their untiring help, advice and cooperation in the initial location and retrieval of much research material. To Joel Crotty, Vincent Plush, Angela Turner and Rhoderick McNeill, special appreciation is due for their valuable ready advice and access to

---

[22] Symons, 'Before *Corroboree*', passim.

their own research materials. In the preparation of the book, an enormous debt of gratitude is owed to Victoria Rogers, who has read successive drafts of the whole text and provided invaluable feedback on its development. Her support over the entire length of this project has been immeasurable. Sincere thanks go to Alan Lourens and Stuart James for their efficient production of the music examples. Finally, appreciation is due to the School of Music, The University of Western Australia for financial support and for providing a congenial academic base for the project.

Chapter 1
Before *Corroboree*

Background

John Antill's creative career spans much of Australia's post-colonial period and just beyond, beginning with his youthful experiments during the years of World War 1 and culminating in his last output of note at the end of the 1960s. As noted in the Introduction, the post-colonial period comprised the years from Federation to approximately 1960, and saw the emergence of Australia's earliest composers of truly musical rather than primarily historical interest. These included Antill's immediate forebears and contemporaries.

The first generation of post-colonial composers included the English immigrants G.W.L. Marshall-Hall (1862–1915) and Fritz Hart (1874–1949), the Australian-born and resident Alfred Hill (1870–1960) and the expatriate Percy Grainger (1882–1961), who nevertheless fiercely declared his 'Australian-ness' throughout his career. While Marshall-Hall's and Hill's musical antecedents were largely nineteenth-century Germanic (Hill's study in Leipzig in the 1880s leading to a strongly conservative bias, whereas Marshall-Hall's musical language owed more to the 'progressive' styles of Wagner and Strauss), both Hart's and Grainger's musical heritage (notwithstanding Grainger's often wide-ranging and adventurous compositional experiments) was basically rooted in British music of the early twentieth century, including, most notably, a style commonly referred to as 'English pastoralism'. This 'pastoral' idiom was prevalent in the work of many English composers from the World War 1 years to roughly the end of the 1920s – composers such as Vaughan Williams, Holst, Delius, Bax, Ireland, Bridge and many others – and comprised an essentially lyrical style, with its roots variously in English folk-song modality as well as post-impressionist harmonies, making use of triadic extensions such as seventh and ninth chords often in parallel or other non-functional sequences, and also incorporating some chromatic dissonance. This idiom resonated strongly in the music of many Australian composers throughout much of the post-colonial period.

Antill's immediate contemporaries of the next generation included the Australian-born and resident Mirrie Hill (1889–1986), Roy Agnew (1891–1944), Margaret Sutherland (1897–1984), Clive Douglas (1903–1977), Robert Hughes (1912–2007), Raymond Hanson (1913–1976), Miriam Hyde (1913–2005) and Dorian Le Gallienne (1915–1963), and the expatriates Arthur Benjamin (1893–1960) and Peggy Glanville-Hicks (1912–1990). The chief cultural and stylistic heritage of these composers was also mainly English. Like that of their English contemporaries, the music of these composers betrayed some survivals of post-Romantic and English pastoral styles, but also (especially among the more 'progressive' composers) incorporated more cosmopolitan influences from the early twentieth century (especially French and Russian), as well as elements of neo-classicism and the influence of such composers as Bartók, Hindemith and Stravinsky. As in the case of all but a few English contemporaries, more radical compositional models, including the atonality and twelve-note technique of the 'Schoenberg School', were eschewed until well after World War 2.[1] In Australia, it was not till the 1950s (occasionally), and especially after 1960, that the influence of more modernist and indeed 'avant-garde' styles were to become dominant. This has led to a popular critical conception that Australian music of the post-colonial period was overwhelmingly outdated and derivative – a view which has for a long time been uncritically accepted, but which has been redressed to some extent in light of more recent studies of Australian music of this period.

A final link with English models may be found in the work of those Australian composers of the period (including Antill) who aspired to the creation of a national identity in their music. The music of the English 'folk-song' and 'pastoral' composers was frequently programmatic or descriptive in character, and the subjects depicted contained a strong portrayal of landscape or the 'spirit of place' (perhaps to a somewhat greater extent than found in the music of other national 'schools'). Examples include Holst's *Egdon Heath*, Vaughan Williams's *Norfolk Rhapsodies*, Bax's *Tintagel* and *November Woods* and Ireland's *Mai-Dun* and *The Forgotten Rite*. Among Australian composers, this may be found not only in similarly programmatic or descriptive works such as Hart's *The Bush* (1923), Alfred Hill's 'Australia' Symphony (1951), Mirrie Hill's 'Arnhem Land' Symphony (1954) and Douglas's tone poems *Carwoola* (1940), *Wongadilla* (1954) and his 'Namatjira' Symphony (1956); but also, during the later post-colonial period, in a spate of theatrical works – especially ballets (including of course Antill's *Corroboree*) – on both Australian Aboriginal legends and post-settlement 'bush' subjects. The notion of 'Australianism' in music (and also literature) – and Antill's engagement with this – will be taken up more fully in Chapter 2, including the role of the evocation of Aboriginal culture in making a meaningful spiritual link with the Australian landscape. As a postscript to this discussion, it is perhaps noteworthy that, following the most aggressive period of avant-garde modernism in Australian

---

[1] It is noteworthy here that even the expatriate Peggy Glanville-Hicks, following her initial studies in Australia with the anglophile Hart, proceeded to England, where she studied with Vaughan Williams. Later, she went on to Vienna where she studied briefly with Egon Wellesz, and then to Paris where she studied with Nadia Boulanger. Nevertheless, she vehemently rejected the Schoenberg-oriented approach of Wellesz, but embraced the neo-classical Stravinsky-influenced teaching of Boulanger, which became her dominant style until she later still sought a simplified pan-consonant style heavily indebted to her studies of Indian and demotic Greek modality. Glanville-Hicks's musical development is covered most extensively in Victoria Rogers, *The Music of Peggy Glanville-Hicks* (Farnham, Surrey: Ashgate, 2009).

music during the 1960s, the role of landscape or environment and its 'spirituality' as subjects for musical compositions has blossomed again during the 'postmodern' period since about 1970, where the influence in particular of the music of Peter Sculthorpe (1929–2014) has been a continuing and definitive factor.

Turning now to Antill's own work overall, perhaps its major and most notable feature is his considerable production of works for the theatre. Further, his work in this area can be seen to fall into two distinct phases. In the pre-*Corroboree* period his preoccupation was with opera, while his later output, from around the time of *Corroboree* or just prior, concentrated on ballet. This will be discussed further in due course. Although Antill makes no comment, in any published sources or in any unpublished statements to be found among the Antill Papers (see below), regarding his awareness of contemporary developments in Australian operatic or ballet composition during his early years, it is noteworthy, first, that his initial engagement with opera (as a teenager) coincided with a period of significant opera production by Australian composers – in particular Alfred Hill (who was to become Antill's chief compositional mentor later), Marshall-Hall and Hart. These and other composers produced, during the first few decades of the twentieth century, a significant number of operas which were performed by local, especially Conservatorium, opera groups in Melbourne and Sydney. In addition, Hill and Hart were instrumental in the formation of the brief and abortive Australian Opera League in 1914, whose aim was specifically the fostering of opera by Australian composers. It is perhaps worth remarking here that this early twentieth-century upsurge in Australian opera composition came at the end of a considerably rich culture of Australian opera performances, especially in Melbourne and Sydney during and since the colonial period by both Australian (notably the Lyster and later Williamson companies) and touring companies, which provided regular seasons of the standard opera repertoire. These included many nineteenth-century operas that achieved performances in Australia not many years after their European premières. However, until the sudden early-twentieth-century efflorescence of Australian opera productions, fully professional (or semi-professional) performances of operas by Australian composers were sparse, but included some early successes such as Isaac Nathan's (1792–1864) *Don John of Austria* (1841) and Stephen Hale Marsh's (1805–1888) *The Gentleman in Black* (c. 1847, but premièred as a Lyster production in 1861). Less significant productions (mostly privately sponsored) occurred during the later decades of the colonial period.[2] In the inter-war years (1918–1939) this significant opera 'culture' declined considerably with the advent of broadcasting in Australia (1923); and especially, following its creation in 1932, the establishment during the 1930s by the Australian Broadcasting Commission (now Corporation) (ABC) of permanent symphony orchestras in all states and the introduction of regular subscription concerts.

---

[2] See Andrew McCredie, *Musical Composition in Australia* (Canberra: Australian Government Printing Office, 1969), pp. 3–4.

Like opera, ballet performances in Australia can be traced back to the early colonial period with the visits of various touring ballet troupes throughout the nineteenth and early twentieth centuries, also often under the aegis of the Lyster and Williamson companies. The advent of the famous tours by Pavlova in the late 1920s inspired the formation of the first Australian ballet company, directed by Louise Lightfoot and Mischa Burlakov.[3] This small company (with which, as will be seen later, Antill had some contact in the early 1930s) commissioned the earliest ballet scores by Australian composers.[4] A further inspiration for Australian ballet production was afforded by the tours, from 1936–1940, of De Basil's troupe formed from the remnants of Diaghilev's Ballets Russes, and the subsequent immigration of various members of his company, and later of refugee ballet dancers from Nazi Germany in the years of World War 2. Detailed accounts of the remarkably sudden emergence of ballet scores by Australian composers from the late 1930s onward may be found in studies by Edward Pask and Joel Crotty.[5] Antill could hardly have been unaware of these developments, which could well have stimulated him to the composition of a major ballet score. His work on *Corroboree* seems to have occupied him from about 1936 to 1944 and, remarkably, this major project appears, on available evidence, to represent his first serious engagement with the medium of ballet. This issue will be discussed in detail later. Now, however, Antill's early development must be examined from a chronological perspective in order to gain as clear a view as possible of the evolution of his musical style in the years leading up to his magnum opus. In particular this will show a style that began as late Romantic and evolved through the 'English pastoral' style, with very few glimpses during this period of the more dissonant idiom of *Corroboree*.

In tracing this development, the following sources have together provided some basic perspectives. The first, Dean and Carell's biography, draws upon reminiscences reported to them by both the composer and his family. Here Antill's reported reminiscences are of course those recalled from near the end of his life and – as was mentioned in the Introduction and will be shown later in this chapter – are not always accurate. A much earlier source, however, a brief document written by Antill himself, comprises a two-page typescript located among the Antill Papers, titled 'Early history'.[6] This autobiographical sketch was quite clearly written around the time of the appearance of *Corroboree* in the mid-1940s since it concludes with a commentary on the ballet (no later works are mentioned) and also

---

[3] Joel Crotty, 'Ballet and Dance Music' in Warren Bebbington (ed.), *The Oxford Companion to Australian Music* (Melbourne: Oxford University Press, 1997), p. 43.
[4] Ibid.
[5] Edward Pask, *Ballet in Australia: The Second Act 1940–1980* (Melbourne: Oxford University Press, 1982); Joel Crotty, 'From Balletic Binge to Cultural Cringe: Choreographic Music in Australia, 1936–1956' in Nicholas Brown et al. (eds), *One Hand on the Manuscript: Music in Australian Cultural History 1930–1960* (Canberra: Humanities Research Centre, Australian National University, 1995), pp. 217–28.
[6] AP, S5/2.

comments on the potential (not yet realised in Antill's view) of the creation of an 'Australian school of musical thought' utilising the materials of Aboriginal music. Although brief, this sketch provides a more reliable perspective of Antill's pre-*Corroboree* output – both as to its extent and chronology – than has subsequently appeared in the literature on Antill published during the composer's lifetime and also in Dean and Carell's biography.

A further source of major significance are Antill's diaries for the years 1925 to the mid-1930s – that is, covering the period following the completion of his apprenticeship with the NSW Railways, his period at the (then) NSW Conservatorium and his early years with the ABC.[7] The diaries from these years in particular provide a detailed record of Antill's musical activities, establishing, as will be seen, a firm chronology for a number of works for which the subsequent sources – even including later work lists and comments by Antill himself – record significantly varied dates.[8] All of the above sources, together with internal evidence provided by surviving manuscript scores located among the Antill Papers, allow one to reconstruct a fairly accurate picture of Antill's work during these early years.

Beginnings

It is clear that Antill was a compulsive composer from his boyhood. According to Dean and Carell, he dates the beginning of his composing music from the time of his first violin lesson at the age of seven (previous piano lessons having been found uncongenial to him). Commenting on his study of the violin he is reported to have said later: 'I took to it naturally and immediately started to write. This was the beginning of my compositional activity. I wrote several pieces for violin and piano, each proudly kept by my mother'.[9] In 'Early history', Antill suggests an even earlier genesis of his creative output, stating: 'It was probably between the ages of five and six when my first melody was produced. I think it was a waltz tune'. He also recalls here: 'my school books always had sketches for future symphonies scribbled on every spare space. Symphonies which did not eventuate'.[10]

Antill's close association with church music also began during these years as he was a member of a local church choir prior to his admission to St Andrew's Cathedral Choir School. Dean and Carell also mention that Antill was immediately drawn to church choral music and in these early years he '"set" various scriptural

---

[7] The diaries referred to here and subsequently are located in AP S4/1–3. Later diaries also held among the Antill Papers contain far less material on Antill's creative activities.

[8] For extended discussion of this issue, see also Symons, 'Before *Corroboree*', passim.

[9] Dean and Carell, *Gentle Genius*, pp. 13–14.

[10] AP, S5/2.

texts and even wrote words and music for anthems'.[11] However it is noteworthy that no major sacred compositions came from his pen until the post-*Corroboree* period, and then only a few.

Another significant event during these years was Antill's trip with his family to La Perouse, a (then) Aboriginal settlement south of Sydney, where performances of 'make believe' corroborees were given for visitors. Antill was fascinated by the rhythms, which he memorised and later wrote down. These he kept for 25 years and incorporated into his famous ballet score.[12]

Perhaps the most significant creative inspiration from this period, however, was his attendance at a 'musical matinee' at a local theatre, which immediately fired what was to become his lifelong fascination for the theatre.[13] Dean and Carell report that he then began writing his own plays and constructed a miniature theatre stage.[14] This, combined with his love of music composition, reportedly led to his first operatic venture – inspired by his father's account of a performance of Puccini's *Madama Butterfly* which he attended in London while a soldier in Europe in 1915.[15] This opera is identified as *Ouida*, and Dean and Carell have provided a full quotation of Antill's own outline of his rather naïve plot concerning the love of a French nurse (Ouida) for a British soldier named Henry during World War 1.[16] No positively identifiable music from this opera – labelled by Antill as 'A Masque Opera in Two Acts' – survives among the miscellaneous early sketches located among the Antill Papers,[17] although the plot outline and extracts from the libretto are located among Dean and Carell's own research papers.[18] It is not clear whether Antill completed this opera. In 'Early history', he states that he wrote his first opera at the age of 15, but does not identify it.[19] This could of course be *Ouida*, which would place the date of this work as 1919. It is possible that he worked on *Ouida* as an extended project over the course of his school years. The extravagant performing resources he is reported to have planned for this work[20] suggests that the task of writing such a large piece would have been a monumental one for a largely untutored teenager with a full school programme as well as his commitments at that time to the St Andrew's Cathedral Choir.

However if *Ouida* was never completed, the reference to his 'first opera' may be to another work titled *Princess Dorothea*, which most probably dates from

---

[11] Dean and Carell, *Gentle Genius*, p. 14. Antill also comments on these early pieces in 'Early history' (AP, S5/2).

[12] Dean and Carell, *Gentle Genius*, p. 15; 'Early history' (AP, S5/2).

[13] Dean and Carell, *Gentle Genius*, p. 15.

[14] Ibid.

[15] Ibid., p. 24.

[16] Ibid., p. 30.

[17] AP, S8k/1.

[18] MLMSS 7804/38, Australian Manuscript Collection, State Library of NSW.

[19] AP, S5/2.

[20] Dean and Carell, *Gentle Genius*, p. 29. Antill also comments in 'Early history' (AP, S5/2) that his first opera (*Ouida*?) required an orchestra of 110 and a stage band of 40.

around 1919–1920 (dates given in the index to the Antill Papers) – that is, from around the end of his school years or during the early period of his apprenticeship with the NSW Railways. This opera survives substantially complete in rough drafts, comprising a short score (labelled 'conductor's score') and parts for both voices and orchestra.[21] The surviving manuscript carries no date, but the opera is quite clearly the product of a youthful and inventive, if naïve imagination. It is a one-act opera and, like *Ouida*, to Antill's own libretto; the plot being set on a mythical island on which the hero, a ship's captain named Edward, and his companions have been shipwrecked. In a dream (although it is not clear as to whether the dream occurs while Edward sleeps on the island or whether the entire plot is a dream narrative), Edward meets Dorothea, the princess of the island who has lived for hundreds of years under the spell of a magician (who is one and the same as one of Edward's companions). She will be released from her immortality if a locket bearing her portrait is found and opened. The locket is found, but meanwhile Dorothea and Edward have fallen in love and Dorothea now wishes to live with Edward for ever. But one of Edward's companions takes possession of the locket and, on Dorothea's refusal to love him, opens it. Dorothea dies – along with Edward and his companions who have drunk a poisonous wine – while Dorothea, now as an angel, bears Edward off to heaven. This plot (like that of *Ouida*) shows Antill's early love of stories of a highly romantic and/or supernatural kind. His preoccupation with Australian materials lay many years in the future.

Of Antill's extant completed compositions, *Princess Dorothea* is clearly one of the earliest available for examination. It amply illustrates Antill's early ambitious aims in the composition of opera during his teenage years – including the writing of his own libretti (as also in the case of *Ouida*); and also the overall handling of operatic form. It is noteworthy that Antill recalled in 'Early history': 'I had written two operas before I ever saw or heard one. My knowledge in this respect being gained by reading and asking'.[22] Whether this 'reading and asking' included an awareness of the scores of Australian operas referred to earlier is unknown. However, the evidence presented by the score of *Princess Dorothea* suggests that Antill was aware of the predominantly through-composed nature of most serious post-Wagnerian opera. Although *Dorothea* is divided into sections called 'numbers', these are not those of Classical 'number' opera, but rather sections or even rehearsal cues, since the work is essentially continuous. Unfortunately a close analysis of the musico-dramatic structure is impossible owing to the often unintelligible or simply sketchy nature of the manuscript. However, the recurrence of particular sections lends thematic coherence to the opera, while the opening theme of the orchestral introduction (see Example 1.1 below) – which, as Antill states in his plot summary appended to the score, 'is the subject the opera is based upon' – certainly appears in various guises throughout and is finally heard as Edward and Dorothea are united in heaven.

[21] AP, S8b/1.
[22] AP, S5/2.

The use of a unifying recurrent theme (though not a specific 'leitmotif') is to be found again in *Endymion*, as will be seen later.

Despite the considerable achievement of a teenage composer in conceiving and realising such a large-scale work, *Princess Dorothea* is essentially an immature piece, of mainly historical interest. Its musical language is largely diatonic, although with some passages which point to Antill's early awareness of late Romantic harmonic freedom. However these musical resources are often handled in a rather awkward manner, while the rhythmic language is unadventurous and foursquare and the notation rough and immature. Example 1.1 quotes the opening bars of the opera which give out the recurring theme referred to above.

Example 1.1   *Princess Dorothea*, opening

Another clearly youthful work, probably dating from the same period as *Dorothea*, is a brief orchestral work titled 'Serenade'. The score survives complete among the miscellaneous sketches located among the Antill Papers.[23] It is formally

---

[23]   AP, S8k/1.

simple (in ternary form) and betrays a basically diatonic idiom comparable to that of *Dorothea* and a musical handwriting of a similarly immature character.

The Railway Years

In attempting to gain an accurate picture of music composed during the Railway years (1920–1925) the most useful source, once again, is Antill's 'Early history'.[24] Here he mentions that during the period at the Railways he 'wrote two more operas'. No other works are mentioned, and the operas are not identified. However, in Dean and Carell's biography (drawn, it must be recalled, from information supplied by the composer decades later), the extraordinary claim is made that Antill composed no less than nine stage works during this period.[25] These are identified as the operas *Heroida*, *Endymion*, *Dorothea* [sic], *The Sleeping Princess*, *Here's Luck*, *The Glittering Mask* and *The Gates of Paradise*; and two ballets, *Capriccio* and *The Circus Comes to Town*. This extravagant programme of compositional activity by a youthful composer aged between 16 and 21 years, as yet without any formal training in the craft – and reportedly only able to compose in his spare time at the Railways as well as on the train travelling to and from work – is scarcely conceivable, and is clearly inaccurate as subsequent evidence will show. However, these works (except *Heroida* and *The Sleeping Princess*), with dates given from this period, are included in a manuscript work list provided by Antill no earlier than 1978.[26] This list includes a date of 1920 for *Endymion* which has appeared in numerous published work lists and confirmed by Antill in various interviews which were published in connection with the performances of this work in 1953 in Sydney and Melbourne. Nevertheless, only *Princess Dorothea* clearly belongs to this early period, while *Heroida* and *The Sleeping Princess* are lost, but may be the 'two more operas' Antill referred to in 'Early history'. As subsequent discussion will show, the remainder of these allegedly early works actually date from the 1930s or even later. It is interesting, therefore, to speculate as to how Antill came, in later life, to list the scores mentioned above as having been composed at such an early date. It was certainly not in his highly moral as well as reticent character to deliberately falsify the dates in order to satisfy a personal agenda, such as to appear a precocious talent. Perhaps the most likely (or least unlikely) explanation, therefore, could be a genuine memory slip during his later years arising from his self-confessed attitude to his early compositions (especially the theatre projects) – namely his habit of packing away completed (or abandoned) scores with no particular expectation as to when, or if, they would ever be performed. In the case of the later premièred *Endymion*, the composition of which was frequently attributed to Antill's teenage

---

[24] AP, S5/2.
[25] Dean and Carell, *Gentle Genius*, pp. 45–6.
[26] AP, S5/1.

years, there are no dates on the original manuscripts that would have reminded him of its true composition date.

The Conservatorium Years

Antill's period of full-time music study, following the completion of his apprenticeship at the NSW Railways in April 1925,[27] saw a temporary abandonment of his youthful pursuit of operatic composition. From 1925 to 1929 – that is, the period covering his private study with Fred Mewton, the St Andrew's Cathedral organist and choirmaster, and his subsequent period as a full-time student at the NSW Conservatorium (from late 1926) – Antill's output consisted only of works of relatively modest dimensions. Presumably his formal study of composition during this time, together with his busy programme of both theoretical and performance studies and practical music making, discouraged him from embarking on such ambitious projects as he had earlier essayed as a youthful amateur. The diaries from the years 1925 to 1929 confirm this, generally telling of his incessant desire to compose, but frequently reporting frustration and illness, together with an ever-increasing determination to further his musical career. There are few references to any completed compositions during these years, but nevertheless constant references to long hours of practice and composition.

It is perhaps noteworthy here that Antill's formal professional training in music – composition, theory and performance – was confined to the four years or so at the Conservatorium, following his period of private study with Mewton. He did not go abroad – especially to England – to gain what a number of his fellow composers such as Margaret Sutherland, Roy Agnew, Miriam Hyde or Peggy Glanville-Hicks would have seen as an essential broader international experience. It is unclear as to whether his own or his family's resources would have been able to provide funds for a period of overseas study; however, in all available biographical sources this question does not even arise. Much later, Antill appears to have made his 'home-grown' musical study a virtue as well as a link with his by then overt 'Australianism'. This is shown in a feature article by Martin Long in the *Sydney Morning Herald* of 25 May 1952, prompted by the announcement of the planned première of *Endymion*, but titled 'His Music is Home Grown'. In this article Antill is quoted as saying 'I am glad that I never went overseas to study as I think it's important that we in Australia should work things out on our own'. However, the musical climate at the Conservatorium at that time, though lively and active, could hardly have been described as 'home grown'. Rather, the range of musical experience and taste was firmly rooted in that prevailing in England – the 'mother country' to which Australia was then linked as an integral part of the Empire, and the preferred destination for those

---

[27] Diary of 1925, AP, S4/1.

Australian musicians who did study abroad! Thus, the music to which Antill and his contemporaries would have been exposed at that time was dominated by the nineteenth-century symphonic and operatic repertoire together with such relatively mild early twentieth-century musical influences as French impressionism; the Russian school from Tchaikovsky and the 'Five' through to Scriabin and Rachmaninov; the English folk-song and 'pastoral' composers such as Vaughan Williams, Holst, Delius, Bax and Ireland; and Scandinavian composers such as Grieg and Sibelius. This orientation was true of the major music schools in Sydney, Melbourne and Adelaide. As mentioned earlier in this chapter, Antill's teacher, Alfred Hill, was a musician whose early overseas study (late nineteenth century) was in Leipzig where he gained a lifelong grounding in conservative nineteenth-century harmony and form, and in his own music this remained basic but also incorporated the milder aspects of English pastoralism.

During his Conservatorium years, Antill's only complete works available for study among the Antill Papers, and firmly dated, are eight songs for voice and piano.[28] These are all brief songs of only one or two stanzas, the musical settings being in simple strophic or sectional forms with very regular phrase structures. The presence of clear dates on each song provides a firm perspective of Antill's work during these still formative years, while the songs suggest a strong influence of his teacher, Alfred Hill. The texts are short lyrics by such poets as Dryden, Browning and Burns, together with lesser-known English (or possibly Australian) poets. The musical styles range from the rich diatonic harmony of early Vaughan Williams (i.e. the period before his study with Ravel in 1908) as found in 'The Garland' and 'My Star' (both 1928), through a bluff English folk-song idiom also reminiscent of Vaughan Williams, in 'Blue Eyed Mary' (1927) (see Example 1.2 below) to a more post-impressionist style as found in the earliest song of the group, 'The Lost Joy' (1926), where Antill makes use of a more subtle harmonic vocabulary including the use of ninth and altered chords together with non-functional progressions, a style redolent of English pastoralism (see Example 1.3 below).

Apart from this small group of songs, Dean and Carell document only one other work – a sonata for bass clarinet and piano – as having been completed during the Conservatorium years.[29] However, this work is untraceable among the Antill Papers and no other works are positively identifiable as having been completed during these years. Nevertheless, miscellaneous manuscripts (mainly early) of mostly incomplete works or fragments[30] include three pieces for orchestra (apparently complete) collectively titled *Nature Studies* and dated 28 October 1925 (while he was still studying with Mewton), together with undated manuscripts, including a fragment from an *Overture to a Chinese Opera*, a set of two pieces for piano titled *Lyric Pieces* and the earlier mentioned 'Serenade'

---

[28] AP, S8j/1.
[29] Dean and Carell, *Gentle Genius*, p. 57.
[30] AP, S8k/1.

Example 1.2   'Blue Eyed Mary', bb. 5–14

for orchestra. As previously discussed, 'Serenade' probably dates from around the time of *Princess Dorothea*, while the other two scores more likely date from 1925 or later. These other manuscripts, along with those of the songs from the Conservatorium period, show a definite advance in notational sophistication as compared with that of *Princess Dorothea* and 'Serenade'. The noteheads are still thick and round as in the earlier rougher manuscripts, but the handwriting here (and the scores are 'fair copies') is much firmer and clearer. The musical idiom ranges from late Romantic to 'English pastoral' as is well illustrated in the following two passages from *Nature Studies* (see Example 1.4 below).

Example 1.3 'The Lost Joy', bb. 1–6

The Operas of 1930–1945 – Chronological Perspectives

It was not until near the end of his Conservatorium years that the composition of stage works again began to occupy Antill; and here may be found the major discrepancies when comparing the dates of these works given by Dean and Carell and in various later work lists with evidence now available from the Antill Papers. This includes most notably the internal evidence provided by the manuscript scores of the works involved, and the entries in Antill's diaries dating from 1929 to the mid-1930s. This evidence clearly shows that the 1930s and early 1940s was a period in which Antill embarked on a number of opera projects – three complete and the others in various stages of completion or in fragmentary form. The first is *Endymion* (1929–1930) based on Keats's poem but to Antill's own libretto. Then follow two 'light operas' titled *Here's Luck* and *The Glittering Mask* (both 1931–1932) to libretti by Margery Browne, an early twentieth-century Australian poet whose works include the libretto for Alfred Hill's early opera *Lady Dolly* (1897). Antill's next opera, *The Gates of Paradise* (1933–1934) was also to a libretto by Margery Browne but only some of the music of Act 1 was completed. A further burst of operatic activity dates from 1938–1943 – years during which Antill was also preoccupied with the composition of *Corroboree*. During this time Antill essayed three opera projects to texts by another Australian poet, John Wheeler – namely *The Serpent Woman* (1938), *The Lost Child* (1940) and *The Scapegoat* (1943). None of these operas was completed.

Example 1.4a   'A Deep Pool' (No. 1 of *Nature Studies*), beginning of middle section

The diaries of 1929 and 1930 make it clear that Antill's only performed early opera, *Endymion*, was composed in these years; and they further imply somewhat mysteriously that the opera was composed, or at least drafted, twice – once in 1929 and again in 1930. While the scores and drafts in the folio dedicated to *Endymion* appear to relate only to a single version of the opera,[31] there are sketches among the miscellaneous manuscripts that contain material clearly related to *Endymion* and may be music composed for a possibly aborted 1929 version.[32] Although it is also not impossible that the opera may have existed in sketch form back in the Railway years, there is no direct reference made in the diary entries to any pre-existing material for *Endymion* or indeed the Margery Browne operas – also claimed (as noted above) to have dated from this earlier period. As to the latter, the fact that Antill records his first meeting with Margery Browne on 7 March 1931 would seem to make it clear that these operas date entirely from the later period.

[31]   AP, S8b/2.
[32]   AP, S8k/1.

Example 1.4b   'To a Waterfall' (No. 2 of *Nature Studies*), bb. 1–10

The diaries of 1931–1932 show clearly that, following the completion of *Endymion*, the two completed Margery Browne operas were composed together in 1931 as entries in a competition organised by a private club called the 'Opportune Club' in Sydney.[33] This competition offered a prize of £100 for the 'best composition, embracing Comic Opera, Light Opera, Musical Comedy or Revue' lasting about 2 hours and 30 minutes, and composed by 'an Australasian, or by any person who has resided in Australia or New Zealand for a period of not less than ten years. The entry shall never have been publicly produced' (similar residential qualifications applied to the librettist when this was not the composer). The conditions further stated: 'It will be counted in favour of entrants if the work has an atmosphere typical of either Australia or New Zealand'. The winning entry would be publicly produced in Sydney 'if unanimously agreed worthy by Judges'. No evidence has yet been uncovered as to the fate of the two works in the competition; however it may be assumed that neither won the award nor was performed.

Further evidence for the later composition of *Endymion* and the Margery Browne operas is provided by the scores themselves,[34] especially when they are compared with those definitely dating from Antill's youth and intervening Conservatorium student years. The sketches and scores of the three completed operas show, first, a similarity of manuscript style – and even the use of identical brand manuscript books for the drafts, while the date 1932 is clearly inscribed on one of the scores of *Here's Luck*. Further, both the musical handwriting, as well as the compositional style, of the works show a sophistication well in advance of that, for example, of *Princess*

---

[33] AP, S8b/8.
[34] AP, S8b/2–10.

Dorothea.[35] A comparison of the preceding examples from *Princess Dorothea*, *Nature Studies*, the songs which survive from the Conservatorium years, and finally (see below) *Endymion*, shows a clear progression in the degree of maturity and compositional expertise consistent with the dates as revealed by the Antill diaries.

Stylistic Development 1930–1945: *Endymion*

Endymion is significant as the only opera from Antill's early period that was both completed and, as previously stated, later performed. Called by Antill a 'lyrical masque', *Endymion* is quite short – in one act and probably no more than 60 minutes in duration (although the lack of recordings or else tempo indications on the score make this conjectural). In its Sydney and Melbourne productions in July and September of 1953 respectively it was performed by the then recently-formed New South Wales National Opera Company as part of an all-Australian 'double bill' with Arthur Benjamin's short opera *The Devil Take Her*.

Although the work shows a considerable advance in compositional sophistication (and, of course, scope) from that displayed in most of the songs of the immediately preceding Conservatorium period, the harmonic language in the more 'progressive' of these songs (cf. Example 1.3 above from 'The Lost Joy') points towards the more complex (though similar) language found in *Endymion*. The 'English pastoral' musical style is admirably suited to the plot of this 'lyrical masque' which is itself a 'pastoral'. Endymion is a shepherd, loved by Diana the moon goddess; and the story tells of the trials Endymion must undergo to become an immortal in order to wed Diana. The original myth had been treated several times in English – as a play by John Lyly and as a novel by Benjamin Disraeli – although it is its best-known incarnation, the 4000-line narrative poem by John Keats, that Antill has identified as the source of his drama. The catalogue of the Antill Papers refers to the libretto as 'by John Keats'. However, the words are not those of Keats's rambling and often diffuse narrative poem, but rather a concise libretto – by Antill himself – of approximately 250 lines. The action is much more firmly delineated and is divided into seven short scenes, played with no breaks except at the end of the second scene, the remainder of the score being labelled 'Part 2' and covering Endymion's trials and triumph.

The musical setting is 'continuous' rather than divided into discrete 'numbers', and the character of the solo vocal writing is largely lyrical arioso, interspersed with a number of orchestral interludes; while in the early and final stages of the work are to be found the only vocal ensembles – a trio of Fates, heard in scene 1, and a mixed chorus involved in the Festival of Pan (scene 2) and in the final scene (7). The musical language throughout is sensuous and soft-edged, ranging from a rich use of diatonic chords, often in parallel triad passages especially in the choral episodes, to a more floating, ambiguous tonality including the use of melodic chromaticism together with seventh, ninth, added note and altered chords. Some of

---

[35] See Example 1.1.

these qualities are well in evidence in the opening bars of the orchestral introduction (see Example 1.5) which begins with a motif heard many times throughout the opera, while the prevailing arioso style of writing for solo voices is well illustrated in Diana's opening monologue following this introduction, in which she declares her passion for the sleeping Endymion (see Example 1.6 below).

Example 1.5   *Endymion*, orchestral prelude, bb. 1–20(2)

Example 1.6 *Endymion*, opening of Diana's arioso

The music for the three Fates and the chorus, both of whom have a commenting role in the drama, largely alternates between homophonic and imitative texture in the manner of a cantata or oratorio, as can be seen in the following examples, the first (Example 1.7) for the Fates in scene 1 in which they proclaim to the enamoured Diana that she can set Endymion's soul free to become immortal in order that he may wed her.

Example 1.7   *Endymion*, opening of Ensemble of the Fates

In the final scene, the chorus enters – near the end of Diana and Endymion's rapturous love duet – in benediction (Example 1.8 below).

Example 1.8   *Endymion*, final scene (chorus)

Example 1.8   *continued*

The music of *Endymion* is of considerable sensuous beauty throughout, and the style remains at all times relatively gentle and sweet-scented within the prevailing English pastoral idiom, even in the most dramatic scene where Endymion raises the spirits of the dead in Neptune's cave. It is this unremitting sweetness and generally static lyricism which undoubtedly led to the most trenchant criticisms of the work at its 1953 performances, alleging its failure to convince as a musical drama. John Moses, writing in a more measured fashion in the *Sydney Morning Herald* (23 July 1953) on the Sydney première, considered the opera, although called a 'lyrical masque', to be too static for an opera, but not spectacular enough to be an effective masque. However there were also a number of favourable comments on the work at this time, and the English publisher, Boosey and Hawkes, was reported to be interested in publishing the work. Unfortunately, this did not eventuate, nor has the work received any subsequent productions.

Stylistic Development 1930–1945: Other Operas

It is perhaps worth noting once again that Antill's preference, in his 'serious' operas during this early period was, as already seen in *Ouida, Princess Dorothea* and *Endymion*, for plots of an essentially romantic type. The serious opera projects of the 1930s and early 1940s continued this preoccupation – being drawn from historical, mythological, Biblical and imaginary sources including much use of supernatural and miraculous elements – rather than from more contemporary, realistic subjects. However, the opposite is true of his two 'light' operas which followed *Endymion* and which are set in colonial (*The Glittering Mask*) and early post-colonial (*Here's Luck*) Australia. The Australian setting of these operas of course reflects the conditions for entries in the operetta competition referred to earlier. These two works, nevertheless, are the first to indicate what was to become a dominant trend in Antill's choice of dramatic and literary themes in his works from *Corroboree* onwards. Such a turn to 'national' subjects in the 1930s and over the next few decades can be traced in part to the encouragement by various artistic authorities – notably the newly-established ABC – for Australian composers, artists and writers to adopt a strongly Australian tone in their work. This upsurge in Australian nationalism was also reflected in the establishment of the Jindyworobak group of writers whose work aspired to an evocation of Australian landscape and Aboriginal imagery, and to reflect what its founder, Rex Ingamells, termed 'an understanding of Australia's history and traditions, primeval, colonial and modern'.[36] Among Australian composers it was notably two ABC 'staffers' – Antill and Clive Douglas – who both began the 'national' phases of their work at about this time following very strong allegiances to Romantic and both Victorian and early twentieth-century English sources of inspiration in much of their earlier output. Moreover, both Antill and Douglas produced works titled 'Corroboree' during this period – Douglas's work being an orchestral tone poem extracted from his short Aboriginal-inspired opera *A Bush Legend* (1938). These developments will be addressed in much more detail in Chapter 2.

Antill's two light operas not surprisingly betray a radical shift of style from that displayed in *Endymion*. Here Antill deliberately adopted a 'light' compositional idiom to suit the 'operetta' or 'revue' nature of the competition's requirements. Both are 'number' operas using spoken dialogue and 'melodrama' (speech against music) as well as songs, ensembles, choruses and instrumental numbers. The settings of both operas are on farm properties in rural Australia. As mentioned above, *The Glittering Mask* is set in the colonial period, whereas *Here's Luck* appears to be set at a later (probably early twentieth century) date, the references to 'the war' by some of the characters referring either to the Boer War (1898–1902) or, more likely, the First World War. *Here's Luck* is a domestic comedy of a rather inconsequential

---

[36] Rex Ingamells, 'Conditional Culture', pamphlet (Adelaide: F.W. Preece, 1938); reprinted in John Barnes (ed.), *The Writer in Australia: A Collection of Literary Documents 1856–1964* (Melbourne: Oxford University Press, 1969), p. 249.

kind, centring on a station owner, Tesler, and his family and employees. The straightforward diatonic idiom and popular, regularly phrased structure of the songs may be clearly shown in two short extracts. Number 4, 'The true Australian way' has a melody which closely resembles a section of the Policemen's Song from Gilbert and Sullivan's *The Pirates of Penzance* (Example 1.9), while the following song, number 5, ('A Sport') is uncomfortably similar to 'Advance Australia fair' (Example 1.10 below).

Example 1.9   *Here's Luck*, No. 4, bb. 1–16

The Glittering Mask largely comprises music of a similar character to that of *Here's Luck*. However a notable shift of tone can be seen in the first number of Act II, titled 'Corroboree'. Here Antill adopts an ostinato-dominated style, while the orchestration is often distinctly shriller and more colourful. The harmonic idiom ranges from relatively diatonic through whole-tone passages to some more dissonant combinations – the general character of the number providing early hints of his more 'primitivist' manner in the more famous work carrying this title (see Example 1.11).

Example 1.10   *Here's Luck*, No. 5, bb. 1–9(2)

The incomplete operas from the 1930s and early 1940s are once more on 'serious' subjects which exhibit the romantic characteristics discussed earlier. Among the Antill Papers,[37] the two-act libretto of the remaining Margery Browne opera *The Gates of Paradise* – written in rather ponderous Victorian English – survives complete. Set in Paris in the early days of the French Revolution, the story is the

---

[37]   AP, S8b/11.

Example 1.11   *The Glittering Mask*, Act II, 'Corroboree', bb. 1–7

time-honoured one of love between members of conflicting factions – in this case the aristocrats and the revolutionaries. Marie, daughter of a count, is in love with Levaux, an 'advocate of the people', rather than Beaulourvaine, a roué who is in favour with the Count. Marie is betrothed to Beaulourvaine but renounces him when she discovers that he has fathered a child with a peasant girl. At the end of the opera Levaux is killed, Marie dies and both are seen, in an apotheosis, as finally united as they pass through 'the gates of Paradise'. Antill appears to have set only part of Act I, but this surviving fragment gives a clear picture of the general style intended for the opera. It is clearly intended to be sung throughout; and although there are distinct arias as 'set pieces', they arise within a context of continuous arioso. The musical style is once more in the late/post-Romantic vein of *Endymion* and the earlier songs.

Of the incomplete operas to texts by John Wheeler, one – *The Scapegoat* – exists as a very short fragment only, comprising some five pages of almost illegible pencil sketches, with no libretto or even synopsis surviving. However, more material exists for the other two operas: *The Serpent Woman* is complete as a draft vocal score up to the final scene, while for *The Lost Child* there survives a fragment of full score. Libretti for both operas survive.[38]

---

[38]   AP, S8b/12–13.

For *The Serpent Woman*, Antill once more turned to Greek mythology for his source. Wheeler's text sets the myth of Lamia, the fabled serpent woman, who seduces men and leads them to destruction.[39] The hero, Lucius, meets Lamia at dusk and is seduced by and becomes betrothed to her. She is unmasked on the day of the wedding by Lucius's guardian, Appolonius, the sage. The symbolism behind this myth is the highly gendered one of male rationality and wisdom delivering man from the darkness of the sensuous, feeling-centred female psyche (the theme is of course similar to the opposition of Sarastro and the Queen of the Night in Mozart's *The Magic Flute*). The opera is in one act and, as stated above, complete in sketch or rough draft (vocal score) up to the final wedding banquet scene. As in the case of *Endymion* and the incomplete *The Gates of Paradise*, *The Serpent Woman* is a 'continuous' through-composed opera, its musical language showing similar sensuous qualities to those of *Endymion*; however, the melodic and harmonic texture is now, in some places, also reminiscent of the more austere style of late Debussy or occasionally of a still more astringent dissonant quality. The manuscript style is somewhat sparer, resembling that of Antill's later works. The date given for this incomplete draft of 1938 is probably fairly accurate, although the score is enclosed in a loose folder dated 1959. Indeed, a diary entry for May 25, 1960, records that Antill 'started The Serpent Woman'; however, it seems likely that the composer may have resurrected the earlier score with the intention of completing and perhaps revising it – only to abandon it once more. The reason may well be similar to that given in a preview of the Melbourne production (2 September 1953) of *Endymion*[40] in which Antill is reported to have said that he originally intended to destroy the score, but subsequently (clearly in light of the planned performance) decided to improve it; however he found that his style had by then (1950s) developed too far and he thus decided to leave it as it was. The music of *The Serpent Woman* has certainly much more in common with Antill's style as seen in his 1930s works than those of the 1950s, and therefore a similar decision as to later completion and revision may well have been made in this case.

The remaining substantial Wheeler opera fragment – *The Lost Child* – carries the following note on the libretto: 'the title is taken from "Das verlorne [*sic*] Kind" – Luther's rendering of John 17:12' (which refers to 'the son of perdition'). The libretto tells the story of Judas Iscariot (the 'lost child' or 'son of perdition') and his repentance and death following his betrayal of Jesus. The typescript of the libretto reads rather like a radio play and raises the intriguing question as to whether this was intended to be a 'radio opera'. However, more conventional stage directions have also been added in a few places in pencil. The musical style follows the general late and post-Debussyan language of *The Serpent Woman* but adds a liberal sprinkling of 'near-Eastern' augmented second/semitone melodic

---

[39] It is perhaps worthy of note that, as well as *Endymion*, Keats wrote a narrative poem on this subject, although there is no evidence that Wheeler and Antill used this as their source.

[40] AP, S5/2.

progressions, together with some stark harmonies of open fifths and fourths – a style which became something of a cliché in scores for such Biblical 'blockbuster' movies from this period as *Ben Hur* and *Quo Vadis*. The use of abrasive bare harmonies of course also points directly to *Corroboree*, in which the 'primitive' style often arises from quite simple relationships of such chords and their combinations in spare dissonant counterpoint, combined with propulsive ostinato rhythms. There are no dates on the manuscripts for *The Lost Child*; but a (later?) scribbled annotation on the cover of one of the sketchbooks 'TAA (?) 9.30a.m. (?) 7p.m.?' appears to refer to a flight with Trans-Australia Airlines (TAA), which was established by the Australian Federal Government in 1946. The presence of this annotation around the time when *Corroboree* was achieving its first performances under Eugene Goossens simply suggests that the score of *The Lost Child* was 'current' among Antill's manuscripts at that time rather than stored away at an earlier period.

Songs and Vocal Ensemble Pieces 1930–1945

During this period Antill also completed a sizeable number of songs and arrangements for voice and piano or for vocal ensembles which he conducted for ABC radio programmes, such as the Melody Makers Quartet (1933), the Mastersingers Male Quartet (1933–1934) and the Wireless Chorus (1936–1941). Of these, the songs for voice and piano, comprising a brief return to the genre during the years 1934 and 1935, continue in a similar vein to those composed during the Conservatorium years. There are some ten of these among the Antill Papers[41] and their styles range from a bland diatonic 'fanfare' style appropriate for the 'Melbourne Centenary Song' (1934), through the bluff English folk-song style of 'To the Heart that Sings Alway' (1935) (cf. Example 1.2), to the more subtle English pastoral idiom of 'If the Heart's Full of Song All Day Long' (1935) (cf. Example 1.3).

The vocal ensemble pieces date mainly from the early 1930s to early 1940s – years during which the ensembles mentioned above existed.[42] The many songs and arrangements Antill produced during these years exhibit a similar range of styles to that of the songs for voice and piano. Among the most notable are settings of two poems by John Wheeler titled 'The Lover's Walk Forsaken' (1941) for unaccompanied vocal quartet (SATB) and 'My Sister the Rain' (1942) for female chorus and string orchestra. These pieces illustrate something of the range of vocal combinations for which Antill composed (the latter work was clearly intended for the Wireless Chorus whereas earlier ensembles were for quartets of solo singers). These songs were of course written while Antill was occupied with the composition of *Corroboree*. However the idiom does not yet betray the more dissonant style that Antill was developing for the ballet score. Clearly, writing

---

[41] AP, S8j/1.
[42] AP, S8i/1+2.

for voices (with presumably fairly limited rehearsal time available) precluded the use of high levels of dissonance and harmonic complexity, while the lyrical texts likewise invited a more sensuous rather than pungent 'soundscape' for such pieces. Both songs are firmly written in the English pastoral manner, including clear-cut tonal centres and a strong modal flavour. However, while 'The Lover's Walk Forsaken' adheres closely to the language of *Endymion*, the idiom of 'My Sister the Rain' contains passages of somewhat more complex harmonic textures, as Example 1.12 demonstrates.

Towards *Corroboree*: Antill and Ballet

The final area to be addressed in this survey of Antill's music prior to *Corroboree* is his creative engagement with the genre of ballet. It was suggested earlier that Antill's preoccupation with ballet composition essentially dates from the time of *Corroboree*. But was *Corroboree* indeed his first essay in the medium, or had he composed other ballet music during these earlier years? It will be recalled in the previous discussion of Antill's Railway years that two ballets are said to date from this period, namely *Capriccio* and *The Circus Comes to Town*. The former work exists complete among the Antill Papers[43] while the latter is a fragment only.[44] However, there are no references to these works in the diaries of the period (i.e. from 1925) which might have provided the firmer chronology such as has been found for the operas discussed in this chapter. Antill's preoccupation with opera composition in his early years rests on a firm foundation of documentary evidence. However his involvement in ballet composition otherwise dates from the time of *Corroboree*, after which there are a number of works in this genre in his output. Apart from the diaries, the only primary evidence from Antill's earlier years – namely his previously mentioned 'Early history'[45] – makes no mention of ballets written during the railway years or the Conservatorium years. However, in the paragraph following the description of the Conservatorium years he writes, 'Followed several exploits – realising that practical experience was the best teacher I went after it in many different ways ...' These include 'learnt and appeared in ballet ...' It is not clear from this document as to just when these 'exploits' took place, but the implication is clearly that it was during and following (but certainly not before) his student years at the Conservatorium – i.e. the late 1920s and early 1930s. Dean and Carell mention his attendance at the ballet classes of Daphne Deane at the Conservatorium and later (?) at the studio of Mischa Burlakov and Louisa Lightfoot.[46] This would suggest that Antill's first attempts at composing ballet music would probably have dated from no earlier than this period – the time,

---

[43] AP, S8d/1.
[44] AP, S8d/1.
[45] AP, S5/2.
[46] Dean and Carell, *Gentle Genius*, pp. 53–4.

Example 1.12 'My Sister The Rain', bb. 1–12

it will be recalled from earlier discussion, that the first Australian ballet scores were commissioned by Lightfoot and Burlakov's fledgling Australian Ballet. It is likely, therefore, that the 'corroboree' scene from *The Glittering Mask* may well have been Antill's first excursion into dance in his theatrical works. Moreover, as will now be seen, a considerably later date for *Capriccio* and *The Circus Comes to Town* becomes more likely than the mid-1920s as given by Dean and Carell and in various work lists. None of the three scores – the piano and orchestral score of *Capriccio* and the incomplete orchestral score of *The Circus Comes to Town* – carries a date.[47] However the score of the latter work, as deposited among the Antill Papers, is attached to a cover lined with two pages of the Sydney *Sunday Sun* magazine dated 24 March 1946, suggesting a composition date as late as the *Corroboree* period. Both *Capriccio* and *The Circus Comes to Town* also display a manuscript style and, as will be discussed below, a musical idiom which appear to be much 'later' than that for the songs of the Conservatorium years or even the three operas from the early 1930s. However, both the short and full scores of *Capriccio* are subtitled 'Background for a mythical Bacchanal' while the short score also appends the words 'from Endymion' to the title – a connection which also appears in some work lists. Its connection with the opera might therefore suggest a composition date in the early 1930s. On the other hand there are no diary entries at the time of the composition of *Endymion* which make any mention of it. Furthermore, as discussed above, the manuscript style (and, to be discussed below, the musical idiom) are clearly much 'later' than that of *Endymion*. Given that the score of the opera was packed away following its completion, as was his habit when moving on to further projects failing any prospects of performances, it therefore appears more probable that Antill wrote *Capriccio* for the 1953 performances since it seems unlikely that he would have composed a work, intended to be connected with such a discarded opera, as a separate project during the intervening period. Antill made it clear in many newspaper interviews at the time of the opera's première that he resurrected the opera only for these performances. No mention of ballet music is made in the reviews of the Sydney première; however Dean and Carell's catalogue of Antill's works notes that *Capriccio* was 'performed Melbourne on programme with *Endymion*' – i.e. at the September 1953 Melbourne performances.[48] Additionally, at least one review of the Melbourne première refers at one point to the 'ballet music' of which there is, of course, none in the original *Endymion* score.[49] The Dana Navytis Creative Dance Group is mentioned in this context as 'lightening the static character of the work'.

Of primary significance is the fact that the musical language of these two ballets is significantly closer to that of *Corroboree* and later works, than to the gentler post-Romantic and 'pastoral' styles of *Endymion* and works already examined from the

---

[47] AP, S8d/1.
[48] Dean and Carell, *Gentle Genius*, p. 201. Interestingly, the full score of *Capriccio* is enclosed in a folder dated 1956! (AP, S8d/1).
[49] Melbourne *Sun*, 3 September 1953.

1930s – and even of the two Wheeler songs of the early 1940s. This discrepancy of melodic and harmonic idiom is strikingly apparent in *Capriccio* as the following examples will show. There is no indication as to its place in an enlarged version of the opera; but the most likely insertion point would seem to be the 'Festival of Pan' in scene 2. Although the probable dramatic context of the interpolated ballet makes the colourful harmony and scoring eminently appropriate, the style is nevertheless considerably more 'hard edged' than that of the opera (cf. Examples 1.5–1.8). The opening passage (see Example 1.13) shows a rather angular melody for oboe accompanied solely by a tambourine.

Example 1.13   *Capriccio*, opening

A later passage (see Example 1.14 below) shows a harmonically dissonant idiom ranging from the use of parallel triads, polytriads and (in the final two bars of the example) the use of chords of bare fifths and octaves moving in dissonant counterpoint.

A similar more astringent use of dissonance may be seen in the surviving opening section of *The Circus Comes to Town*. The style is lighter and the texture sparer, in keeping with the subject, but the level of dissonance is nevertheless greater than in works of the 1920s and 1930s as can be seen in the opening bars of the prelude (Example 1.15 below).

It is clear, from perusal of these examples, that Antill has now moved into a sound world closer to that of *Corroboree* and, as subsequent chapters will show, of Antill's post-*Corroboree* output – a sound world more directly related to the idiom of ballet scores written around the time of the First World War by such composers as Bartók, Prokofiev and Stravinsky. Interestingly, the most direct prior glimpse of something approaching this style, in Antill's output definitely of the pre-*Corroboree* period, was in the 'corroboree' scene from *The Glittering Mask* back in 1931. This music (see Example 1.11) was at a substantial remove from the

Example 1.14   *Capriccio*, second section

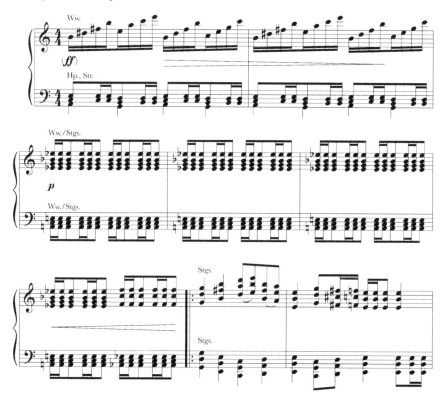

otherwise diatonic simplicity of the rest of the opera – and indeed is somewhat more overtly dissonant than any of the music Antill was otherwise writing during the 1930s. This suggests that Antill was aware of this 'primitivist' style from this time at least, but chose not to adopt it for his other (vocal) music. The 'corroboree' subject clearly evoked such a response even here and this makes the apparently sudden adoption of such an idiom in the later ballet more understandable. Indeed, if the sketch of *The Circus Comes to Town* dates – as seems likely – from the mid-1940s, and if *Capriccio* dates from the time of the première of *Endymion*, then this early 'corroboree' – and perhaps some passages from the incomplete Wheeler operas – appear to show the only definite evidence of anything remotely prophetic of the 'corroboree' style in Antill's previous output. Of course the lack of definitive dates for *Capriccio* and *The Circus Comes to Town* makes this point conjectural, but it would seem that Antill's turn to the more dissonant style of *Corroboree* had few precedents in his output and was the result of a deliberate shift of emphasis which had much to do with both the turn to the more overtly rhythmic vitality appropriate to ballet composition and also to the sense of stylistic appropriateness for such a 'primitive' form of musical expression (to Western ears) as a corroboree. A detailed examination of the strikingly more dissonant and abrasive style of *Corroboree* will be made in the following chapter.

Example 1.15   *The Circus Comes to Town*, opening

Chapter 2
Corroboree – The Turning Point

Introduction

> *Corroboree* was the first breakthrough for an Australian contemporary style. I hope it was, without being presumptuous, one step ahead in the right direction. Don't let us get away from the fact that we're Australians and we don't want to get into European ways, or any other ways. We want something distinctly Australian. I hoped that *Corroboree* began this contemporary style.[1]

Thus commented Antill to his biographers, Dean and Carell, some four decades after the première of his music for the ballet *Corroboree* in 1946. This comment highlights two centrally important issues surrounding Antill's music from the time of *Corroboree*: first, his aspiration to produce a musical art that was distinctly and exclusively Australian; and second, his claim that *Corroboree* was a work that inaugurated such an art, as well as originating a style that was distinctively 'contemporary' in Australian terms. While there is no doubt that the advent of *Corroboree* was a landmark in the history of Australian art music, the above claims need to be examined critically in order to accurately evaluate *Corroboree* both in its proper historical context as well as in the context of Antill's development as a composer and his place in the history of Australian art music generally. This chapter will attempt such an evaluation, first addressing the two aspects of Antill's statement: the issue of his aspiration to create an Australian national identity in his music, and the genesis of *Corroboree* as a reflection of this new artistic commitment; and the question of *Corroboree* being written in – and pioneering – a 'contemporary style' in Australian art music.

'Australianism' in Music

The genesis of a sense of 'Australianism' as expressed in musical terms might be said to date from the earliest years of permanent white settlement in New South Wales, with the advent of patriotic songs such as 'The Trumpet Sounds Australia's Fame'[2] – and here one might note the identification of the colony as 'Australia' long before any notion of nationhood existed. Likewise, the fascination of composers with Aboriginal music, which was later to form such

---

[1] Dean and Carell, *Gentle Genius*, p. 91.
[2] Covell, *Australia's Music*, p. 10.

a significant aspect of perceptions of an Australian musical identity, can also be said to date from these early colonial years with the appearance of transcriptions and arrangements of Aboriginal melodies by Isaac Nathan and John Lhotsky (1795–1865). Although a song by Lhotsky (1834), said to be based on an Aboriginal woman's song from southern NSW, was 'humbly inscribed as the first specimen of Australian music',[3] this fascination was at that time simply for an exotic musical culture rather than as a means to an 'authentic' expression of an Australian musical identity. The latter was not to develop until the early years of the twentieth century. A major catalyst for a more serious engagement with Aboriginal culture on the part of Australian artists, writers and composers was provided by the pioneering anthropological work of Sir Baldwin Spencer (1860–1929), F.J. Gillen (1856–1912) and others. The deeper awareness of the nature of Aboriginal culture arising from these researches, and the desire of creative artists to identify with its link with the landscape and 'Dreamtime', was first demonstrated in the works of the poet Bernard O'Dowd (1866–1953), whose poem *The Bush* (1912) was also to become the inspiration for a tone poem of the same name (1923) by Fritz Hart (cf. Chapter 1). This period also saw the writings and compositions of Henry Tate (1873–1926), who advocated the creation of a distinctly Australian music based on the imitation of bush sounds, bird calls and Aboriginal music.[4] Even the expatriate Percy Grainger, who throughout his life fiercely proclaimed his Australian musical identity, maintained theories regarding the 'unbroken' nature of the Australian landscape and the need for a musical expression that would reflect its special character. These developments were all part of a noticeable upsurge in nationalistic sentiments in the arts of Australia from the period just prior to Federation (1901), but especially following the First World War. By 1933, the newly formed Australian Broadcasting Commission was to proclaim its aim to 'lay the foundations of an essentially "national musical literature"'.[5] During the 1930s there were similar calls among musicians and critics – calls which increased over the next two decades, including suggestions to make use of Aboriginal music as a means to create an Australian school of composition.

The equation of Aboriginal and landscape evocation with the notion of a genuine Australian national art found perhaps its most striking expression with the founding, in 1938, of the Jindyworobak Club by the South Australian poet Rex Ingamells (1913–1955). A small group of writers soon joined Ingamells's movement, including Ian Mudie (1911–1976), Flexmore Hudson (1913–1988), William Hart-Smith (1911–1990) and Roland Robinson (1912–1992). The poems and essays by these writers and others formed the substance of a series of annual

---

[3] David Symons, 'Composition in Australia (1): From European Settlement to 1960' in Warren Bebbington (ed.), *The Oxford Companion to Australian Music* (Melbourne: Oxford University Press, 1997), p. 138.

[4] Henry Tate, *Australian Musical Possibilities* (Melbourne: Edward A. Vidler, 1924); and compositions such as *Dawn: A Bush Rhapsody* (1922).

[5] Hill, 'Clive Douglas and the ABC', pp. 239 and 242 (n. 32).

collections titled *Jindyworobak Anthology* (1938–1953). Ingamells announced his new movement in a pamphlet titled 'Conditional Culture'.[6] Borrowing the Aboriginal word 'jindyworobak' and its meaning 'to annex or join' from a volume of short stories by James Devaney (1890–1976) titled *The Vanished Tribes* (1929), Ingamells announced the aims of his newly established literary movement in the following terms: 'The Jindyworobaks, I say, are those individuals who are endeavouring to free Australian art from whatever alien influences trammel it, that is, to bring it into proper contact with its material'.[7] For Ingamells, the 'conditions' referred to in the title of his manifesto were threefold:

1. A clear recognition of environmental values;
2. The debunking of much nonsense;
3. An understanding of Australia's history and traditions, primeval, colonial and modern.[8]

The most basic of the above 'conditions' is the first, in which 'environmental values' refers to the aspiration of the Jindyworobak artist to form a spiritual identification with the Australian landscape; and the main (though not the only) pathway to this identification would be via the Aboriginal myths and legends of their 'Dreamtime'. A similar sentiment had been expressed by Bernard O'Dowd some 25 years earlier in his poem, *The Bush* (referred to previously). The second 'condition' – 'the debunking of much nonsense' – concerned Ingamells's desire to rid Australian poetry of Victorian English 'poeticisms' – that is, of the use of archaic pronouns such as 'thou', 'thy' and 'thee' and such pastoral imagery as 'wood', 'brook' or 'dale' in favour of 'Australian' landscape terms such as 'bush', 'scrub' or 'creek'. Ingamells also made copious use in his poetry of Aboriginal words, which he considered would evoke an authentically Australian flavour through their use and sheer 'sound value' – an approach that was less true of other Jindyworobak poets. The third 'condition' was the wish to embrace the entire heritage of Australia – 'primeval [Aboriginal], colonial and modern' – in order to create a total cultural and artistic identity. From today's perspective, the Jindyworobak philosophy may be seen in terms of 'cultural appropriation', as the preoccupation with things Aboriginal was not primarily for the sake of Aboriginal culture itself, nor yet did it engage with the social problem of that culture's relationship with a white displacing culture. It was rather a means for the white Australian to achieve a similarly deep spiritual link with the unique Australian environment. In the Jindyworobak period, however, the concept of 'cultural appropriation' would not have occurred to non-indigenous artists, and certainly not as an ethical issue.

---

[6] Ingamells, 'Conditional Culture', pp. 245–65.
[7] Ibid., p. 249.
[8] Ibid.

The nature of 'Jindyworobakism' has been discussed elsewhere at much greater length, particularly in terms of its link with the work of a number of composers who were active in the years of the Jindyworobak literary movement – i.e. from the late 1930s until the mid- to late 1950s.[9] These composers included Clive Douglas, Alfred and Mirrie Hill, James Penberthy (1917–1999) and, of course, Antill. Of these it was Douglas and Antill, both ABC employees, who were the first, during the mid- to late 1930s, to turn to a major preoccupation with Australian subjects – especially Aboriginal – and to consciously aspire to an Australian musical idiom. This followed the earlier allegiance of both composers to late Victorian and early twentieth-century English literary sources and late Romantic and English 'pastoral' musical styles (cf. the discussion of Antill's early works in Chapter 1). Both Douglas and Antill were to confirm this new Australian orientation in later statements which forthrightly espoused Jindyworobak-like artistic aims. Antill's statement at the beginning of this chapter clearly recalls his aim in *Corroboree* to produce a music that was overtly Australian rather than European; and it is consistent with Ingamells's reference to 'free Australian art from whatever alien influences trammel it'. The subject of *Corroboree* unmistakably implies the choice of an Aboriginal subject as a means to this end. Douglas, in 1956, published an even more direct and comprehensive statement clearly paralleling the spirit of Jindyworobakism:

> The absence of a national music in the white man's idiom adds to the difficulties which confront an Australian composer who attempts to infuse his music with a recognisably Australian identity. Unless some link can be forged which will serve to connect the composer's thought to the land itself, the music written will be strongly derivative of what has been recorded in some other country earlier.
>
> A musical idiom must be found which is so entirely Australian that no other influence can be felt. In this arduous search the imported traditions of the white man disappear in the mists of long ago before he came to this country; and only there, in the mystical "dream-time" of antiquity can be found the all-important link – the tribal ceremonial chants of the brown man.[10]

The question of an 'Australian musical idiom' will be taken up later in this chapter. As a general observation here, one may discern a remarkable naïvety in the aspirations of both the Jindyworobak writers and like-minded composers to

---

[9] David Symons, 'The Jindyworobak Connection in Australian Music c. 1940–1960', *Context: Journal of Music Research*, 23 (Autumn 2002), pp. 33–48; David Symons, 'Words and Music: Clive Douglas and the Jindyworobak Manifesto' in Fiona Richards (ed.), *The Soundscapes of Australia: Music, Place and Spirituality* (Aldershot: Ashgate, 2007), pp. 93–116.

[10] Clive Douglas, 'Folk-song and the Brown Man – A Means to an Australian Expression in Symphonic Music', *The Canon*, 10/3 (1956), p. 81.

produce an art independent of European culture. The poetry of the Jindyworobaks was, of course, English lyric verse, as at least one commentator has pointed out,[11] while the musical idioms of Douglas, Antill and other composers with similar aims in this period were firmly based on the styles and techniques of early twentieth-century Western art music – impressionism, English 'pastoralism' and finally the 'primitivism' of early Stravinsky and others.

Despite the clear commonality of aims between these composers and those of the Jindyworobaks, it is curious that there has been an almost complete lack of acknowledgement of any link between the composers and the writers: none on the part of the composers and only a few oblique references to music on the part of the writers.[12] It is perhaps not surprising, however, that such nationalist aspirations should be shared between creators working in different artistic media during the same period. Indeed, it is the commonality of aims referred to above that has led Covell[13] and later writers to refer to Douglas and others as 'Jindyworobak composers'. Clearly Antill's *Corroboree* and (as will be seen in the following chapters) later works with related subject matter resonate with this commonality.

The Genesis of *Corroboree*

Antill's diaries and other available sources provide no direct statement as to the immediate impetus behind the composition of *Corroboree* on which, as noted in Chapter 1, Antill worked from around 1936 to 1944. This period of course directly coincides with the previously noted calls for Australian composers to pursue a recognisably 'Australian' character in their choice of subject matter as well as musical idiom. This led Clive Douglas to first investigate Australia's post-settlement history, and only subsequently to study Aboriginal culture. The first fruit of this study was his one-act opera *A Bush Legend* (1938), from which two orchestral pieces – titled *Carwoola* and *Corroboree* – were extracted for concert performance. Douglas's work was a direct response to an article by the critic Thorold Waters which appeared in 1937 directly encouraging the ABC to 'foster a distinctive national creative school'.[14] It is unlikely that Antill, as a fellow ABC staffer with Douglas, would have been oblivious to this and similar calls, and it is significant that it was around this time that he began serious work on his own *Corroboree*. His study of Aboriginal culture was possibly even more intensive than that of Douglas, as is evidenced by the copious descriptive and illustrative

---

[11] Brian Elliot, 'Introduction' in Brian Elliott (ed.), *The Jindyworobaks* (St Lucia: University of Queensland Press, 1979), pp. xxvii, xxx.

[12] See discussion of this issue in Symons, 'The Jindyworobak Connection', pp. 35–8.

[13] See Covell, *Australia's Music*, p. 150.

[14] Thorold Waters, 'Australia Tunes a Strange Lay', *The Listener In* (6 February 1937), p. 16; quoted in Hill, 'Clive Douglas and the ABC', p. 238 and n. 29.

material to be found in Antill's two autograph full scores[15] – veritable (if amateur) anthropological documents as well as music scores.

It is, of course, not difficult to account for the choice of a corroboree as the subject of a musical work depicting Aboriginal culture. The term 'corroboree' first came to be used by Europeans in the very earliest years of settlement in the colony of New South Wales as a corruption of an Aboriginal word from the Dharug language of the Sydney region, denoting all kinds of Aboriginal dancing and ceremonial. As Chris Sullivan has noted in *Currency Companion to Music and Dance in Australia,* '[t]he corroboree became the archetype of Aboriginal musical culture for Europeans, and it quickly entered the realm of public entertainment'.[16] As was also noted in the Introduction to this book, Antill had been impressed by his witnessing, as a boy (probably in 1913), one such piece of public entertainment – a 'make believe corroboree' by an Aboriginal troupe – and had written down some melodic and especially rhythmic ideas which he had kept over the ensuing 25 years or so. In Chapter 1 it was also noted that Antill's earliest practical involvement with ballet occurred in the late 1920s or early 1930s; and by 1931, he had composed a 'corroboree' dance scene in his light opera *The Glittering Mask* (cf. Example 1.10) – a work that has never been performed. Meanwhile, in 1933, there was premièred a musical play titled *Collitts' Inn*, with music by Varney Monk, which also contained a corroboree scene. This play, set in colonial NSW, was immensely popular, while the corroboree scene, reportedly based on material 'taken down by Harry Jacobs ... from an Aboriginal woman of the Illawarra tribe'[17] was regarded by critics as 'an impressive and weird sight' and 'easily the most spectacular feature of the show'.[18] It could therefore be argued that the idea of the corroboree as the typical representative of Aboriginal culture for Europeans continued to be alive and well in the public consciousness at this time. In this overall context, then, the choice, by both Antill and Douglas (each apparently oblivious of the other), of the corroboree as a fitting and striking manifestation of their new found allegiance to musical 'Australianism' can be seen as hardly surprising.

Finally, the medium of ballet is, of course, the obvious one for the depiction of a corroboree. Moreover, as pointed out in Chapter 1, Antill's significant turn from opera to ballet composition at this time may also have been spurred by the

---

[15] There are two extant manuscript full scores in Antill's hand, complete with these illustrations: one among the Antill Papers (AP, S8a/1) and the other in the State Library of NSW (MLMSS7072, Safe 1/249).

[16] Chris Sullivan, 'Indigenous Adaptations' in John Whiteoak and Aline Scott-Maxwell, *The Currency Companion to Music and Dance in Australia* (Sydney: Currency House, 2003), p. 333.

[17] Hill, 'Clive Douglas and the ABC', p. 241.

[18] Bronwen Arthur, 'The Pub with no Peer, or *Collitts' Inn*: The First Australian Musical Romance' in Nicholas Brown et al. (eds), *One Hand on the Manuscript: Music in Australian Cultural Life 1930–1960* (Canberra: Humanities Research Centre, Australian National University, 1995), p. 131.

upsurge of interest in the medium by Australian artists and musicians – eventually including composers – during the late 1930s and early 1940s when ballet scores by Australian composers began to appear in significant numbers for the first time.

It is now time to examine Antill's music for *Corroboree* in order to address the remaining issue in his statement quoted at the beginning of this chapter – that is, the degree to which this work was a 'breakthrough for an Australian contemporary style', and why his *Corroboree* became so celebrated as such a notable landmark in Australian artistic history.

A 'Breakthrough for an Australian Contemporary Style'

The first point to address regarding Antill's claim to create – indeed originate – an 'Australian contemporary style' is precisely what he meant by this phrase. Nowhere, in the statement quoted at the beginning of this chapter, does he define or describe what he means by the term 'contemporary'. However, in a comment made later apropos of his later ballet *The Unknown Land* (1956), Antill stated:

> It is written in the contemporary style. I always write anything to do with Aborigines in the contemporary style. Why? Because there's nothing new, and the contemporary style is so old, it is primitive.[19]

The equation of 'contemporary' and 'primitive' here provides the all-important clue – namely that Antill's conception of 'contemporary' had nothing to do with the more 'progressive' developments of twentieth-century Western art music such as the atonal and twelve-note music of the Viennese School, let alone the even more radical modernism of Varèse, early Cage and others; but rather the ostinato-dominated, abrasively dissonant idiom which is clearly derived from the so-called 'primitivist' ballet scores of the World War 1 years by Stravinsky, Bartók, Prokofiev and others. This style, though aesthetically different, is technically closely related to Debussy's emancipated, non-narrative approach to tonality and form – a situation recognised by Constant Lambert in his now famous characterisation of *The Rite of Spring* as 'the logical outcome of a barbaric attitude applied to the technique of impressionism'.[20] Thus the origins of Antill's 'Australian contemporary style' in *Corroboree* lie deep in the early twentieth century, more or less contemporary with both impressionism and English pastoralism. From a purely historical point of view, then, the leap from the post-impressionist and pastoral styles of Antill's 1930s compositions – *Endymion*, the later Wheeler songs and opera fragments and the 'Corroboree' from *The Glittering Mask* (cf. Chapter 1) – is not such a huge one. The idioms of the two reportedly early ballets discussed in Chapter 1 – *Capriccio*

---

[19] Dean and Carell, *Gentle Genius*, p. 145.
[20] Constant Lambert, *Music Ho! A Study of Music in Decline* (London: Faber, 1934), p. 34.

and *The Circus Comes to Town* (fragment) – are, as was shown, even closer to the language of *Corroboree* in their freer use of dissonance; although, as also previously discussed, it seems likely that neither of these works actually antedated *Corroboree*. Therefore the now predominantly dissonant idiom of *Corroboree* was indeed for Antill a 'breakthrough' in terms of his musical style, if not of basic compositional technique. In terms of its relationship to wider contemporary European and American trends, there had been a number (admittedly small) of earlier Australian works that, if less strikingly dissonant, are nevertheless at least as harmonically 'progressive' – for example, some works dating from the 1920s and 1930s by Margaret Sutherland and Roy Agnew (who, incidentally, wrote a 'primitivist' dissonant piano piece called *Dance of the Wild Men* as early as 1919). The idiom of such works extends from late Scriabin, Cyril Scott and later Frank Bridge through to later Bartók and between-the-wars neo-classicism. Nevertheless it was the confronting dissonance, striking rhythmic energy as well as brilliant orchestration, together with its colourful Australian theme that ensured *Corroboree*'s deserved local and international success as truly a 'breakthrough' in the history of Australian art music. Indeed, it was a work that, more than any other single composition, brought new perspectives to the Australian scene which had hitherto been dominated by more conservative styles – principally influenced by late Romanticism and the milder sounds of English pastoralism. Even Douglas's *Corroboree*, not yet performed at this time, spoke a far less dissonant – albeit post-Debussyan – musical language than Antill's ballet. The following musical analysis of *Corroboree*, therefore, is intended to provide as clear a perspective as possible of its distinctive character.

Corroboree – An Analysis

Although much has been written about *Corroboree* – principally its overall character and historical significance in Australia's musical development, as well as its reception history and accounts of the 1950 and 1954 choreographic productions – very little analysis has been undertaken of its formal structure or its musical style or language. To begin with, it is quite clear that Antill had a stage production (as well as his own basic scenario of varying detail) for *Corroboree* in mind from its conception: given his preoccupation with compositions for the theatre from his early years, this is hardly surprising. The seven movements that make up the complete 45-minute score[21] are given specific titles and also indications of 'characters' involved in the respective 'numbers' as follows:

---

[21] Goossens's performances of the work in 1946 in Sydney and elsewhere were of the 'suite' of approximately 16 minutes extracted from the full score. The precise origin and content of this and the 'second suite' made in 1950 will be discussed later.

1. Welcome Ceremony: Witchetty Grub men assisted by members of the Emu Totem
2. Dance to the Evening Star: by the Thippa Thippa and Bellbird people
3. A Rain Dance: by the Frog Totem assisted by Fish men
4. Spirit of the Wind: demonstrated by the Snake Totem
5. Homage to the Rising Sun: Kangaroo men
6. The Morning Star Dance: by the Hakea Flower Totem
7. Procession of Totems and Closing Fire Ceremony: in which representatives of the Lace Lizard, Cockatoo, Honey Ant, Wild Cat and Small Fly Totems participate. Much usage of Boomerang, Spear and Fire Stick.

There are also numerous 'stage directions' indicating the presence and actions of particular participants in the first and last movements (and very briefly in movements 3 and 5) given in the following sources: a choreographic outline and commentary provided by Antill, located among the Antill Papers (and also in a collection of material relating to *Corroboree* in the State Library of NSW) and reproduced in Dean and Carell's biography,[22] as well as in Appendix 2 to this book; and also in the manuscript piano and full scores. In the subsequent analysis of the movements, these sources will be collectively referred to as 'Antill's scenario'. As mentioned earlier, the manuscript full scores also contain a wealth of descriptive and illustrative material – but all the above material has been omitted (save for the full movement titles) in the published full score.[23] The elimination of the copious illustrations may have been an economic, or even a cultural, consideration;[24] however the total elimination of any reference to Antill's scenario makes the final published score (presumably with the composer's approval) essentially an autonomous concert work, the descriptive titles of the movements acting as some kind of imaginary 'programme' as for a 'tone poem'. The 'programme' is introduced by the composer, on the title page preceding the list of movements, as a brief background description of the phenomenon of the corroboree as the traditional dance ceremony of the Australian Aboriginal.

It is clear from the above, however, that there was never any narrative-type scenario envisaged for *Corroboree*, and that the work was conceived as a suite

---

[22] AP, S8a/1; Dean and Carell, *Gentle Genius*, pp. 193–4; also State Library of NSW, MLMSS7072 (safe 1/249).

[23] Score published by Boosey and Hawkes, London, in 1953.

[24] Although the idea of Europeans representing an indigenous subject was not seen as 'cultural appropriation' at this time, the publishers may well even then have wished to avoid any cultural sensitivities regarding the public dissemination of representations of material possibly deemed sensitive or even 'secret' by indigenous people. After Antill's death, when the illustrated manuscript score of *Corroboree* was deposited in the NLA, protests were made by indigenous people on just these grounds. The score was therefore restricted to viewing by special permission only. See Vincent Plush, 'A Timeline of Corroboree' in Vincent Plush et al. (eds), *Encounters: Meetings in Australian Music: Essays, Images, Interviews* (South Brisbane: Queensland Conservatorium Research Centre, 2005), p. 30.

of discrete dances evoking the general character of the corroboree as a kind of stage pageant. Indeed, in all the manuscript scores as well as the first page of the published score (a facsimile reproduction of a manuscript copy score), the work is subtitled 'A Ballet Suite for Orchestra', and it is only on the cover and printed title page of the published score that this designation has been altered to 'Symphonic Ballet'. This subtitle evokes similar designations affixed to early twentieth-century ballet scores such as 'choreographic symphony' (as for Ravel's *Daphnis and Chloe*) or 'dance poem' (cf. 'poème dansé' for Debussy's *Jeux* and Dukas's *La Péri*). However, despite this now more 'organic' title, *Corroboree* is essentially episodic in its construction with a minimum of thematic or motivic links between movements, and no traditional thematic development. Although the stage directions and identification of certain 'characters' in Antill's scenario sometimes refer to specific musical sections or themes, there is little or no evidence (save in one instance to be identified later) of any obvious 'leitmotivic' connections between them.

As to the general character of the work's structure, thematic material and harmonic idiom, the music is, like its early twentieth-century 'primitivist' antecedents, cast in static, 'block'-type sections articulated primarily through the devices of ostinato and pedal point. There is very little scope for thematic expansion: rather, the melodic material is largely built from brief, repetitive motifs. Many critics have noted this as well as the widespread use of abrasive dissonance and propulsive rhythms as most closely related to Stravinsky's *The Rite of Spring*. However, Antill has maintained that he had not heard Stravinsky's famous ballet when he composed *Corroboree*.[25] Nevertheless, Antill's diaries for 1936 record his attendance at performances that year of the earlier Stravinsky ballets (*The Firebird* and *Petrushka*), performed in both Sydney and Melbourne during the Australasian tours of De Basil's Ballets Russes (cf. Chapter 1).[26] Both the above scores contain the use of polytonality as well as varying degrees of 'primitivism', most evident in the 'Danse infernale' from *The Firebird*. Other works which Antill most likely would have heard in Sydney during the 1920s and 1930s include Holst's *The Planets* (with its abrasively dissonant, ostinato-driven opening 'Mars' movement), which was performed by Arundel Orchard with the NSW Conservatorium orchestra in 1925;[27] and Vaughan Williams's ballet *Job*,

---

[25] Brown, 'John Antill' p. 49. Ironically, Goossens conducted the first performance in Australia of *The Rite of Spring* only five days after the *Corroboree* première! See Martin Buzacott, *The Rite of Spring: 75 Years of ABC Music Making* (Sydney: ABC Books, 2007), p. 207.

[26] The programme details for all the Ballets Russes performances during these tours may be found in an archive based in the National Library of Australia titled 'The Ballet [*sic*] Russes in Australasia 1936–1940', catalogue no. aus-vn 143713.

[27] Orchard, W. Arundel, *Music in Australia: More than 150 Years of Development* (Melbourne: Georgian Press, 1952), p. 78.

also performed by the Conservatorium orchestra, under its later director Edgar Bainton in 1937.[28]

A further aspect of Antill's musical language may also be noted here – that of the evocation of Aboriginal music – as this bears directly upon not only Antill's, but also like-minded composers' aspirations to create an independent Australian idiom. It will be recalled that a principal technique of the Jindyworobak poets was the use of specifically Australian imagery, including the liberal use of Aboriginal words (especially in Ingamells's case) to create not only an Australian frame of reference, but also an Australian 'sound'. The response of composers such as Douglas and both Alfred and Mirrie Hill during the Jindyworobak period was to make use of literal transcriptions of Aboriginal melodies – with their characteristic 'song descent' and 'terminal recitative' on the lowest note – to create as direct an association as possible with a uniquely Australian sound. Notwithstanding this, the actual surrounding harmonic style tended to dilute any sense of 'authenticity' to varying extents. In Antill's case, no use is made of such direct quotation of Aboriginal melodies; but there is ample evidence of his attempt to evoke a 'soundscape' redolent (at least for Europeans) of the corroboree, via his use of rhythm and especially orchestral texture.

What follows is a general examination of the chief stylistic (melodic, rhythmic, harmonic and textural) and formal characteristics to be found in the seven movements of *Corroboree* in turn. References will be made to Antill's scenario (see Appendix 2) only where there are descriptive links to specific themes, which are otherwise treated quite autonomously.

Welcome Ceremony

This substantial opening movement (of approximately eight minutes' duration) is cast in a loose ternary form with an extended introduction. The introduction contains perhaps the best example in the entire score of Antill's direct evocation of the Aboriginal 'soundscape' referred to earlier. This is achieved through the use of intermittent drones by the contrabassoon and bass clarinet, imitating the didjeridu, together with the typical accompanying clapping sounds, here played on actual Aboriginal trora sticks introduced into the orchestra. During this opening section there is at least a hint of the melodic descent typical of much Aboriginal singing, although these are brief, repeated semiquaver flourishes and are not literal transcriptions of actual Aboriginal melodies. Further evocation of the characteristic sounds of the corroboree may be heard in the brief 'shrieks' in the upper strings and woodwinds during this opening. However the main theme that emerges in the first and last sections of the movement is a distinctly non-Aboriginal, modal and, uncharacteristically, more or less periodic melody with a rather 'jazzy' flavour played initially by the trumpet, and later by horns and

---

[28] Helen Bainton, *Remembered on Waking: Edgar L. Bainton* (Sydney: Currawong Publishing, 1960), pp. 74–5.

flutes. This theme (see Example 2.1), which Antill has labelled the 'Witchetty Grub Theme' in the scenario, is striking in its character, since the melodic material of the whole ballet otherwise consists of brief repetitive motifs or, in the case of more extended themes, melodic and/or rhythmic patterns which are open ended, but internally repetitive.

Example 2.1   *Corroboree*, 'Welcome Ceremony', bb. 66–68

As can be seen from the above example, the 'Witchetty Grub' theme is heard over a dissonant ostinato based on a pitch platform of A held throughout. However, periodically during the ensuing repetitions of the theme, there also appears a brief dissonant descending figure comprising the notes B, F and E♭. This figure, identified by Antill as representing movements of the medicine man, presages the main ostinato motif of the 'Procession of Totems' (cf. Example 2.10 below). Indeed, the final movement also recapitulates the brief semiquaver melodic descents referred to above (see also Example 2.9); and while these are the only two obvious recollections of the 'Welcome Ceremony' in the final movement, the two movements are similar in character; and this similarity imparts an overall sense of closure to the ballet's structure. The tonal centre of A, underpinning the main theme of the 'Welcome Ceremony', periodically recurs, for instance in the second movement (see below) and again in the two final movements; and is the tonal centre on which the entire work concludes.

The 'Welcome Ceremony', together with the even longer 'Procession of Totems and Closing Fire Ceremony', are the most substantial movements in the score as well as the most abrasively 'barbaric'; they also use the most extended resources of the orchestra, especially the large percussion section. Example 2.2 quotes a typical example of the more propulsive as well as complex, layered rhythms, to be found in the more lively middle section of the 'Welcome Ceremony'.

The five central movements are all much shorter (lasting in total around the same time – 18 minutes – as the 'Procession of Totems and Closing Fire Ceremony') and are mostly more lightly (though no less colourfully) orchestrated.

Example 2.2 *Corroboree*, 'Welcome Ceremony', bb. 196–202(1)

Dance to the Evening Star

This short, lightly-scored movement is in rondo form, the principal material comprising a melody for oboe, appearing twice in full and finally as a brief reminiscence, interspersed with episodes of delicate, colouristic material highlighting celeste and high strings (in one passage playing harmonics, perhaps evoking the sound of the bellbird, whose totem is represented in this movement). The tonal centre of A is emphasised especially in the principal theme (Example 2.3), which in its initial presentation (it is later accompanied by timpani and triangle only) is heard against the static pedal notes A and E in muted strings.

Example 2.3   *Corroboree*, 'Dance to the Evening Star', bb. 2–5(2)

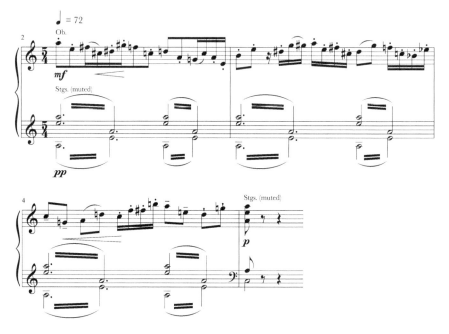

The delicate, colourful textures heard throughout impart a typically 'impressionist' character to the movement.

A Rain Dance

This movement is once again ostinato-dominated after a long introduction accounting for approximately a quarter of its four-and-a-half minutes' duration. The introduction is, like 'Dance to the Evening Star', sparsely scored; but the scoring is harder edged, with much use of percussion (notably including the thunder sheet at its climax), interspersed with brief motifs which are described in Antill's scenario as the croaking of frogs – a reference to the 'Frog Totem' given in the title. The main body of the movement comprises two alternating, ostinato-accompanied sections: A–B–A^1–B^1. The A section highlights an extended vibraphone solo (Example 2.4) accompanied by a 'stamping' ostinato on low woodwinds, piano, horns and harp (in the A^1 section joined by strings).

Example 2.4 *Corroboree*, 'A Rain Dance', bb. 98–105

In the A^1 section (at a slightly faster tempo), the scoring is similar, but the vibraphone melody is new, the melody shown in Example 2.4 reappearing later in the strings and winds. At its first appearance, the ostinato is identified in the scenario as the continuous croaking of the frogs; while the A♭ tonal centre shown in Example 2.4 moves to C in the recapitulation, on which centre the movement closes.

The B sections are likewise ostinato-accompanied, but notably interspersed with tremolandi for high strings and woodwinds as well as vibraphone and triangle (described in the scenario as 'incantations to the clouds'). In the final climactic section these are joined by fortissimo low wind, piano and percussion, notably including the thunder sheet – the scenario commenting 'Incantations are answered – thunder crash and coda'. For the coda, Antill injects a delightfully witty touch by concluding incongruously with a very thinly disguised perfect cadence in C major, following the dissonant climax preceding it.

Spirit of the Wind

The title of this movement is musically evoked by swiftly rising and falling semiquaver chromatic scales largely for flutes and violins (Example 2.5), while the whole movement is a *perpetuum mobile* in 7/8 metre, with a characteristic accompanying motif for timpani, joined by various other sections of the orchestra.

Example 2.5   *Corroboree*, 'Spirit of the Wind', bb. 1–12

This material dominates almost completely save for three brief episodes (thus imparting a rondo-like form to the movement) in which the rhythmic motif drops out but the *perpetuum mobile* effect is maintained by a continuous rhythmic figure of three quavers and two crotchets. The third of these episodes (Example 2.6) is the most densely scored, dissonant climactic section in which the 'wind' semiquavers are absent for the only time in the movement.

Example 2.6 *Corroboree*, 'Spirit of the Wind', bb. 83–90(1)

The tonal centre of this movement is ambiguous, but the persistence of the rhythmic motif of Example 2.5, at mostly the same pitch throughout, obliquely suggests C once again (cf. the previous movement).

Homage to the Rising Sun

This brief movement (approximately two and a half minutes) is also dominated by a single motif which is extended and continuously varied in an open-ended manner. As can be seen in Example 2.7 below, the basic tonal centre is clearly C, which is stated at the outset in a brief ostinato, followed by a flourish in upper strings and winds prior to the initial appearance of the main motif in cellos, double basses and bassoons, identified in the scenario as the hopping of kangaroos.

Example 2.7   *Corroboree*, 'Homage to the Rising Sun', bb. 1–11

The movement is in two broad sections, the first alternating the material quoted in Example 2.7 with a tonally and texturally contrasting episode. This episode varies the main motif beneath the flourishes of bars 4–8 of Example 2.7 (which however provide an inverted pedal of high Cs) and culminates in a return to the C tonal centre hammered out by the strings. The second main section largely comprises an expansion of the main motif, first scored as in Example 2.7 and later as an extended solo for muted trumpet. Material from the first section gradually reappears and the texture rises to an emphatic climax once again culminating in hammered out C-based chords in the whole orchestra. The scenario identifies the general movement towards the climax as 'Dawn – and brighter to conclusion'.

The Morning Star Dance

This is the shortest of the seven movements of *Corroboree* (at just under two minutes) and leads without a break into the final movement. It is quieter and slower than the three preceding movements and forms a relatively contemplative prelude to the long, energy-charged finale to come. It is scored for bass clarinet, bassoons, harp and strings, together with an ostinato figure for the only percussion instrument, the tambourine. Formally it is cast in a simple rondo-like alternation between two thematic sections, the principal one being a melody for bass clarinet, sometimes alternating with, or joined by, bassoons, while the harp provides an ostinato which emphasises the tonal centre of A, the figure heard at the outset of the movement (Example 2.8 below) continually recurring throughout.

This material is briefly interspersed with related melodic passages for the strings, while the harp abandons the figuration of the principal sections. The A tonal centre is clearly confirmed at the end of the movement, while the tambourine ostinato has continued throughout without a break.

Procession of Totems and Closing Fire Ceremony

This final movement is by far the longest of the whole ballet (at 604 bars and around 18 minutes) and is also the most loosely episodic in construction. There is no clear overall formal structure, but rather a series of thematically separate sections or 'sub-movements' which follow without a break. In the published score there are no indications as to the designation of these sections. However, Antill's scenario refers to them specifically in terms of their association with various totems, successively depicted, and also the dramatic stages involved. These are: Lace Lizard Totem (bars 1–75); Cockatoo Totem (bars 76–102); Honey Ant Totem (bars 103–110); Wild Cat Totem (bars 110–181); transition (bars 182–186) to Small Fly Totem (bars 187–245); transition (bars 246–249) to 'Procession of Totems' (bars 250–423); and finally the 'Closing Fire Ceremony' (bars 424–604).

Each of the early sections, which depict totems not hitherto mentioned in the scenario as being involved in earlier movements, is thematically independent, with its own chief motivic idea(s) repeated virtually throughout the section. The Lace Lizard is symbolised by an arpeggic 6/8 motif interspersed with 1/8 bars noted in the scenario as 'shake of the head'. The Cockatoo is represented by an extended cor anglais solo lightly accompanied. The brief Honey Ant section comprises an incisively accompanied lively melody shared between trumpets and oboes; while the Wild Cat section features a *perpetuum mobile* melody in rapid 3/8 metre.

Viewed retrospectively, the Lace Lizard, Cockatoo, Honey Ant and Wild Cat sections appear to function structurally and dramatically as a series of relatively lightly scored introductions. With the advent of the Small Fly section, the trora sticks re-enter and create a 'soundscape' very reminiscent of the opening of the ballet (save for intermittent three-note figures in the 'Homage to the Rising Sun' movement, they have been silent since the 'Welcome Ceremony'). Here also begins a process of recapitulation of material heard in, or derived from, the 'Welcome Ceremony'. Two repetitive figures are direct recapitulations – namely, the brief descending semiquaver flourishes (see earlier comment in the 'Welcome Ceremony' section) played by bassoons and cellos; and also a brief horn motif. These figures are shown in Example 2.9 from near the end of the Small Fly section.

Example 2.8   *Corroboree*, 'The Morning Star Dance', bb. 1–13(2)

Example 2.9   *Corroboree*, 'Procession of Totems', bb. 230–237

From bar 234 of Example 2.9 the horns switch to a motif first heard some 20 bars earlier, and which comes to dominate the entire 'Procession of Totems' and to a lesser extent the 'Closing Fire Ceremony'. This motif is clearly derived from the three-note figure B-F-E♭ earlier identified in the 'Welcome Ceremony' as being associated with the medicine man, who is also now mentioned in Antill's scenario as being very much in charge of both the 'Procession' and also the 'Fire Ceremony'. This appears to be a rare (and possibly the only) example in the entire score of a thematic association that might be seen as linked leitmotivically. The motif here has been expanded from three to five notes that are extended repetitively in various permutations. Example 2.10 shows the expanded motif, now prominently blazed forth by woodwind and brass (bars 277ff.) at the 'original pitch' of the three-note motif from the 'Welcome Ceremony' – i.e. B-F-E♭-F-B (etc.).

Example 2.10   *Corroboree*, ' Procession of Totems', bb. 275–284(2)

Example 2.11   *Corroboree*, 'Closing Fire Ceremony', bb. 464–467

Example 2.12   *Corroboree*, conclusion of 'Closing Fire Ceremony'

The rhythm of this motif was first hammered out by the bass drum early in the Small Fly section (bars 198ff.) There are also two prominent timpani solos – one in the 'Procession of Totems' and the other near the end of the 'Closing Fire Ceremony' (see Example 2.12) in which the original three-note motif – B-F-E♭ – is given out *fff*.

The 'Procession of Totems' section, dominated by the motif of Example 2.10, could perhaps be seen as cast once again in a very loose rondo form, in which the above motif is separated by contrasting episodes. As can also be seen in Example 2.10, the ballet's main tonal centre of A is again prominent (brass and strings from bar 281).

Considerable dramatic tension is built up throughout the 'Procession of Totems', which explodes into the final 'Closing Fire Ceremony'. Antill's scenario refers to 'absolute frenzy to bar 600. Concluding bar – prostration'. The thematic ideas previously identified from the 'Welcome Ceremony' and shown in Examples 2.9 and 2.10 continue throughout this closing section, which also features a new fanfare-like melody (see Example 2.11 above) prominent in the early stages of the section.

In the last climactic passages, the orchestra is joined by the bullroarer, and the five-note motif of Example 2.10 returns prominently. In the final bars of the ballet (see Example 2.12), the fundamental tonal centre of A is reiterated while the three-note 'medicine man motif' at its original B-F-E♭ pitch is loudly proclaimed, including the timpani solo preceding the shattering crescendo on the final A unison tutti.

The Musical Language of *Corroboree*: Concluding Reflections

The foregoing discussion has presented a general picture of the style and techniques of Antill's *Corroboree* music. The analysis of its large-scale formal organisation has shown clearly its allegiance to early twentieth-century static or 'block-like' structural procedures, built around tonal 'platforms' created chiefly by the devices of ostinato and pedal point. As has been observed, this places *Corroboree* firmly in the orbit of the 'primitivist' ballets of the World War 1 period, and Stravinsky's *The Rite of Spring* has been habitually identified by critics as some sort of 'exemplar' for *Corroboree*. Notwithstanding this, Antill's assertion that he did not know Stravinsky's work when he composed *Corroboree* is, in part at least, supported by the fact that his own dissonant harmonic organisation is not, as in *The Rite*, built from superimposed or interlocking triads and seventh chords, but rather principally from harmonies ranging from fairly simple aggregates based on fourths, fifths and tritones as well as minor and major seconds. More chromatic dissonances result from the frequent layering of such intervallic materials. The technique of harmonic layering (including bitonality and polytonality) is not, of course, peculiar to *The Rite of Spring*, but emerged in the work of many composers from the early decades of the twentieth century. Antill's avoidance, in large part, of full triadic constructions gives *Corroboree* an essentially stark, hard-edged sound entirely appropriate to the 'hollow' as well as percussive 'soundscape' of the corroboree. Examples of Antill's harmonic thinking are plainly evident in almost every musical example presented in the preceding analysis. This harmony is also intervallically 'of a piece' with his mostly angular melodic writing. An excellent example of the latter may be found in Example 2.3 from 'Dance to the

Evening Star'. Even in this gentle piece, the principal solo melody for the oboe is chromatically dissonant overall, yet clearly oriented towards its A tonal centre and also built principally from juxtaposed fourths and fifths interspersed with conjunct tones and semitones. Some melodies in the work are more obviously modal, especially the 'Witchetty Grub' theme (Example 2.1), while the tritone figures perhaps most prominently in the 'medicine man' motif (Example 2.10). Other examples quoted in the analysis give a representative impression of the intervallic unity of *Corroboree*'s melodic and harmonic idiom. While the total effect is often abrasively dissonant and chromatically complex, the materials creating such complex textures are themselves simple and elemental. In no sense is *Corroboree* an example of modernist atonality, and it is emphatically 'instinctive' rather than 'theoretical' or 'constructivist' in its conception.

Corroboree as Ballet and Concert Suite

Since its première in 1946, *Corroboree* has been performed in its full version during three seasons of stage productions in 1950/1951, 1954 and 1970. In concert performances (including the 1946 première) and recordings, the work has been mostly heard in the form of one or other of the two concert suites arranged from the full score, which will be discussed below.

The first stage production, with choreography by Rex Reid, was given by the National Ballet during a season of ballet productions at the Empire Theatre, Sydney, the première taking place on 2 July 1950, followed by five further performances. In 1951, as part of the Jubilee Year celebration commemorating 50 years since Federation, this production was taken on tour to all the state capital cities and finally to Broken Hill, NSW. These performances were conducted by the composer.

A detailed description of this first stage production is given by Dean and Carell.[29] Reid's choreography, produced at very short notice, followed Antill's non-narrative scenario, but, 'added concepts which his own instincts for theatre requirements dictated'.[30] Although the audience and press reactions were wildly enthusiastic, it was observed, nevertheless, by some critics that Reid's choreography was far removed from a truly authentic representation of Aboriginal dance. The writer Colin Simpson, in his book *Adam in Ochre*, while praising Antill's score and William Constable's stage décor, went so far as to label the choreography and Robin Lovejoy's costume design as 'no more than a gaudy, circus-like travesty of corroboree'.[31] However, Dean and Carell point out that Reid was 'following guidelines laid down by the composer who was not himself a choreographer, and who had never personally seen a traditional corroboree'.[32] It should be

---

[29] Dean and Carell, *Gentle Genius*, pp. 106–16.
[30] Ibid., p. 107.
[31] Quoted in Ibid., p. 110.
[32] Ibid.

remembered that the 'make believe' corroboree that Antill had witnessed at La Perouse during his boyhood was a 'touristy' affair and far from 'authentic'. Antill himself defended the production in these words:

> *Corroboree* should not be mistaken for a ritual corroboree, which is something I never attempted. Rather it was an "entertainment" corroboree ... done on stage for theatre audiences.[33]

A new ballet production was mounted in connection with the first Royal Visit by Queen Elizabeth II and the Duke of Edinburgh in early 1954 and presented at the Tivoli Theatre, Sydney on 6 February, followed by nearly 100 performances on tour around Australia – once again conducted by Antill. A new ballet company was formed for the performances, called the Arts Council Ballet Company; and a new choreography was commissioned from Beth Dean who, with her husband, Victor Carell, spent some eight months, as preparation for this, in Arnhem Land and central Australia studying Aboriginal culture – especially their dances and ceremonies.[34] Carell wrote a completely new scenario for the new production; and while Dean's resulting choreography was deemed to be closer in spirit and action to traditional Aboriginal dance than Reid's earlier choreography, their new version created a narrative scenario which was never envisaged by Antill. This scenario, however, presumably approved by the composer, comprises a representation of the various stages of initiation of a young boy who has reached puberty and must undergo the trials attendant upon being accepted as a man and a full member of the tribe. These trials commence at dawn ('Welcome Ceremony') and continue throughout the day, culminating in the final stages ('Procession of Totems and Closing Fire Ceremony') which occur at night and in which the Initiate undergoes the final ordeal by fire. In Antill's original conception, the whole corroboree takes place throughout one night. Dean and Carell have provided a detailed account of this scenario and choreography in their biography of Antill.[35] For this version, the score was apparently slightly abridged, with cuts made to the Welcome Ceremony and the Procession of Totems and Closing Fire Ceremony.[36]

Since the 1954 performances, *Corroboree* has been revived only once as a complete staged ballet. This occurred in 1970 in an 'all-Antill' season as part of the Captain Cook Bicentenary celebrations, organised by the Sutherland Shire south of Sydney – appropriately since the shire encompasses the Botany Bay area where Cook had made his original landfall in Australia. *Corroboree* was performed, along with the ballet *G'Day Digger* and a balletic realisation of the oratorio *The*

---

[33] Ibid., p. 111.
[34] Ibid., p. 127.
[35] Ibid., pp. 129–33.
[36] Personal communication from Joel Crotty who recalls that Beth Dean requested cuts to the first and last movements at the time of producing her choreography for this production.

Song of Hagar to Abraham the Patriarch (see Chapters 3 and 5 for details of these works) in a specially constructed outdoor amphitheatre. The Dean/Carell version was once again used for the 1970 production.[37]

Since this time there have been no further stage productions of the original ballet score. However, a further choreography was devised, apparently to the suite only (cf. below – it is not clear which one) by Stanton Welch, and performed by ten members of the Australian Ballet in San Francisco in 1995 during a festival to celebrate the 50th anniversary of the signing of the United Nations Charter. It was later restaged by the Atlanta Ballet (under the title *Wild Life*) in 2001. This version has never been staged in Australia.[38]

Notwithstanding the enormous publicity and critical success enjoyed by the Australian ballet productions of *Corroboree*, it is – for reasons which will be suggested later – in the concert hall and on recordings that music from the work has been most often heard; and here, performances have largely been of one or other of the concert suites extracted from the full score. There are two such suites, the original one performed by Goossens for the work's première in 1946 and subsequently taken on tour overseas and finally recorded in 1950 by the Sydney Symphony Orchestra conducted by Goossens.[39] For this first suite, the 'Welcome Ceremony' was cut to its first section only, highlighting the first presentation of the 'Witchetty Grub' theme after the initial didjeridu evocation, the orchestral 'shrieks' and brief descending 'Aboriginal' melodic flourishes (see earlier analysis). The longer middle section and the recapitulation of the 'Witchetty Grub' theme (comprising approximately three quarters of the movement) are omitted, reducing the playing time of the movement from its original eight minutes to around two and a half minutes. The movement thus gains a much more introductory character, but at the expense of its original formal balance. Then follows the 'Dance to the Evening Star' (No. 2), more or less complete, and 'A Rain Dance (No. 3) minus its introduction (97 bars) and some 40 bars from the middle section. The suite then concludes with a considerably abridged version of the 'Procession of Totems and Closing Fire Ceremony' (No. 7), which begins with the final bars of the Small Fly Totem section (modified to effect an introductory character), omitting the Lace Lizard, Cockatoo, Honey Ant and Wild Cat sections which begin the full version. A further cut of some 135 bars is made from the 'Procession' leading into the 'Closing Fire Ceremony' (the final 180 bars). The result is a shortened movement of approximately seven minutes dominated by the 'medicine man' theme (cf. Examples 2.10 and 2.12). The original suite lasts for approximately 16 minutes in total.

It is not clear as to whether Goossens or Antill arranged this original concert suite. Dean and Carell report that when Goossens told Antill that he would perform *Corroboree*, he announced that he would 'make a suite out of it'.[40] However, the only sources for this suite are cuts made, in Antill's hand, to the manuscript full

---

[37] Dean and Carell, *Gentle Genius*, p. 167.
[38] Details of these productions are given by Michelle Potter in her article '*Corroboree*, from a Dance Perspective' *NLA News*, 14/6 (March, 2004).
[39] HMV LP OALP7503.
[40] Dean and Carell, p. 91.

score held among the Antill Papers. This would indicate that Antill arranged the suite himself. Nevertheless, it is possible that Antill made the cuts at Goossens's direction, or else wrote them into his score following the première. A score for this suite was published by Boosey and Hawkes, who also published the full score of the ballet. However at the time of writing, the author has only been able to locate the score of the final movement, labelled 'No. 4' (i.e. according to the movement sequence of the original suite), held in the Australian Music Centre library in Sydney.

In 1950, a second (or rather, revised and extended) suite was arranged. Once again, it is not clear as to whether this 'second suite', as it has been called, was arranged by Goossens or by Antill himself; although undoubtedly both composer and conductor were actively involved. It is this version that has since featured on both subsequent commercial recordings – by Goossens with the London Symphony Orchestra in 1958[41] and by Antill conducting the Sydney Symphony Orchestra in 1967.[42] This 'second suite' comprises all the items of the original suite outlined above, but adds the 'Homage to the Rising Sun' (No. 5) and 'The Morning Star Dance' (No. 6) as well as restoring the introduction (though not the 40-bar cut to the middle section) to 'A Rain Dance' (No. 3). The revised suite's duration is approximately 22–24 minutes. No separate score appears to exist for this 'second suite', which has also received numerous performances. As recently as 2005, this suite was performed in Brisbane, and the score and parts were provided in a 'kit' from Boosey and Hawkes, the score simply comprising that of the complete published ballet score with cuts marked.[43] However, from a perusal of the annotations provided for the preparation of this performance, it is clear that only the movements of the original suite were played.

In light of the above, it is perhaps less than surprising that, in each of the recordings of this second suite, the accompanying liner notes provide inaccurate information as to its content. The 1958 Goossens recording with the London Symphony Orchestra lists and describes all seven movements of the complete *Corroboree* score. However, the notes state that only movements 1, 2, 3 and 7 are to be found on the recording – that is, only the movements of the original suite – namely: 'Welcome Ceremony'; 'Dance to the Evening Star'; 'A Rain Dance'; and 'Procession of Totems and Closing Fire Ceremony' – thus omitting 'Homage to the Rising Sun' and The Morning Star Dance', the added movements for the second suite. Furthermore, the 1994 CD transfer of this recording lists the movements only as per the original suite, but misplaces these movements on the respective track numbers as follows: 'Welcome Ceremony' (correctly identified); 'Dance to the Evening Star' (which also includes 'A Rain Dance'); 'A Rain Dance' (actually 'Homage to the Rising Sun'); 'Procession of Totems' (actually 'The

---

[41] Everest LP, SDBR 3003, re-released on CD in 1994 (Everest EVC9007).
[42] HMV LP OALP7554.
[43] Plush, 'A Timeline of Corroboree', p. 30. Grateful acknowledgement is made to Vincent Plush and to Angela Turner for providing detailed information regarding the performing resources used for this performance.

Morning Star Dance'); and 'Closing Fire Ceremony' (actually the entire abridged 'Procession of Totems and Closing Fire Ceremony'). The notes to Antill's 1967 recording lists the movements of the second suite correctly save for the omission of 'The Morning Star Dance'; while another recording by Antill and the Sydney Symphony Orchestra on an ABC LP produced for educational use only,[44] claims to include – like the Goossens recording – only the movements of the original suite (Nos 1, 2, 3 and 7). Finally, in Dean and Carell's biography, the movements of the second suite (including their titles) are given even more inaccurately – namely 'Ceremony of Welcome', The Spirit of the Wind' [not in either suite], 'Dance to the Morning Star' and 'Dance of the Kangaroo Men'.[45]

At the time of writing, there also exist two recordings of the complete *Corroboree* score. The first recording was made as late as 1977 by John Lanchbery conducting the Sydney Symphony Orchestra,[46] while a second recording was made in 2008 by James Judd conducting the New Zealand Symphony Orchestra.[47] The existence of these recordings – as well as those of the concert suites – has made it possible for a wider musical public to assess the relative merits of the complete score and the suites in a non-theatrical context. There will no doubt continue to be differences of opinion as to the effectiveness of the complete score as a concert work compared to either of the two suites. The latter provide a pleasingly concise presentation of *Corroboree*'s essentially episodic material; while the full score has been considered by some commentators as unable to effectively sustain sufficient musical interest without its stage setting. On the other hand, the severe pruning of the music for the suites, while skilfully done, adversely affects the formal balance of both the 'Welcome Ceremony' and 'A Rain Dance'; although in the case of the 'Procession of Totems and Closing Fire Ceremony', the omission of the introductory episodes provides a much 'tighter' treatment of its climactic material.

Corroboree – Impact and Aftermath

John Antill's *Corroboree* must lay claim to being the most celebrated and best known single work by any Australian resident composer of the first half of the twentieth century. As noted in the Introduction, its initial performances as a concert suite were greeted with tremendous ovations by audiences in Australia,[48] as well as during Goossens's subsequent tours with the work in London and in Cincinnati (where he had been for many years principal conductor prior to his appointment

---

[44] ABC LP RRCS133.
[45] Dean and Carell, *Gentle Genius*, p. 112.
[46] EMI LP OASD793060 and CD CDOASD793060.
[47] Naxos CD 8.570241.
[48] Dean and Carell quote Goossens as reporting in his programme notes to his performance of *Corroboree* in Cincinnati that the ovation following the Sydney première lasted eight minutes (Dean and Carell, *Gentle Genius*, p. 93).

to the Sydney Symphony Orchestra in 1947). During these years *Corroboree* was also heard in other British cities as well as in Holland and Sweden.[49] It was also taken up for broadcast by the BBC and recorded for international distribution by the BBC Transcription Service.[50]

Audiences were even more enthusiastic when *Corroboree* was finally staged as a ballet in 1950 and 1954. Enormous excitement and expectations surrounding these eventual productions had been generated since the earlier successes of the concert performances; and Dean and Carell report that, at the 1950 première, over 2,000 people were turned away at the theatre doors, while the performance itself received unprecedented and 'tremendous applause'.[51] Similar accolades are reported for the 1954 performance before the Queen and during the subsequent Australia-wide tour of this production. According to Dean and Carell, the Arts Council report for 1954 described it as 'the most successful tour of this type yet sponsored by the council'.[52]

Since the euphoric days of its mid-century performances, the music of *Corroboree* has continued to receive concert performances, though of less frequency. Nevertheless, as late as 1982, the Australasian Performing Right Association (APRA) presented Antill with an award for 'the most performed Australian Classical Composition;[53] while, as mentioned earlier, compact disc recordings of the entire *Corroboree* score were made in 1977 and as recently as 2008. As previously noted, performances of the suite (labelled 'Suite No. 2' in the concert programme) were given in 2005 in Brisbane, while still more recently – in 2013 – there were concert performances of the complete ballet score in Sydney and Canberra.[54] Nevertheless, there is a certain irony in the fact that the status of *Corroboree* as a staged ballet production is likely to become that of a 'historical icon' rather than an active part of contemporary ballet repertoire, owing to the change in cultural climate since the period of its heyday. It will be recalled from discussion earlier in this chapter of the Jindyworobak influence on perceptions of 'Australianism' via the evocation of Aboriginal culture, that the question of this practice as constituting 'cultural appropriation' did not then arise as a significant factor. However, in more recent years, there has developed considerable sensitivity surrounding the idea of non-Aboriginal Australians directly portraying features of Aboriginal culture, perhaps especially visually. Here, *Corroboree* suffers from the fact that, as a staged ballet, it is undoubtedly the most prominent example of such direct visual 'invasion' of Aboriginal culture (the same is true of a number of now lesser known theatre works – including some by Antill to be discussed in the next chapter – of the 1940s and 1950s, directly portraying Aboriginal subjects). This

---

[49] The Dutch and Swedish performances are reported in ABC Annual Report 1946–1947 and quoted in Buzacott, *The Rite of Spring*, p. 205.
[50] Dean and Carell, *Gentle Genius*, p. 93.
[51] Ibid., p. 109.
[52] Ibid., p. 127.
[53] Ibid., p. 181.
[54] See Australian Music Centre website.

almost guarantees that future ballet productions – certainly as Antill envisaged his scenario and also the versions by Reid and Dean – are unlikely in the present political and cultural climate, and that the 'survival' of *Corroboree* will be sustained by concert performances and recordings, where the link with Aboriginal culture lies at a more 'abstract' evocatory level. Although performances of *Corroboree* have become fewer during the last couple of decades, the 'iconic' status of the work is still attested to, as witnessed by composers of a later generation. Peter Sculthorpe, who has assumed the mantle of Australia's most prominent 'national' composer previously worn by Antill, made the following comment on Antill's ballet as recently as 2006:

> *Corroboree* is one of the great landmarks of Australian music. For the first time, people in the outside world knew that there was somebody in Australia writing music. John may have written better pieces, but *Corroboree* has tended to outshine them all.[55]

Another contemporary composer and writer on Australian music, Vincent Plush – also as recently as 2006 – stated that

> … [*Corroboree*] represents a watershed moment in our musical history, an event that had no precedent or peer, and one which no future Australian composer can escape. *Corroboree* is fundamental to our history. It is the first important musico-dramatic work that we could present to ourselves and the world as truly Australian. "Here it is and here we are" it says and shouts even after 50 years.[56]

Conclusion

The foregoing chapter has attempted to provide a comprehensive examination of Antill's famous ballet score, which has reached – and as suggested above, maintained – a truly 'iconic' status in the history of Australian art music. Given the work's exceptional profile, it might be assumed that Antill's subsequent output could potentially be seen as something of an 'anticlimax'; and – as will be discussed in the following Interlude section of this book – this point of view has been expressed in different ways by a number of commentators on Antill's music over the ensuing decades. The remaining chapters will therefore attempt to provide as clear as possible a perspective of the 'second stage' of Antill's creative career in order to address these views and to place Antill's total corpus of works in its proper context within Australian art music of the post-colonial era.

---

[55] Interview with Martin Buzacott, quoted in Buzacott, *The Rite of Spring*, p. 207.
[56] Vincent Plush, programme note to performance of *Corroboree* Suite No. 2 in *Encounters – Program Booklet – Orchestral Music* (South Brisbane: Queensland Conservatorium Research Centre, March 2005), p. 19; quoted by Martin Buzacott in ibid.

Interlude
Antill After *Corroboree*: An Overview

The remainder of this book examines the works of the 'second stage' of John Antill's creative career referred to in the Introduction. Although Antill lived for some 40 years after the première of *Corroboree*, and was composing up to the year before his death in 1986, he produced a very small number of works – and none of any substance – during the years after his retirement from the ABC in 1969. His last significant work was the *Cantate Domino*, composed for the ecumenical service on the occasion of the visit to Australia of Pope Paul VI, and performed in the Sydney Town Hall in December 1970. However, in the 25 years from the time of *Corroboree* until his retirement, Antill's output was quite voluminous. Overall, the Antill Papers, and also Dean and Carell,[1] list over 100 items dating from after *Corroboree*, ranging in scope from relatively sizeable works for theatre, orchestra, solo voice and choir, through film scores and incidental music for television, radio and live plays, to a large volume of brief pieces comprising fanfares, anthems, carols, part songs, solo songs, one short piece for organ and various arrangements. The bulk of this output is in the 'public' genres of theatre, orchestral and choral music, nearly all of which was the result of specific commissions – many by Antill's employer, the ABC. Non-commissioned works include a number that, like nearly all of Antill's pre-*Corroboree* works, were left unfinished or unperformed. As the above summary of his output indicates, there are practically no works – and none of significance – in the genres of either chamber or keyboard music (apart from piano or organ accompaniments to some theatre and choral works).

That Antill was able to produce such a large corpus of works while employed full time in the demanding role of Federal Music Editor for the ABC (from 1949–1969) shows a remarkable degree of creative energy. However, the relative size and scope of much of Antill's post-*Corroboree* output raises a fundamental issue with respect to critical opinions of it. A basic theme among critics of Antill's music refers to the fact that so many of his later works are of either modest dimensions or slender substance, and that *Corroboree* is his one and only work of real stature and significance. While it is true that Antill never wrote another work that made such an impact upon audiences, it would be misleading in the extreme to assert that he never produced any further works of stature. Nevertheless such prominent writers on Australian music as Roger Covell, Patricia Brown and James Murdoch have, either directly or indirectly, made this claim. Covell's comment that Antill's later works were 'the diligent makeweights of an extremely competent musician'

[1] Dean and Carell, *Gentle Genius*, pp. 200–202.

was mentioned in the Introduction.[2] Covell, together with Brown and Murdoch, have raised the image of Antill as a 'one work composer'. Covell asserted that '*Corroboree* was the work Antill had to write ...',[3] while Brown maintained that 'if it is possible for a composer's reputation to be sustained chiefly by one composition, then Antill is a one-work composer'.[4] Murdoch also used the 'one work composer' epithet and compared Antill with such composers as the two expatriate Australians Arthur Benjamin and Percy Grainger, whom he also saw as 'one work composers', although (unlike Antill) on the basis of minor rather than major works ('Jamaican Rhumba' and 'Country Gardens' respectively).[5] In commenting on the nature of Antill's post-*Corroboree* output, Murdoch, together with Harold Hort and Pauline Petrus, have noted his situation in relation to his employment by the ABC. Murdoch observed that Antill's commitments involved 'incessant requirements to write and arrange small pieces' and speculated that if the ABC had provided him with more time and commissions for major works, Antill might have produced more significant and 'exportable' output.[6]

Both Hort and Petrus, also accepting the idea that Antill's post-*Corroboree* works were largely of lesser scope and stature, have shared Murdoch's view as to the reason for this. Hort (as quoted by Dean and Carell) noted the sparseness of Antill's output after his retirement from the ABC, remarking, however, that '... had John had the opportunity earlier in life, and not just near its end, I feel he might have written a great deal more music of significance'.[7] Hort's position as a colleague of Antill at the ABC allowed him direct observation of Antill's extremely busy work schedule with the broadcaster and the lack of time offered to him for any sustained compositional activity. Petrus commented similarly on Antill's situation post-*Corroboree* as follows:

> [Antill's] employment with the ABC led to several commissions to write music for state occasions.[8] But he did not receive the necessary support to enable him to devote himself entirely to composition, and therefore did not fully realise the enormous potential that he showed so early in his life.[9]

In addition to criticisms regarding the relative scope or substance of Antill's post-*Corroboree* works, much of the critical commentary on the music itself has appeared

---

[2] Covell, *Australia's Music*, p. 154.
[3] Ibid.
[4] Brown, 'John Antill', p. 44.
[5] Murdoch, *Australia's Contemporary Composers*, p. 9.
[6] Ibid., p. 12.
[7] Dean and Carell, *Gentle Genius*, p. 173.
[8] Cf. Covell's comment referred to in the Introduction, that 'as a musician employed by the ABC, [Antill] seemed to be at times a kind of composer-laureate for state occasions' (Covell, *Australia's Music*, p. 155).
[9] Petrus, 'Antill, John Henry', p. 25.

negatively toned – its main thrust being the perception that Antill retreated into a more conservative style and did not follow up on the stylistic breakthrough he had achieved in *Corroboree*. Covell, in his summing up of Antill's later output, commented that '(l)istening to the mildness of his other works makes it possible to wonder if he wrote *Corroboree* by accident'.[10] Similarly, Brown asserted that '… *Corroboree* stands like Ayers Rock among the soundscapes of the gentler works which both precede and follow it'.[11] She also wrote of Antill's conservatism and allegiance to the English choral tradition, stating that

> [t]he bulk of [Antill's] music is firmly established in traditions such as the English choral movement and the more readily accessible styles of European orchestral writing of the late nineteenth and early twentieth centuries.[12]

Petrus likewise wrote of Antill's conservatism, his 'strong leaning towards the English choral tradition' and his 'docile, melodic approach to composition' (which she linked with his studies with the strongly conservative Alfred Hill); but she also pointed to 'his fascination with the rhythmic drive of Russian composers from Mussorgsky to Prokofiev'.[13]

Murdoch has been perhaps the most outspoken critic of Antill's post-*Corroboree* style. His comments – and indeed those of Covell, Brown and Petrus – appear heavily coloured by the prevailingly modernist critical climate of the 1960s, where music of the previous post-colonial period was seen as backward and totally out of touch with contemporary trends in Europe and America. For Murdoch, as well as a number of commentators at this time, any Australian work, in order to be at all respected, needed to be seen above all as 'contemporary' in style – 'contemporary' referring to the style of the European and American avant-garde of the 1950s and 1960s. Murdoch was a staunch supporter of the modernist trends in Australian music after 1960. There is therefore some irony in his classification (in 1972) of *Corroboree*'s musical language – based firmly, as has been amply demonstrated in the previous chapter, on early twentieth-century 'primitivism' – as 'advanced'. Murdoch opined that *Corroboree* 'is the most advanced work by Antill and he has written nothing since to approach its virile idiom'.[14] Earlier in the same chapter on Antill, Murdoch lamented Antill's failure (after *Corroboree*) 'to become a standard bearer for a follow-up body of other Australian advanced composition'.[15] In the same vein he deplored the inclusion of Antill's *Five Australian Lyrics* (1953) in a set of recordings

---

[10] Covell, *Australia's Music*, p. 154.
[11] Brown, 'John Antill', p. 49.
[12] Ibid., p. 47.
[13] Petrus, 'Antill, John Henry', p. 25.
[14] Murdoch, *Australia's Contemporary Composers*, p. 11.
[15] Ibid., p. 9.

of Australian contemporary music[16] with the curtly dismissive comment that the work 'is pleasant enough but has nothing to do with contemporary music'.[17]

Andrew McCredie had earlier offered a rather more measured assessment, but also addressed the unique position of *Corroboree* and its status as an Australian musical icon:

> [Antill] has had to bear the distinction and notoriety of being hailed as the creator of Australian music … *Corroboree* remains a unique work both in Antill's own production and for Australian composition.[18]

McCredie then commented on Antill's later work, and identified *Symphony on a City* (1959) as the best essay for orchestra since *Corroboree*, capturing 'some of the vivid style of *Corroboree* but with greater epic sweep and symphonic design'.[19] He also offered an assessment of *Five Australian Lyrics* that is far more complimentary than that of Murdoch, commenting on Antill's 'sensitivity to word and tone and to declamatory possibilities which at best invite comparison with Britten'.[20] These two major works will be discussed in detail in Chapters 4 and 5 respectively.

McCredie's assessment provides a more accurate clue to Antill's later style, as the following chapters will attempt to show. This style, far from retreating into the late nineteenth century, has more to do with that of a large body of English and European music between the two world wars, encompassing some survivals of English pastoralism, but within a predominantly neo-classical and neo-tonal frame of reference – a pathway also followed by the more progressive of Australian composers during the 1940s and 1950s. It is only the more radical trends of twentieth-century modernism that are avoided in this music; but this nevertheless coincides with the styles and techniques of a very large percentage of significant Western music of the second quarter of the century.

The remainder of this book, then, will seek to address the foregoing critical perceptions of Antill's post-*Corroboree* works. To achieve an overall perspective of this numerically voluminous output, the respective chapters covering his theatrical, orchestral, choral and vocal works will first provide a comprehensive survey of his work in these genres, followed by more detailed analyses of the most significant compositions in each category. As stated in the Introduction, the works selected for more detailed treatment will be those more substantial pieces that have achieved, in most cases, public performance and/or recordings; while a more comprehensive catalogue of Antill's surviving output will be provided in Appendix 1.

---

[16] *Australian Music Today, Vol. 1*, LP recording A/601 (Sydney: World Record Club, 1966?).
[17] Murdoch, *Australia's Contemporary Composers*, p. 13.
[18] Andrew McCredie, *Musical Composition in Australia* (Canberra: Australian Government Printing Office, 1969), p. 10.
[19] Ibid., p. 11.
[20] Ibid.

Chapter 3
After *Corroboree* (1) – Theatre Works

Introductory Perspectives

Any examination of Antill's post-*Corroboree* works must first highlight those in the medium of ballet and opera, since, as noted in the Introduction, music for the theatre formed Antill's major preoccupation throughout his creative career. Within this sphere – as also previously noted – Antill's primary attention shifted, after the overwhelming success and fame of *Corroboree*, from his earlier concentration on opera, to ballet composition. This shift of emphasis was, circumstantially at least, the result of numerous commissions Antill was to receive for ballet scores following the enormous publicity surrounding *Corroboree*, and more especially the two highly successful stage productions of the work in 1950 and 1954 (as discussed in Chapter 2).

Of Antill's post-*Corroboree* output for theatre, only two works are operas (both one-act): one, *The Music Critic* (1952), which has never been performed; and the other, *The First Christmas* (1969), commissioned by the New South Wales Government for an Australian opera to be performed during the celebration of the soon-to-be-completed Sydney Opera House. In any event, the work never achieved performance in this venue, but was premièred in a broadcast performance by the ABC on Christmas Day, 1970. These operas – both on Australian subjects – will be discussed later in this chapter.[1] There is also a quantity of incidental music for television, radio and stage plays, which will be documented in Chapter 4.

Turning now to Antill's output of ballet scores after *Corroboree*, there are some six items – all commissioned – dating from 1956 to 1963. These are: *The Unknown Land* (1956), *Wakooka* (1957), *G'Day Digger* (1958), *Burragorang Dreamtime* (1959), *Black Opal* and *Snowy!* (both 1961). In addition to these ballets of the

---

[1] Apart from these two complete post-*Corroboree* operas, the Antill Papers include one further opera project in Antill's total output – uncommissioned and incomplete – titled *Body Politic* (S8b/20). This work comprises a full libretto and synopsis (by Antill) and some ten pages of orchestral score – a fragment of the first scene only. Both the score and script are untitled and undated (the title appears only in the AP catalogue) – a creative situation more typical of Antill's pre-*Corroboree* period than of his later works of the 1950s and beyond. Antill's highly fanciful romantic plot – it is a romance in a political context set in a mythical country of the future – is also more reminiscent of those of his early operas discussed in Chapter 1 rather than those of his post-*Corroboree* theatre works on exclusively Australian subjects. However, references in the story to past atomic explosions imply a (perhaps early) post-World War 2 (i.e. post-Hiroshima) date, unless these references were prophetic rather than topical!

1950s and 1960s, it will be recalled from Chapter 1 that two earlier essays in the medium, *Capriccio* and the fragmentary *The Circus Comes to Town*, cannot be dated with any certainty, but, on the available evidence, seem most likely to have post-dated *Corroboree*.

Ironically, Antill's first intended ballet project following the 1950 and 1954 stage productions of *Corroboree* proved to be stillborn. This was to be a ballet with a scenario devised by Beth Dean and Victor Carell based on C.J. Dennis's (1876–1938) *The Songs of a Sentimental Bloke*. Antill had provided all or most of the score before it was discovered that another composer, Albert Arlen, held the rights to any musical setting of Dennis's work. Although Arlen's version was a musical play, he would not permit the separate composition of a ballet on the subject. Antill thereupon 'recycled' the music as an orchestral suite for concert performance, titled *A Sentimental Suite* (1955).[2] This work will be discussed in Chapter 4.

The commissioned ballets of 1956 to 1963 illustrate vividly an aspect of Antill's situation as a composer in the post-*Corroboree* years – namely the severely limited resources with which he often had to work, as well as the frequently tight time constraints and other compositional limitations accompanying the commissions. Due to financial constraints, *The Unknown Land* (a short ballet commissioned by the choreographer and dancer Coralie Hinkley for her solo performance) and *G'Day Digger* (commissioned expressly for ABC TV production) were scored for piano only (*G'Day Digger* also incorporating a brief 'musique concrète' interlude of recorded sound effects); while *Wakooka* (commissioned by the small Elizabethan Opera Ballet Company) was written for two pianos. *The Unknown Land* was subsequently rescored for string orchestra,[3] in which form it has had several concert performances and a recording.[4] *Snowy!*, a dance drama with narration, based on the story of the Snowy Mountains Hydro-Electric Scheme and commissioned by Margaret Barr of the Sydney Dance-Drama Group, was originally choreographed to the music of Mahler. It was only toward the final stages of the project's development that Antill was asked to provide in its place original music to the existing choreography. Antill's score for the stage première was again written for piano only; however, as will be discussed later, for its television productions by the ABC – including its entry for the 1962 Italia Prize – Antill provided a version for a small orchestra of 11 players. *Black Opal*'s commission, by Ballet Australia, also placed severe limitations on performing resources; but here Antill decided to write for a small female choir and percussion. Finally *Burragorang Dreamtime*, a balletic depiction of two Aboriginal legends – that of the creation of the world and the birth

---

[2] Dean and Carell, *Gentle Genius*, p. 139.

[3] There is a record of the strings version being published in facsimile by H.E. Garraway in Sydney in 1957. However no trace of this score has been located, and subsequent musical examples from this work have been copied from the manuscript score held in the NLA (AP, S8a/21).

[4] Dean and Carell, *Gentle Genius*, p. 145.

of the waratah (the floral emblem of New South Wales) – was commissioned by the New South Wales Government for performance at pageants associated with the royal visits of Princess Alexandra in 1959 and the Queen and Duke of Edinburgh in 1963. The latter royal visit was in connection with celebrations to mark the 175th anniversary of white settlement in Australia. For this later occasion, *Burragorang Dreamtime*, composed for the 1959 royal visit, was then incorporated, along with further music (hurriedly commissioned from Antill) and an overall narration, to form *Music for a Royal Pageant of Nationhood*. These scores were written for full symphony orchestra, and the performances (to a recording of the music) were on both occasions given in the open air of the Sydney Showground with some five hundred dancers. Despite the size and prestige of the projects, the commissions once again allowed severely limited time, and the composition was undertaken under very artificial circumstances. In this instance Antill was required to provide – piecemeal in brief sections – a rhythmic skeleton to the choreographer, Beth Dean, and then hurriedly put together a full score,[5] with little opportunity to plan a large overall musical structure. Roger Covell was later to describe the 1963 presentation as 'a diffuse and often pointless pageant'.[6] A further version of *Burragorang Dreamtime* was arranged by Antill for a television performance in 1964; and its title, as found among the Antill Papers, is *Dreaming Time Legends*.

Viewing Antill's output of completed operas and ballets after *Corroboree*, it can be seen from the above brief synopsis that, in contrast to his pre-*Corroboree* stage works, the composer had now shifted his attention to the depiction of Australian subjects – indigenous, colonial and post-colonial; and furthermore, all these works are one-act pieces of relatively modest dimensions. The strongly Australian flavour of these works coincides with a similar orientation in stage, texted and programmatic works by many other Australian composers in the 20 years or so following World War 2. The frequent use of Aboriginal themes in much of the music of Alfred and Mirrie Hill, Clive Douglas, James Penberthy and others during this period – and here of course, Antill's *Corroboree* stands as something of an archetype or exemplar – resonates clearly with the contemporary Jindyworobak literary movement, as was pointed out in Chapter 2.

The Ballets 1956–1963

The Unknown Land (1956)

The scenario of this short ballet for solo dancer as presented to Antill by Coralie Hinkley, is based on poetry by Rex Ingamells, the founder of the Jindyworobak literary movement. Its subject therefore shows some continuity with that of *Corroboree*, although there is a far wider Australian reference than the purely

---

[5] Ibid., p. 151.
[6] Covell, *Australia's Music*, p. 155.

Aboriginal, and spans Ingamells's declared identification of Jindyworobakism with Australia's 'environmental values' – 'primeval [the landscape and Aboriginal culture], colonial and modern'.[7]

The choreographer, Coralie Hinkley, studied dance with the pioneer of the modern dance movement in Australia, Gertrud Bodenwieser, and subsequently became the first Australian dancer to be awarded a Fullbright Travel Grant for graduate study in New York, where she studied with such luminaries of the modern dance movement as Martha Graham, Merce Cunningham and others.[8] Her choreography for *The Unknown Land* was therefore made in the 'modern dance' genre rather than that of classical ballet, the basis of the two danced versions of *Corroboree*. Dean and Carell quote Hinkley at length regarding the genesis and scenario of the work, stating that 'her aim was to create a modern dance work portraying a perspective of Australia'.[9] Hinkley would also seem here to have wished to present herself as something of an ambassador for Australian dance since, as Dean and Carell state, she danced *The Unknown Land* a number of times during her period in the USA, including a performance as her audition piece for entry to the Dance Division of the Juilliard School of Music.[10] However, there appears to be no record of the work ever being mounted publicly as a ballet production in Australia;[11] whereas, as mentioned earlier, the version for string orchestra has received a number of concert performances as well as a recording.

Hinkley's scenario for *The Unknown Land* quotes the following extracts from Ingamells's poetry (which Hinkley intended to be recited by the dancer in performance[12]), together with her own comments, upon which she based her choreography:

> *Unknown Land* [*sic*] is a modern dance, approximately 20 minutes, in four movements.
> *The Red Heart*:
> 'Withdrawn from men, superb, aloof, alone,
> brooding eternal secrets on her own'.

---

[7] Ingamells, 'Conditional Culture', p. 249.
[8] 'Hinkley, Coralie', National Library of Australia Biographies, <http://trove.nla.gov.au/people/488345> accessed 4 April 2014.
[9] Dean and Carell, *Gentle Genius*, p. 144.
[10] Ibid.
[11] A report in *The ABC Weekly* (23 October 1957), p. 10, mentions a projected TV production of *The Unknown Land* (strings version to be conducted by Antill) by the ABC 'some time next year' (i.e. 1958); however, since Hinkley took her scenario and choreography to USA and did not return to Australia until 1960, such a production is unlikely to have eventuated.
[12] See 'A New Antill Ballet' in *The Sydney Morning Herald* (22 December 1957).

The first section symbolises the vastness and solitude of the Australian landscape, its fierce beauty; we are permitted a glimpse of its mysteries, communing in secret with its soul.

From a Dying People:
'I caught the echo of a faint coo-ee crying
I glimpsed a vision of a people dying'.
The image is a cry for the forgotten people, the Aborigines; their pleas, dreams, hopes; NOT to be torn away from their land.

Women of the Outback:
'Through arduous days they shaped a dream-made world
to their strong purposes'.
This depicted the physical struggles of the settlers who endured in the outback – harsh difficulties – the restlessness of conflict resolved through the functional movement of work – the building of an imaginary house.

Riverina Celebration:
'My heart would give you joy of this
that riots in the air,
The vibrant colour, warmth and sound,
Australia everywhere'.
The dynamic is joyful expression; man dancing his new vision for the unities of the land.[13]

Hinkley's scenario is thus an 'abstract' non-narrative one. For the purposes of examining the music of *The Unknown Land*, the above therefore provides only a descriptive 'programme' but does not entail any prescription for the music's organisation. According to Dean and Carell, Antill stated that Hinkley 'gave me a suggestion of what she wanted and I wrote the suite with that in mind'.[14] Antill would therefore seem to have been allowed a basic structural autonomy by Hinkley, and an examination of the music confirms this. *The Unknown Land* is, like *Corroboree*, a non-narrative ballet – in this case in the form of a suite of four structurally self-contained movements, which, if episodic, nevertheless make perfect sense when heard as a concert suite. Furthermore, for concert performances of the work, Antill provided his own 'programme' (together with the Ingamells verses) as follows:

> Section (1) *The Red Heart*: The music reflects in a broad, majestic, sweeping movement, something mysterious, guarding, reflecting the colours and qualities of the ancient land – earth-brown, red, the fierceness of the sun-drenched ridges, the silence, the primeval rocklike hardness.

---

[13] Dean and Carell, *Gentle Genius*, pp. 144–5.
[14] Ibid., p. 145.

Section (2) *From a Dying People*: He senses danger, alert-curious, afraid; he is an outcast, lonelier and lonelier, wandering into banishment.

Section (3) *Women of the Outback*: They are purposeful, pioneering women, steeling themselves against the forces of defeat, drought, bushfire and despair – but emerging triumphant in their lives of dedication.

Section (4) *Riverina Celebration*: At first we are aware of the sameness of the land, the monotony; we feel the drama of the vital soil and suddenly the bursting forth of a promised land – its problems conquered, its far-reaching gifts to man revealed.[15]

It will be recalled from the discussion of *Corroboree* in Chapter 2 that Antill identified the musical language of *The Unknown Land* as also being 'in the contemporary style'.[16] On the other hand, the work immediately strikes the listener as definitely 'milder' in sound than *Corroboree* – both in its scoring for piano and (soon afterwards) for strings.[17] The work's more expansive melodic and rhythmic language relies somewhat less obsessively on ostinato and propulsive rhythms – both of which are well in evidence, however. The harmonic vocabulary ranges from simple bare octaves and fifths, through some dissonant contrapuntal passages, to some more complex layering and parallelism as in *Corroboree*. However there is a greater use of full triads, both alone and in layered textures. The overall 'soundscape' (especially in its string orchestra garb) suggests strong affinities with such composers as Bartók, Martinů or Honegger.

The work's four movements are, as stated above, largely episodic, the first and third being loose alternations of sections, while a firmer constructive logic is applied to the second and fourth. The first movement, 'The Red Heart', presents both slow and faster ostinato-dominated sections alternating with a slow chromatic melody for solo viola (Example 3.1).

This melody imparts a sense of mystery appropriate to the movement's scenario. In the piano score it opens the movement. However, in the version for string orchestra it is preceded by a slow to moderate-paced, soft introductory passage for pizzicato strings providing a throbbing ostinato as accompaniment to supple melodies for solo violin, then solo cello, and finally solo viola, presaging the unaccompanied viola solo to come. The latter functions as a kind of 'refrain' between the fully scored sections, in some cases 'infiltrating' these as in a passage near the end of the movement quoted in Example 3.2.

---

[15] Ibid., p. 166.

[16] Ibid., p. 145.

[17] Indeed the latter, 'mellower' string (or some orchestral) version might appear to have been envisaged from the outset, since the piano score clearly resembles a 'short score' or 'piano reduction' rather than one written expressly for piano.

Example 3.1   *The Unknown Land*, I, b. 1

Example 3.2   *The Unknown Land*, I, bb. 47–55

The most characteristic contrasting motif is first heard immediately following the initial appearance of the solo viola 'refrain' (Example 3.3).

Example 3.3   *The Unknown Land*, I, bb. 2–3

Here its ostinato accompaniment consists of chords built from perfect fourths, while later ostinati are based on triadic, polytriadic or more dissonant textures. The movement ends with an enigmatic, incomplete restatement of the solo viola theme, underlining the 'lonely' character of the movement's scenario.

The second movement, 'From a Dying People', falls into two repeated sections in the form A–B–B^1–A^1. The final A^1 section is an almost exact retrograde of the A section, which illustrates Antill's awareness of so-called 'constructivist' procedures found in some early twentieth-century music as, for example, in Bartók's *Music for Strings, Percussion and Celesta* and elsewhere, as well as, of course, in much twelve-note music of the Vienna School. The opening of the A section (Example 3.4) also shows Antill's wider textural frame of reference, which here ventures into the distinctly neo-classical area of dissonant melodic and contrapuntal writing.

The slow dirge-like character of the A section illustrates the lamenting nature of this movement's scenario. The tempo is predominantly slow and the dynamics soft; yet at the end of section B, the music rises to a fast and highly dissonant climax before subsiding once more into the sombre mood of the opening (Example 3.5 below).

The third movement, 'Women of the Outback' is once more loosely structured, although its overall shape suggests a roughly ternary feeling, with its outer sections fast and 'busy' suggesting the vigorous activity of the scenario. These sections are loosely related melodically and rhythmically, while enclosing a strongly modal, 'English pastoral' middle section.

Between this movement and the finale, 'Riverina Celebration', there is an interlude titled 'Monotone'. In the original piano score, this interlude comprises a slow ostinato based entirely on repeated B naturals, either in bare octaves or filled in by varying harmonies. In the final string orchestra version, Antill has substituted another, more melodically active passage, though still of a relatively slow, contemplative character. It is interesting that the two newly composed sections for the string orchestra version – namely the introduction to the first movement, and this interlude (still titled 'Monotone') – are of a very similar character and texture, although not using the same thematic material. Given Antill's own 'programme'

Example 3.4 *The Unknown Land*, II, bb. 1–8

for this movement with its opening reference to 'the sameness of the land, the monotony', it seems clear that he intended this 'Monotone' to remind the listener of the mood of the opening movement – both these newly composed passages relating to the 'unknown' or 'aloof' nature of the landscape depicted in the ballet's title.

The finale, 'Riverina Celebration', as befits its title and scenario, is a highly energetic movement exhibiting the fastest tempo of the entire ballet. It is cast in an informal rondo form (the movement is actually labelled thus by Antill, though only in the piano score). The opening (see Example 3.6, bars 1–4 below) returns several times literally repeated, and separated by episodes loosely related to bars 5ff. of Example 3.6.

The movement concludes with a rumbustious coda led off by a passage in which triads and bare fourths and fifths are layered in a dense two-part counterpoint of a style distinctly reminiscent of passages from the orchestral works of Honegger or Martinů (Example 3.7 below).

The Unknown Land follows, as has been seen, an abstract or descriptive scenario, and the music works satisfactorily as a concert suite for string orchestra, which, as stated earlier, appears to be the only form in which the work has been performed in Australia. This may possibly account for the fact that the various

Example 3.5 *The Unknown Land*, II, bb. 27–33

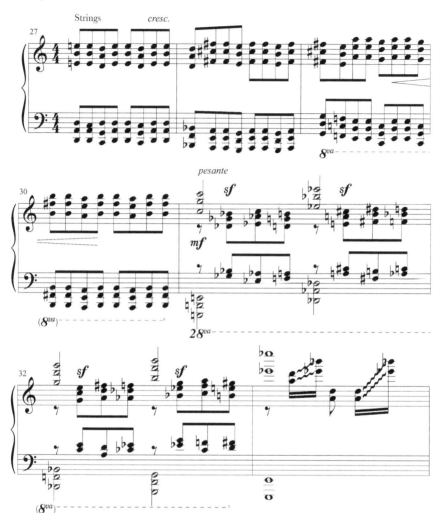

manuscript scores of the work held among the Antill Papers are catalogued under 'Orchestral Music' rather than 'Ballet'. By contrast, the remainder of Antill's ballets carry narrative scenarios; their scores are less structurally independent of their stage settings; and no concert suites have been extracted from them. They have received no performances since the ballet productions of the late 1950s and early 1960s;[18] nor (unlike *The Unknown Land*) has the music of the ballets been heard in the concert hall or received any commercial recordings.

---

[18] One exception is an isolated performance of *G'Day Digger*, along with *Corroboree* and a balletic version of *The Song of Hagar to Abraham the Patriarch* (cf. Chapter 5) at the

Example 3.6   *The Unknown Land*, IV, bb. 1–9

Example 3.7   *The Unknown Land*, IV, bb. 29–35(1)

Wakooka (1957)

Like *The Unkown Land, Wakooka* is a short ballet of approximately 30 minutes' duration. It was premièred in Brisbane by the small Elizabethan Opera Ballet Company in July 1957, followed by seasons in Newcastle, Sydney, Melbourne and Adelaide. The choreography was by Valrene Tweedie (1925–2008), who had been acquainted with Antill while she was a dance student at the Lightfoot/Burlakov Dance Studio in the 1930s, and again from the early 1950s when Tweedie arranged dance programmes that were presented at Antill's home amphitheatre to small invited audiences.[19] Tweedie had an illustrious career as a dancer – at first in Australia, and then for over ten years as both dancer and eventually prima ballerina in USA and Cuba, where she worked with Fokine, Massine, Balanchine and others.[20] By 1955 she had retired from the stage to concentrate on teaching and choreography.[21] Tweedie's dance pedigree was thus in the field of classical ballet and choreography, as distinct from Coralie Hinkley's work in the modern dance genre.

Tweedie's scenario for *Wakooka* is set on a sheep station[22] in the contemporary (i.e. post-World War 2) period and is divided into two scenes – the morning and evening of a single day. Edward Pask provides a concise summary of the ballet's action as follows:

> Wakooka is a sheep station; the ballet's action opens in the early morning with the entrance of a rouseabout, three shearers and the station owner's daughter. Flirting with the men, the girl can't decide which of them she prefers, and the situation is further complicated by the appearance of a young engineer from a nearby project who wishes to obtain information from the girl's father. Interested in the young man, the girl invites him to a barbecue that evening. The second scene depicts the preparations for the barbecue and the arrival of the girls, after which everyone joins in dancing. The station owner's daughter is anxious as the engineer has not arrived. Finally he reappears, and the barbecue is a tremendous success for everyone concerned.[23]

Joel Crotty has commented on the choice of this slight subject in terms of the strong 1950s 'defence' of Australia's hitherto largely homogeneous, 'monochrome Anglo-Celtic culture' in the face of the early influx of post-war migration from

---

'all-Antill' presentation as part of the Captain Cook Bicentenary celebrations in 1970. See Chapter 2 for details of this performance.

[19] Dean and Carell, *Gentle Genius*, pp. 54, 121, 145.
[20] Edward Pask, *Ballet in Australia: The Second Act, 1940–1980* (Melbourne: Oxford University Press, 1982), p. 54.
[21] Ibid., p. 56.
[22] 'Wakooka' means 'kookaburra' and is the name of the station at which the ballet's action takes place (cutting, AP, S14/5).
[23] Pask, *Ballet in Australia*, p. 219.

non-English, especially southern European, countries at this time.[24] The Australian rural setting of the scenario and its lightweight character are qualities that obviously appealed to Antill. The first manifestation of such characteristics in his work has already been noted in the two 'light operas' produced in the 1930s, *Here's Luck* and *The Glittering Mask* (see Chapter 1). Other rural, colonial or 'light' subjects can be found in the fragmentary *The Circus Comes to Town* (cf. Chapter 1), *G'Day Digger*, *The Music Critic* and *The First Christmas* (all to be discussed later in this chapter). All preserve this essentially 'monochrome Anglo-Celtic culture' identified by Crotty in relation to *Wakooka*, and provide a striking 'foil' among Antill's 'Australian' works to those with Aboriginal subjects or incorporating Aboriginal references.

Musically, as will be seen shortly, this led, in the case of the 'lighter' works, to a different approach by Antill from his 'Aboriginal' works (*Corroboree*, *The Unknown Land*, *Black Opal* and *Burragorang Dreamtime*). It will be recalled that Antill referred to works such as these as 'written in the contemporary style' (i.e., as we have already seen in the case of *Corroboree* and *The Unknown Land*, a style involving, to varying extents, the 'primitivist' idiom of early twentieth-century ballets by Stravinsky and others). In contrast to this avowed 'contemporary style', Antill's approach to works of a lighter, comic character, such as *Wakooka* and *G'Day Digger*, is, not surprisingly, to adopt a simpler melodic and harmonic language. In the two early 'light operas' of the 1930s, this had involved a return to largely traditional diatonic functional tonality. After *Corroboree*, however, Antill's approach, when adopting a simpler style, is more influenced by neo-classicism. Passages of functional diatonicism lie embedded in a context which is predominantly modal or 'pandiatonic' – that is, the use of diatonic melodic and harmonic materials in a free, non-functional manner. Further, as in the case of neo-tonal works of this nature, the simple diatonic materials are frequently spiced with sharp dissonances or disjunct harmonic progressions to create a cool, fresh musical flavour redolent of so much neo-classical and neo-tonal music being composed in Europe and America between the wars and just after.

The score of *Wakooka*, as held among the Antill Papers,[25] offers the analyst only occasional and indirect indications as to the way in which the music links with the action of the scenario. The score is divided into 16 'numbers', of which there are eight in each scene (called 'acts' in the score). Within the scenes, the numbers are played without a break. While all the numbers are marked in scene 2 (the barbecue scene), only numbers 4,5,6 and 8 are marked in scene 1, the continuity between the sections and subsections making accurate pinpointing of the remaining numbers problematic. Further, only a few of the numbers are accompanied by titles, and these refer in only general terms to the point in the action at which they occur. The score numbers are as follows: Scene 1: opening scene (no number); 2–3 – unidentified;

---

[24] Joel Crotty, 'Ballet Australia between 1961 and 1962: A Microcosm of Musical Change', *Brolga: An Australian Journal about Dance*, 1 (December 1994), p. 43.

[25] AP, S8d/1.

4 – Engineer's Entrance; 5 – Off to Work; 6 – untitled; 7 – unidentified; 8 – untitled; Scene 2: 9 – Noctorn [sic]; 10–11 – untitled: 12 – Five Girls; 13 – City Dance; 14 – Engineer's Dance; 15–16 – untitled. To further complicate matters, Antill provided a fuller list of titles for the numbers in his handwritten worklist from the late 1970s[26] which identifies only 12 numbers rather than 16; and these titles in most cases do not coincide with those in the score. They are: Scene 1: 1 – Opening Scene; 2 – Off to Work; 3 – The Rouseabout's Return; 4 – Pas de deux; Scene 2: 5 – Noctorn [sic]; 6 – Five Girls; 7 – Girls' Dance; 8 – City Dance; 9 – Engineer's Variation; 10 – Concert Music; 11: Barmaid's Entrance; 12 – Finale.

Example 3.8   *Wakooka*, No. 1, bb. 1–5(1)

---

[26]   AP, S5/2.

The two scenes are introduced by slow introductory numbers, both marked 'slowly with much expression', while the opening of the second scene – the evening barbecue – is appropriately titled 'Noctorn' [*sic*]. Clear tempo markings are lacking in the remainder of the score, although it must be assumed that the succeeding dances are generally of a moderate to fast tempo in keeping with the character of the scenario and of the music itself. These opening sections contain some of the more complex harmonic passages in the score as can be immediately seen in the opening bars of the work (Example 3.8).

Another example of quite dissonant harmony can be found in the second-last number of the ballet – during the rowdy barbecue celebration. Here Antill adopts his familiar chromatically sliding parallel chords of bare fifths and octaves in piano 2 accompanying a disjunct melody in piano 1 (see Example 3.9).

Example 3.9   *Wakooka*, No. 15, bb. 25–32

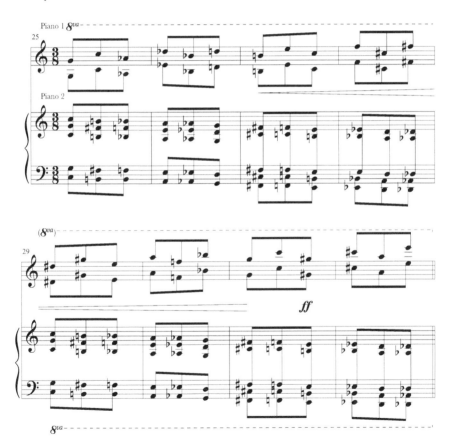

Much of the music, however, is basically diatonic or modal. Rhythmically, Antill, not surprisingly, makes liberal use of ostinato, while the phrase structure of much of the melodic writing is extremely regular, often employing melodies of a popular cast, with traditionally balanced phrases, appropriate to the 'light' or 'popular' character of the work. This evocation of a popular or 'country dance' style even extends to the quotation of the well-known country tune, 'Click go the Shears' immediately following the introduction to scene 2 (see Example 3.10).

Example 3.10   *Wakooka*, No. 10, bb. 13–20

Antill's treatment of this tune well illustrates the point made earlier regarding pandiatonicism. Instead of harmonising this melody with its simple functional progressions, the accompaniment comprises a harmonically inert ostinato, using alternating tonic and leading note seventh chords. This technique is typically pandiatonic and strongly resembles Aaron Copland's treatment of the Shaker hymn 'Simple Gifts' in his 1940s ballet *Appalachian Spring*.

Finally, Example 3.11, from the following number in the barbecue scene, illustrates Antill's periodic adoption of quite straightforward functional harmony as well as a balanced phrase structure.

Example 3.11   *Wakooka*, No. 11, bb. 3–7(1)

As mentioned earlier, *Wakooka* is scored for two pianos; and, as in the case of *The Unknown Land*'s original piano version, the writing strongly suggests that Antill was thinking orchestrally rather than pianistically.[27] The scoring of *Wakooka* for this rather 'monochrome' medium – whether from economic necessity or choice – in any case lends a cool, crisp-edged quality which is entirely appropriate to the musical idiom as outlined above.

The critical reaction to *Wakooka* was varied, though mainly positive, ranging from Constance Cummins's comment on the Brisbane première, that 'Antill's fresh, vigorous music seems to flow through the piece like a melodious little creek'[28] and Roland Robinson's enthusiastic remark on the Sydney première that 'this ballet dances and sings with the springtide of youth and love and happiness',[29] to Curt Prerauer's dismissive comment, on a later (1962) performance, that the music is 'out of date'.[30] Prerauer, a central European émigré, was writing at a time when the modernist bias in Australian music criticism, coinciding with the advent of the younger avant-garde generation of Australian composers such as Richard Meale, Nigel Butterley, George Dreyfus and Larry Sitsky, was strongly in vogue. As observed elsewhere in this book, this bias involved an almost apologetic dismissal of most pre-avant-garde Australian music as artistically irrelevant.

---

[27]   See n. 17 above.
[28]   Constance Cummins, '"Wakooka" Jolly as a Bush Picnic', [Brisbane] *Telegraph*, 29 July 1957.
[29]   Roland Robinson, 'Australian Ballet About Station Life Presented', *The Sydney Morning Herald*, 4 September 1957.
[30]   Curt Prerauer, 'At the Local', *Nation*, No. 105, 20 October 1962, p. 18.

G'Day Digger (1958)

This short ballet (also of approximately 30 minutes' duration) follows the essentially 'light' style of *Wakooka*. It was commissioned by the Arts Council of Australia to a scenario by Victor Carell and choreography by Beth Dean; and it was the first ballet created specifically for Australian television. The première by ABC Television took place on 11 February 1958. Later, in April of that year, a staged version was toured throughout New South Wales and Queensland by the Arts Council Ballet Company. The work is scored for piano only, save for a brief episode of tape recorded 'musique concrète' or 'sound effects' which will be discussed later. The ballet was originally titled *Hello Diggers!*, the title found on the manuscript score and accompanying script (see below). However, the eventual title, *G'Day Digger* – reflecting, as Dean and Carell point out, 'the familiar greeting among Australian troops in World War 2'[31] – was well established before the TV première, as is clearly evidenced by various media announcements of the forthcoming production.[32]

The ballet's action was supplemented by a narrator outlining the story. The script for this narration has been lost, but in the folio containing the score among the Antill Papers[33] there is a detailed typescript, presumably of Carell's scenario, with numbered annotations in pencil linking points in the action to specific cues in the otherwise continuous, through-composed score. The action is in two scenes, played without a break in the music – the first, a brief scene set in a foxhole in wartime Tobruk, and the second in a bar in King's Cross, Sydney, after the war. The action is succinctly summarised by Edward Pask as follows:

> [G'Day Digger] evolved around two Australian soldiers who were mates in Tobruk. During the dirt, dust and danger of warfare [first scene] their thoughts drift back to Sydney, the girls and the cool beer, and they make a pact to meet in Sydney after their return. The ballet records their meeting [second scene] – their exuberance and fun on the town with a couple of girls [portrayed in the première by Beth Dean and Valrene Tweedie], and encounters with a jovial drunk and a pugnacious bodgie.[34]

As in the case of *Wakooka*, the musical idiom ranges from simple diatonic, through modal and pandiatonic, to somewhat more dissonant textures, as is well illustrated in the opening scene in Tobruk where the 'digger' and his mate are expressing their boredom and dreaming of the girls at home. The opening loud chord illustrates a

---

[31] Dean and Carell, *Gentle Genius*, pp. 148–9.
[32] For example, 'Antill Ballet Tells Story of Diggers', *The Sydney Morning Herald*, 20 January 1958; also 'Concrete' (a reference to the taped episode referred to above), *The ABC Weekly*, 5 February 1958.
[33] AP, S8d/2.
[34] Pask, *Ballet in Australia*, pp. 218–19.

nearby bomb blast and the hurried entrance of the two soldiers (Example 3.12), while later in the scene, as the digger imagines his girlfriend, the music adopts an overtly popular 'dance hall' style (Example 3.13) – a style which pervades much of the music of the second scene.

Example 3.12   *G'Day Digger*, bb. 1–8

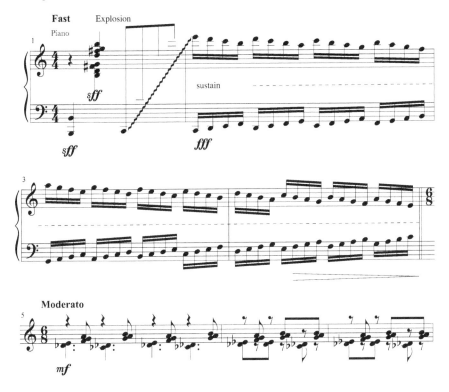

Example 3.13   *G'Day Digger*, bb. 25–30

The ballet's episodic music is effectively 'closed' near the end, where, in the King's Cross bar, a crash is heard offstage, which recalls to the soldiers the air raid at the opening, at which point they rush for the doorway and crouch as in the opening scene. This episode almost literally recalls the opening music (see

Example 3.12) before the light character of the immediately preceding music is resumed in a brief coda.

Perhaps the most noteworthy feature of this score is the passage accompanying the 'dream sequence' when the digger's mate is briefly knocked out in a fight with the bodgie. The blow is accompanied by yet another appearance of the same chord that opened the ballet (the 'bomb blast' – cf. Example 3.12) which introduces a section of 'musique concrète' – a short (approximately two-minute) interval of recorded sounds manipulated in the manner of the studio tape recording techniques of the 1950s. There are varying accounts of the sound sources used, for example by Dean and Carell and also in newspaper announcements of the ballet's coming production. The sound sources described in the typescript scenario among the Antill Papers are:

> Automobile brakes screech ... train whistles ... motor car rev up ... clang of a tram bell ... fire engine ... jet plane ... finger nails scratching across blackboard ... wood sawing ... ships whistles ... siren ... etc. [*sic*] factory machine monotonously running ... (voices running fast) [added by Antill in pencil].

The music of *G'Day Digger* is otherwise scored for piano only. Like *Wakooka*, the medium is appropriate to the character – in this case the predominantly 'music hall' atmosphere – of the scenario.

As was the case with *Wakooka*, *G'Day Digger* seems to have received a mixed reception. Dean and Carell report that, on the tour of the stage performance by the Arts Council Ballet Company,

> *G'Day Digger* touched a chord in the heart of audiences over the five months' tour and the Arts Council termed it "very successful" and announced a small profit.[35]

However, the initial television production elicited a negative review, mainly of the choreography that was considered 'unballet-like'; while the music was, rather oddly, given the predominantly popular cast of much of the melodic writing, deemed 'untuneful'.[36]

Burragorang Dreamtime (1959/1963)

Burragorang Dreamtime, along with *Black Opal* (see later discussion), marked a return to the depiction of an Aboriginal subject and, predictably, the adoption of a musical approach somewhat closer to the more dissonant style of *Corroboree*. A further commissioned collaboration between Beth Dean, Victor Carell and Antill, this ballet is, as previously mentioned, based on a scenario depicting two Aboriginal legends: the creation of the world and the first boomerang; and the birth of the waratah. *Burragorang Dreamtime* was first composed for the visit of Princess

---
[35] Dean and Carell, *Gentle Genius*, p. 149.
[36] 'Look at TV', *Daily Mirror* (Sydney), 18 February 1958, p. 27.

Alexandra to Sydney in September 1959. For the later visit by the Queen and Duke of Edinburgh in 1963, it was again performed, but in an abridged version, followed by a series of danced and mimed tableaux, with additional music depicting episodes in Australia's post-settlement history. The circumstances of both productions, and the severe constraints placed on Antill in producing the score for full orchestra (and, for the later pageant music, also a choir), have been referred to earlier. For both productions, the stage performances were accompanied by an extended narration.

As also noted earlier, the 1959 and 1963 performances were extremely elaborate and prestigious public spectacles produced for mass audiences in the open air. It is interesting to compare the critical reactions to the two performances. The more unified and coherent production of *Burragorang Dreamtime* alone in 1959 elicited an enthusiastic review in the Sydney *Daily Telegraph* of 12 September 1959, calling the performance a 'unique, intensely animated and thrilling presentation'. By contrast, the longer presentation of 1963 – with its abridged performance of *Burragorang Dreamtime*, followed by additionally narrated and enacted scenes from Australia's post-settlement history, to hastily commissioned additional music from Antill, provoked the earlier mentioned description from Roger Covell of a 'diffuse and often pointless pageant'.[37]

Dean and Carell provide a succinct summary of the two legends that make up *Burragorang Dreamtime* as follows:

> *The Boomerang Legend* has its origin in the story of Yondi, a warrior of great strength, who used a stick to lift the sky from the earth. In the Dreamtime, the earth and sky were so close together, that man and beast could only crawl and creep. The terrific strain bent the stick, and thus the boomerang was created. *The Waratah Legend* describes how a beautiful young lubra, Krubi, heartbroken at the death in battle of her warrior lover, died on a peak high above the Burragorang Valley [south-west of Sydney]. Where she fell, the first waratah grew, taking its principal colour from her robe, made of the skin of a red rock wallaby, and from brilliant gang-gang feathers she wore in her headdress.[38]

As was the case with *Wakooka*, the sources for *Burragorang Dreamtime*,[39] while considerable, offer the analyst only scant clues as to the musico-dramatic structure of the ballet and its relationship to the extended narrative scripts. The latter were provided for both the 1959 and 1963 versions of *Burragorang Dreamtime* and also Antill's additional music for the post-settlement tableaux for the 1963 *Royal Pageant of Nationhood*. The narration for *Burragorang Dreamtime* tells the stories of the two legends in detail and is accompanied in the scripts by general notes of the stage action, music and lighting. However, the music is only identified in general descriptive terms, such as: 'music in ... suggests aboriginal

---

[37] See n. 6 above.
[38] Dean and Carell, *Gentle Genius*, pp. 151–2.
[39] AP, S8a/40.

subject ... music up a little ... music picks up drumbeat to suggest corroboree dancing ... music drops little ...', etc. These descriptive notes are linked to the narration, but there are few indications in the orchestral score as to what specific passages of music coincide with the narration and these accompanying notes. Indeed the music itself, episodic and through-composed, generally lacks clear structural divisions, and appears somewhat rambling and diffuse – perhaps not surprising in view of the extremely artificial constraints under which Antill was expected to compose.[40] There is an indication of where the first 'creation' or 'boomerang' legend ends and the waratah legend begins. However, there is no sense, even here, that one section or 'act' has been concluded. Rather, there is a ten-second pause marked, during which the horns hold a pedal point on A, against a steady rhythmic pattern on the snare drum. The narration, coinciding with the transition between the legends, effectively links them together thus:

> Such was the beginning of the world, of the boomerang and of many things, but not yet of the Waratah. In the story the Aborigines tell, the Waratah did not come till well after the beginning ...

Apart from this indication, there are very few points in the score to guide the analyst as to what specific stages in the narration are being depicted. Two of these occur near the beginning and illustrate clearly the stylistic and expressive range of much of the music of the ballet. The first indication is found on page 7 of the (incomplete?) 72-page score, where the words 'the Corroboree, the Picture ... and dance' can be found. This reference coincides with the first part of the narrative that introduces the legends, and proceeds thus:

> Out of these legends has grown the corroboree ... the picture story, the history book of song and music and dance.

The mention of 'corroboree' here evokes, not surprisingly, something of Antill's *Corroboree* style. Thus the opening of *Burragorang Dreamtime* begins softly with Antill's own familiar 'corroboree' sounds – such as 'shrieks', here depicted by piccolo, flutes and clarinets; 'croaks' by bassoon and contrabassoon; and a continuous rhythmic ostinato for drums, punctuated by other percussion. This introduction gradually builds to denser passages culminating at the point of the above narrative cue, and well illustrates the more complex dissonant style to be found in much of the ensuing music (Example 3.14).

As a 'foil' to this more dissonant writing, there are passages where Antill adopts once more an 'English pastoral' manner – a more lyrical, consonant, modal idiom redolent of the music of Vaughan Williams and the English 'national school'. An example of this style occurs in the gentle, ruminative passage somewhat later in the first part of the ballet, where there is an inscription, on page 22 of the score,

---

[40] In addition it appears that some final pages of the score are missing.

Example 3.14 *Burragorang Dreamtime*, Rehearsal Letter C

reading 'Burragorang Valley' and, a few bars later, 'the waters of the Warragamba'. This coincides in the narration with the following passage:

> The waters of the Warragamba Dam are now rising high in the Burragorang Valley ... the hunting grounds of the Burragorang aborigines have gone forever.

Here the writing (see Example 3.15), while evoking an essentially lush, 'green' landscape, is also expressive of the rising waters of the Warragamba River in the formation of the dam.

Example 3.15 *Burragorang Dreamtime*, Rehearsal Letter J+

The severely artificial circumstances of composition as outlined earlier, and the occasional nature of the commission, understandably militated against the achievement of a work of potentially major stature, while the required piecemeal nature of the writing ensured a less than effective overall structure. This is regrettable, since the score contains much attractive music in an idiom in which Antill was clearly at home. It is interesting therefore to speculate that Antill, now working once more with the full range of instrumental colour afforded by the symphony orchestra, might have been able, with greater time at his disposal, to have created an even more colourful as well as structurally 'tighter' composition; and even – as in the case of *Corroboree* – to have extracted a suite for future concert performances. As it stands, *Burragorang Dreamtime*, too, has enjoyed no revivals since its initial performances in its various guises in the late 1950s and early 1960s.

Black Opal (1961)

Black Opal provides a final example of Antill's engagement with an Aboriginal choreographic subject. It was created for the newly formed Ballet Australia to choreography by Dawn Swane, an Australian ballerina and choreographer who became a prominent make-up artist following a back injury which terminated her dancing career. Ballet Australia was yet another small ballet company, formed in 1960 by Valrene Tweedie, which had as its principal aim 'to further the appreciation of ballet'[41] – notably through the encouragement of new works by Australian choreographers and composers. *Black Opal* was premièred at the Elizabethan Theatre, Sydney on 28 July 1961 in a multiple bill of five new Australian ballets.

The scenario of *Black Opal* is yet another version of the familiar 'Romeo and Juliet' theme about forbidden love between members of antagonistic families. Choreographer Dawn Swane is reported to have 'based her story on a tale told to her in childhood by an old opal prospector from Lightning Ridge'.[42] Alan Brissenden and Keith Glennon recount the story, presumably related to them by Swane herself, as follows:

> Two lovers, Euroka and Amaroo, break taboos because they are from different tribes; they are discovered by Euroka's promised bride and flee across the desert to escape punishment. Amaroo soon becomes exhausted and when the lovers appeal to the wind spirit, he sends a storm of rolling grass balls to hide them. They are found by their pursuers but as the warriors raise their spears there is a lightning flash and Amaroo and Euroka are transformed into a black opal, known afterwards as the love stone.[43]

---

[41] Pask, *Ballet in Australia*, p. 220.
[42] 'Special Music by Antill for New Ballet', *The Sydney Morning Herald*, 20 July 1961.
[43] Alan Brissenden and Keith Glennon, *Australia Dances: Creating Australian Dance 1945–1965* (Kent Town, South Australia: Wakefield Press, 2010), p. 101.

The only manuscript source for *Black Opal* among the Antill Papers comprises a full score;[44] but it is accompanied by no detailed scenario, and there are only a few references in the score to the dramatic context of the music. As to the music itself, Antill was once again hampered by financial constraints, and thus had only limited performing resources available. Instead of piano, however, he chose here to write for an unusual and more colourful ensemble of SATB choir and percussion.[45] According to Brissenden and Glennon, the ensemble is placed 'offstage',[46] although this direction does not appear on the score itself.[47] The choir's textless part comprises only vocalising, shouting and speaking. The percussion comprises a varied array of colourful non-pitched instruments (save for a pair of timpani) including bass drum, snare drum, claves, triangle, tambourine, cymbals, woodblock and Chinese block. At no point in the score are more than two of the above played simultaneously, and for the most part there is only one instrument involved. This allows the percussion component to be performed by one player, in keeping with the modest performing resources at Antill's disposal. In addition, there is a wind machine – heard at what clearly appears to be the climactic episode of the ballet, while the dancers provide an addition to the percussion accompaniment, being periodically directed to clap hands or strike their thighs 'in corroboree fashion'.

As in the case of the previous ballets considered in this chapter, the story and music of *Black Opal* called forth varied critical reactions. Dean and Carell comment on the 'atmosphere of lyrical beauty and mystery, in keeping with the drama of thwarted love and its dramatic denouement', but comment further on the relative lack of intensity in this 'slight story'.[48] Roger Covell, reviewing the five ballet premières, singled out *Black Opal*, along with Nigel Butterley's *The Tell-Tale Heart*, as the most significant of the new works, commenting that

> it was only in [these] ballets that a sympathetic spectator could feel that anything important or original was being attempted in the marriage of music and movement; and it was significant that both these ballets were danced to the most interesting sounds of the evening: new scores by John Antill and Nigel Butterley respectively.[49]

Later in the same review, Covell commented thus on the performing resources of *Black Opal*:

---

[44] AP, S8d/4.

[45] Joel Crotty notes that this was 'the first Australian choreographic composition to have been scored for choir' (see Crotty, 'Ballet Australia Between 1961 and 1962', p. 46).

[46] Brissenden and Glennon, *Australia Dances*, p. 101.

[47] Roger Covell, reviewing the première performance, noted that the choir was placed 'in one of the boxes' rather than behind the scenes as is normally denoted by the phrase 'offstage'; but does not state where the percussionist was located (see Roger Covell, 'New Ballets at Elizabethan', *The Sydney Morning Herald*, 29 July 1961, p. 7).

[48] Dean and Carell, *Gentle Genius*, p. 153.

[49] Covell, 'New Ballets at Elizabethan', p. 7.

The resulting sounds ... were highly interesting in themselves, but not completely
successful in terms of this ballet. The chorus sounded in character when singing
in unison or shouting shrieking [*sic*] in quasi-aboriginal fashion; but some of
Antill's choral harmonies had too many greenly pastoral associations to match
the parched and blazing desert conjured up on the bare boards of the stage.

These criticisms have some resonance in relation to the character and language of Antill's music for *Black Opal*. Dean and Carell's reference to the 'relative lack of intensity' and Covell's reference to 'greenly pastoral associations' are all too apparent in many pages of the score, which, nevertheless, as will be seen shortly, is not lacking in some more astringent passages. The 'contemporary style' that Antill maintains he adopts in works with an Aboriginal subject may be seen once more in the general idiom of *Black Opal* which, like *Burragorang Dreamtime*, is essentially based on the same early twentieth-century post-impressionist and 'primitivist' sources which are found, though much more abrasively, in *Corroboree*. As to Aboriginal associations, this work is notable for containing the most direct evocation in Antill's music of the traditional 'song descent' style of much Aboriginal chant. However, it is unlikely that Antill made use, as did Alfred and Mirrie Hill or Clive Douglas, of a direct transcription of a particular Aboriginal melody. Antill's 'song descent' melody appears a number of times in the first of the two scenes (or 'acts' as indicated in the score) and is first heard in the introduction (see Example 3.16) where the lower voices of the choir chant on repeated bare fifths evoking the drone of the didjeridu, while the first sopranos sing the descending melodic line.

Example 3.16   *Black Opal*, Introduction, bb. 21–28

Later, the melody reappears in a more dissonant bitonal setting as the accompanying chant/ostinato shifts to B♭/F, while the melody is sung (as in all its appearances) at the original pitch (see Example 3.17).

Example 3.17   *Black Opal*, Scene 1, Rehearsal Letter F

The score at this point – the choir is here accompanied by claves – is annotated with the word 'corroboree' in parentheses, clearly indicating Antill's intention as to the ritual association of the chant. At the end of the first scene, its further repetition leads to a general pause following which one of the very few stage directions may be found, reading 'scream of the medicine man' – at which point the curtain falls.

The 'greenly pastoral' style is well represented in a passage heard in scene 1 following the introduction (see Example 3.18).

This music, and similar material following it, returns near the end in a passage just preceding the lightning strike (another of the occasional scenario cues in the score). At this later point, it presumably typifies the peace of the hidden lovers, which is then violently interrupted by a series of barbaric shouts from the choir, against a snare drum roll, when the warriors surround them. The final passage, clearly associated with the appearance of the transfigured lovers now fused in the form of the black opal, returns to the 'pastoral' music heard at the beginning of the ballet.

Example 3.18   *Black Opal*, Scene 1, Rehearsal Letter AA

By contrast, the most 'primitivist' or abrasive passages of the ballet are to be found, as noted by Covell, in the percussive shouts of the warriors; while the choral writing, not surprisingly, does not lend itself to the level of complex dissonance much more easily realised by instruments. The most astringent passages are, predictably, to be found in scene 2 which clearly follows the desperate pursuit of the lovers; but even here, the harmony rarely moves beyond fairly simple parallel triads, sometimes chromatically adjacent and against static and dissonant pedal points held by the basses (see Example 3.19 below).

The sound world of *Black Opal* is thus of considerable novelty and interest; but the choice of performing forces creates a more colourful, rather than confrontingly abrasive, effect. *Black Opal* nevertheless clearly belongs in the same stylistic and theatrical 'family' as *Corroboree*, *The Unknown Land* and *Burragorang Dreamtime*. It also marks, for Antill, the end of his evocation of Aboriginal subjects in the theatre. Joel Crotty has recalled a personal communication with

Example 3.19   *Black Opal*, Scene 2, Rehearsal Letter M

Dawn Swane, in which the choreographer asserted that Antill was actually reluctant to undertake this latest project for fear of being exclusively typecast as a composer of 'Aborigiana'.[50] Crotty offered an alternative, though related, explanation – namely that Antill may have considered such theatrical subjects as 'passé' by the early 1960s.[51] This interpretation would seem to be supported by

---

[50] Crotty, 'Ballet Australia Between 1961 and 1962', p. 45.
[51] Ibid.

the fact that the considerable post-World War 2 effusion of ballets, operas and programmatic orchestral pieces on Aboriginal themes by such composers as the Hills, Douglas, Penberthy and others had effectively ceased by the early 1960s. Antill remained committed to Australian subjects in his remaining theatre works, to be considered in the rest of this chapter – but none are on Aboriginal themes.

Snowy! (1961)

Antill's last ballet score, *Snowy!*, was composed to a scenario of a type very different from any of his previous ballets, notwithstanding its Australian theme. As an account, in poetic, balletic and musical terms, of a major historical event – namely the development of the Snowy Mountains Hydro-Electric Scheme in New South Wales in the early 1950s[52] – the subject has much of the nature of a documentary; and it is perhaps worthy of note that by this time Antill had already composed scores for a number of documentary films. The subject is nevertheless treated – and subtitled – as a 'dance drama'; and the format is the (by now) familiar one for Antill of a choreographic scenario with accompanying narration – the latter, however, being in verse form.

The scenario and choreography are by Margaret Barr (1904–1991), an exponent, like Coralie Hinkley, of the modern dance genre. Barr was born in Bombay, India, to English and American parents and studied dance in the USA, where she subsequently worked at the studio of Martha Graham in New York. From the 1930s she moved to England, then to New Zealand during the war, and finally to Australia in 1949, where, in the early 1950s, she established her Dance-Drama Group in Sydney. Subsequently (1958) she also became the foundation Director of Dance at the newly formed National Institute of Dramatic Art (NIDA) based at the University of New South Wales, remaining in that position until 1975.[53] Her choreographic scenarios include, unusually, a number of subjects based on historical, political and biographical themes, of which *Snowy!*, as well as *Mexico!*[54] – another historical ballet produced on a double bill with *Snowy!* at their stage premières – are notable examples.

---

[52] The Snowy Mountains Scheme is arguably one of the most notable engineering achievements in Australia's history and involved the diversion of the easterly-flowing Snowy River and some tributaries in south-eastern New South Wales through a series of tunnels and reservoirs to both generate hydro-electric power for a large area of south-eastern Australia and also irrigation for the drier pastoral regions west of the Great Dividing Range via the Murray and Murrumbidgee river systems. As the project's enormous workforce included a large proportion of post-World War 2 immigrants from many parts of Europe, it also marked something of a defining stage in the social development of a more multicultural Australia.

[53] 'Barr, Margaret (1904–1991)', National Library of Australia Biographies, <trove.nla.gov.au/people 487668> accessed 17 March 2014.

[54] This ballet was written to a score by another Australian composer, Bruce Hembrowe.

The narrative poem written for *Snowy!* is by the Australian poet, playwright and social activist, Mona Brand (1915–2007), who began collaborating with Margaret Barr and her Sydney Dance-Drama Group in some projects in the early 1960s including, notably, *Snowy!*. A version of the poem was published in a collection of her poems titled *Coloured Sounds* (1997).[55] However, this version is far from the complete narration that Brand provided for the ballet production.

As mentioned at the beginning of this chapter, Antill's final ballet score was composed under unusually restrictive conditions – to Margaret Barr's already fully developed choreography originally based on the music of Mahler (there is no indication as to which Mahler score was involved). The composition of Antill's score must have begun at least by early 1961, while he was also involved with *Black Opal*. The stage première of *Snowy!*, now to Antill's music, followed hard on the heels of that of *Black Opal* – at the Science Theatre, University of New South Wales (the headquarters of NIDA) on 2 September 1961. A repeat performance was given of the double bill (*Snowy!* and *Mexico!*) on 9 September.

As also mentioned earlier, the music for the stage première was, as in the case of previous Antill ballets, scored for piano only. However a television production by the ABC followed almost immediately afterwards – on 4 October; and for this production, Antill provided a version of the music for a small orchestra comprising two flutes, oboe, horn, two trumpets, two trombones, piano/celeste and timpani. There is also a short section for vocalising soprano voice (found also in the piano score) at the narration lamenting the coming inundation of the town of Adaminaby for the hydro project (see scenario headings below). Dean and Carell state that the orchestral version (shortened to 35 minutes from the original piano version of 45 minutes) was especially commissioned from Antill and Barr for the ABC's entry of the work for the 1962 Italia Prize.[56] However, an examination of a number of ABC inter-office memos and correspondence at the time[57] shows clearly that the orchestrated version for the TV productions was planned at least as early as 21 April 1961, where mention is found of the ABC's plan to engage Margaret Barr's dance group to perform the work for television. Here, Antill's music was said to exist

> so far in piano score, but Mr. Antill has indicated that he would be pleased to score it for an unusual combination, consisting mainly of brass and percussion instruments, consisting of some eleven players.

By 29 May, a letter to Margaret Barr from the ABC's NSW Music Supervisor, Werner Baer, in making firm plans for the telecast, was referring to the

> hope that Mr. Antill will have scored his composition, which should be pre-recorded at least some four weeks before the date of transmission.

---

[55] Mona Brand, *Coloured Sounds: Poems* (Sydney: Tawny Pipit Press, 1997).
[56] Dean and Carell, *Gentle Genius*, p. 153.
[57] Copies of these memos and letters are to be found in AP, S8d/2.

Finally, an inter-office memo of 23 August acknowledged receipt of Antill's (orchestral) score 'for urgent copying'. It is to be assumed, therefore, that the stage première in September for piano only was due to the inability of the orchestral players – all members of the Sydney Symphony Orchestra – to perform at this venue, for either financial, contractual or logistical reasons. Following the initial TV production and the Italia Prize entry, there appears to have been at least one further ABC telecast of *Snowy!* – on 8 May 1963. ABC inter-office memos of February and March 1963 also refer to a fresh recording of the music at this time.[58]

The scenario for the television production is as follows:

Part 1: (a) Lamentation for the drought-stricken country; (b) March of the Commission.

Part 2: (a) Slopes of snow; (b) The game of chess: "My fathers fought this land. I shall fight for it"; (c) Adaminaby: (i) Farewell to the homestead; (ii) The rising waters; (iii) Regatta; (d) Dance night; (e) Happy Jack camp; (f) The tunnel.

Part 3: Rejoicing for the fruitful land.

The general idiom of *Snowy!*'s music ranges widely from Antill's 'Corroboree' style (although milder in texture) through to his 'light' idiom as found, for example in the 'Dance Night' episode. Reviews of the work were again mixed, with Dean and Carell commenting that the ballet was 'well received' at its Italia Prize performance,[59] while Roger Covell, reviewing the stage première, commented thus:

Snowy! [was] danced to a predictably accomplished but disappointing new score by John Antill ... [and later] ... It was unfortunate that Antill's music had to be restricted to the palette of a piano, for a subject of this kind obviously calls for the clash and colour of an orchestra.[60]

Antill's restricted task in composing a ballet to a scenario and choreography previously devised for another score must have surely inhibited him in producing what otherwise might have been a more effective composition. Also, in light of Covell's above comments, it is unfortunate that there is no record of his response to Antill's orchestrated version. Furthermore, it is regrettable that later generations have not had the opportunity of reassessing *Snowy!*, which, like Antill's other ballets of this period, has received no performances since its 1960s productions.

---

[58] AP, S8d/2.
[59] Dean and Carell, *Gentle Genius*, p. 153.
[60] Roger Covell, '"Snowy" Theme Dance-drama', *The Sydney Morning Herald*, 4 September 1961.

The Operas 1952 and 1969

The Music Critic (1952)

As stated in the introductory section of this chapter, Antill completed two operas during the post-*Corroboree* period. The first of these is *The Music Critic* – its title in full: 'The Music Critic; or, The Printer's Devil: A Burlesque Opera in One Act and Scene'. The title page of the vocal score[61] states that it was 'commenced in Perth W.A. June 1951' and 'completed Sydney N.S.W. Oct. 1952'. This opera has never been performed. Such a situation would seem to hark back to Antill's pre-*Corroboree* days in which his primary creative activity was centred upon the composition of operas, uncommissioned and with no definite prospect of a production.[62] In light of Antill's post-*Corroboree* situation, in which he was besieged by commissions – most notably for ballets – this apparent 'throwback' calls for comment. The situation becomes clearer, however, when it is realised that Antill composed *The Music Critic* with a definite performance in view. Numerous press announcements from as early as December 1951 refer to the composition of a new opera; and subsequently it is made clear that its envisaged première was to be as the companion piece in a planned double bill with *Endymion* (see Chapter 1). The stimulus for this composition appears to have been given by the then newly-formed opera company called 'New South Wales National Opera Incorporated'. This company, and Antill's work on his new opera, were discussed at length (but without reference to the planned double bill with *Endymion*) in December 1951 in an article in *The ABC Weekly*.[63] Curiously enough, however, by May 1952 Antill was reported to be writing a new ballet for performance by the same company on the planned *Endymion* double bill. In an article in *The ABC Weekly* of 17 May 1952, Antill was reported to be composing a ballet 'specially commissioned by the NSW National Opera' for this occasion, and said to be based on 'a little known Grimm's [sic] fairy tale'. It was further stated that at this time Antill had planned a scenario but had not written any music.[64] By 25 May, the Sydney *Sun-Herald* was still referring to this planned ballet.[65] However, two weeks earlier, on 10 May, an article by John Moses in the Sydney *Sun* was once again referring to Antill's opera, 'a short one-acter with a witty but so far secret title' (clearly referring to *The Music Critic*). Here Moses reported that Antill 'wrote it to fill the second part of a program with *Endymion*' and that the opera was 'completed except for the final scenes and the orchestration'.[66] On 18 October of that year, the same writer

---

[61] AP, S8b/14.
[62] Cf. n. 1 above.
[63] M.C., 'John Antill ... Writes an Opera', *The ABC Weekly* (1 December 1951), p. 7.
[64] M.C., 'NSW Opera Plans New Antill Ballet Production', *The ABC Weekly* (17 May 1952), p. 9.
[65] Martin Long, 'His Music is Home Grown', *The Sun-Herald*, Sydney (25 May 1952).
[66] John Moses, 'Music', *The Sun*, Sydney (10 May 1952).

reported on the opera, now 'just finished, except for the final orchestral scoring', in more detailed terms, including the announcement of its title and plot line.[67] Once again, the opera was stated to be 'designed' to go on a double bill with the composer's *Endymion*, but no actual commission is mentioned. However earlier, on 25 August, another notice in the Sydney *Sun* was already announcing the double bill as it finally eventuated in 1953 (see Chapter 1) – namely with Arthur Benjamin's *The Devil Take Her* as *Endymion*'s companion piece. All subsequent announcements of the planned 1953 double bill that the author has been able to trace refer to this final programme.

Regarding the question of *The Music Critic*'s commissioning by the NSW National Opera, it is curious that, while the projected ballet score was referred to as a 'commission', no such term was directly reported at the time for *The Music Critic*; although it was, as previously stated, also referred to in the context of the planned double bill with *Endymion* by this company. It can therefore be inferred that the NSW Opera had an arrangement of some kind with Antill for its composition. While there is no evidence that Antill ever wrote any music for the planned ballet, the completion of the opera – as shown by the full set of vocal, orchestral scores and orchestral parts among the Antill Papers[68] – begs the question of its fate as a fulfilled commission – if a formal commission was involved. The reasons behind the rejection of *The Music Critic* in favour of the Benjamin opera are unknown, as are any details of contractual arrangements for the opera that must have been made with Antill by the NSW National Opera Company – arrangements that would have induced the composer to write the opera.

The libretto for *The Music Critic* is Antill's own. John Moses's extended commentary on the then projected opera quoted Antill as saying 'I've never been happy writing music to fit other people's words'.[69] Among his earlier operatic essays, the youthful *Ouida* and *Princess Dorothea*, as well as *Endymion*, are set to Antill's own libretti.[70] However, the remaining pre-*Corroboree* operas (most incomplete), were, it will be recalled from Chapter 1, written to texts by Margery Browne and John Wheeler respectively; while the libretto of his final completed opera, *The First Christmas* (to be discussed later), is also not by Antill.

Antill's plot for *The Music Critic* was inspired by an actual event which is said to have occurred in Hobart around the year 1840:

[d]uring the performance of an opera at the Royal Victoria Theatre, Hobart, one of the singers [the prima donna] rightly complained that at the critical moment, a sharp report from a rifle disturbed the atmosphere causing disastrous complications to her top note.[71]

---

[67] John Moses, 'Music', *The Sun*, Sydney (18 October 1952).
[68] AP, S8b/14.
[69] See n. 66 above.
[70] Also the incomplete *Body Politic* (see n. 1 above).
[71] Antill, introduction to the libretto of *The Music Critic*, AP, S8b/14.

Around this incident, Antill fashioned an amusing story. The scene is the bar room of a tavern called 'The Shades' which is situated beneath the Royal Victoria Theatre in which the opera is being performed. A staircase backstage leads from the tavern up to the theatre. The characters are: Robert, a 'printer's devil' from the local newspaper office (tenor); Mildred, a barmaid (mezzo-soprano); Bill, a barman (bass-baritone); 'Madam Soprano', the prima donna; and 'Signor Baritone', from the cast of the opera. The chorus is made up of soldiers, townsfolk and (later) the chorus of the opera. Robert has become enamoured of the opera's prima donna, causing his former sweetheart Mildred's jealousy and despair. Bill ridicules Robert in an endeavour to win Mildred's affections, but his advances are rebuffed by her. Further hoping to win her, Bill shows off with a rifle borrowed from one of the soldiers of the chorus and accidentally fires it just at the precise moment that Madam Soprano is singing her 'top C' in the opera upstairs. Robert meanwhile, a would-be poet, having been writing damaging criticisms in verse of the opera performance, has dropped off to sleep, and upsets a glass of red wine which trickles on to the floor. Bill drops the gun by Robert's side, the spilt wine making it appear that he has been shot. Following the end of the opera performance, Madam Soprano and the cast of the opera descend to the tavern demanding revenge on the culprit who had thus ruined the final scene. Madam Soprano, seeing the gun lying beside Robert, presumes him to be the guilty one and vows retribution until she sees the red wine stains and concludes that Robert has killed himself. As the company debate a suitable epitaph for the supposed corpse, Mildred, still in love with Robert, protests that he was more than just a 'printer's devil', but truly a 'poet who loved music', and pleads that he be posthumously deemed a 'music critic'! At this point, a crumpled piece of paper (thought to be a suicide note) is found in Robert's hand, which discloses his disparaging criticisms of the operatic performance. Robert then awakens and the hostile prima donna demands that Robert be given 50 lashes for his supposed interruption of her performance and his negative criticisms. Mildred pleads on his behalf, while Bill confesses that it was he who fired the rifle shot. All ends happily when Robert confesses his rekindled love for Mildred, the couple are reunited and Madam Soprano announces that she has just married the opera conductor.

It will be recalled from Chapter 1 that Antill's basic approach to opera composition from his earliest youthful essays was to adopt a 'through-composed' or 'continuous' rather than 'number opera' format. This was true of all his pre-*Corroboree* operas with the exception only of the two 'light operas' written for the Opportune Club competition – *Here's Luck* and *The Glittering Mask*, where an 'operetta' format with numbers and spoken dialogue was required. In *The Music Critic*, Antill again follows a 'through-composed' style. His intention to compose in this way is highlighted in a previously quoted interview in *The ABC Weekly*[72] where his method of composition for the then only sketched opera was commented upon by the interviewer thus:

---

[72] Cf. n. 63 above.

Example 3.20   *The Music Critic*, bb. 37–46

Any comparison with Wagner he brushed aside with a laugh, but allowed that his method was Wagnerian rather than Italian in so far as his opera was continuous with words and music closely integrated. "Any applause must come at the end", he stipulated, "not after every aria as you so often hear at performances of Italian opera".

Notwithstanding the 'Wagnerian' reference, *The Music Critic*, as a sparkling comedy, is written in a manner appropriate to an 'opera buffa' rather than a

Example 3.21   *The Music Critic*, bb. 232–237(2)

'music drama'. Its continuity resembles, to a far greater degree, an extension of the 'chain finale' form found in opera buffa – that is, a series of clearly phrased episodes ranging from solos to ensembles of varying numbers of characters. The predominantly regular (though changing) metres of the successive sections of the libretto lend themselves to this kind of setting, and the pace is generally taut, as appropriate to a light hearted comedy of the opera buffa type. The musical language is, not surprisingly, similar to that of the two 'light' ballets already considered – *Wakooka* and *G'Day Digger* – i.e. clearly tonal or modal, but liberally spiced with dissonances of a neo-classical character.

Robert's opening solo, in which he is composing his poem for Madam Soprano, illustrates the neo-classical style as well as the comic arioso singing found throughout most of the opera (see Example 3.20 above).

The first, and one of the few isolated pieces of Italian style recitative – creating a suitably dramatic change of pace at a critical point in the action – occurs at the entrance of Madam Soprano after the gunshot (see Example 3.21).

Example 3.22   *The Music Critic*, bb. 558–561

Following this recitative, she insists upon repeating her hitherto interrupted cadenza, which she does, to the accompaniment of a solo flute, comically echoing the style of the Mad Scene from Donizetti's *Lucia di Lammermoor*. Another Italian operatic touch occurs when both Signor Baritone and Madam Soprano are confronted with Robert's criticism of their performances, at which each sing an aria which is greeted with shouts of 'bravo' from the cast and chorus. Madam Soprano's aria is in the late Classical/early Romantic slow-fast rondò format, the two sections resembling the cantabile-cabaletta pair common in operas from Rossini to Verdi. The opening of the swift stretta-like 'cabaletta' is shown in Example 3.22.

All in all, this as yet unperformed opera is an attractive work with highly infectious music. Its rejection by the NSW National Opera in 1952 would seem inexplicable, at any rate on purely musical grounds. The opera nevertheless deserves to be heard, along with a number of the now too many neglected works by Antill and other composers from this hitherto unfashionable period of Australia's musical development.

The First Christmas (1969)

Antill's last opera was completed at the time of his retirement from the ABC and, apart from *Cantate Domino* (1970 – see Chapter 5) and his contribution to the collaborative *Variations on a Theme of Alfred Hill* (1969–1970 – see Chapter 4), was his last composition of substance.

The opera resulted from a commission by the New South Wales Government in 1966 for an Australian opera that could be performed at the Sydney Opera House when completed. The grant of $1500 was offered to Antill in September 1966 as was widely reported in the press at the time. The commission was for a one-act opera on an Australian theme, preferably depicting an Australian Christmas. The Sydney *Daily Telegraph* of 13 December later reported somewhat more fully on the details of the commission as follows:

> Mr. Cutler [NSW Deputy Premier] said the Advisory Committee recommended that the opera have an Australian flavour, preferably based on an Australian Christmas. It should be in a lighter vein, suitable for both professional and amateur performance. Mr. Antill would choose his own librettist.

It is clear that Antill had some misgivings about the project – mainly, it appears, regarding the Christmas theme – before he finally accepted it. This can be seen in an article in *The Australian* newspaper of 9 September 1966, titled 'Antill may reject $1500', where Antill was quoted thus:

> … The bit about the Christmas theme makes me wonder whether I'll accept. It's a peculiar idea, to say the least … Whether I accept the commission will depend on the Government's stipulations regarding theme, and the time allowed for writing the opera.

Antill did, nevertheless, accept the commission, and on the Christmas theme as recommended by the commissioners. The question of the 'lighter vein' will be discussed shortly, in relation to the opera's final plot. *The First Christmas* was completed in full score by November 1969.[73] However, the work was never performed live, as intended, at the Sydney Opera House, which finally opened in 1973; but it was broadcast by ABC Radio on Christmas Day 1970, and a subsequent broadcast was aired on Christmas Eve 1971.[74] It has received no further performances – either broadcast or staged.

Antill's commission offered an additional grant of $500 for the librettist of his choice. Antill's chosen collaborator was Pat Flower (1914–1977), an English-born Australian novelist, playwright, film and television script writer. Her work unusually encompassed crime and 'psychological' novels as well as plays and scripts of an often lighter or comic character. At the time of her collaboration with

---

[73] An annotation on the first page of the piano score reads: 'completed full score November 1969' (AP, S8b/16).

[74] See annotation on piano score title page (AP S8b/16). These dates contradict Dean and Carell's dates of the two broadcasts of a year earlier – viz. Christmas Day 1969 and repeated in 1970 (no date) (see *Gentle Genius*, p. 165).

Antill she was awarded the Dame Mary Gilmore Award (1967) for a television comedy titled *Tilley Landed on Our Shores*,[75] which was set at the time of the First Fleet settlement under Governor Arthur Phillip at Sydney Cove in 1788. This may well have suggested the period setting of *The First Christmas*, which is during the time of Phillip's governorship, on Christmas Day 1788. The comic nature of Flower's television play may also have resonated with both librettist and composer in keeping with the commissioners' request that the opera be 'in a lighter vein'. However, examination of the plot outlines, multiple versions of the libretto and the final scores of the opera reveals a change of direction from a happy to a tragic ending.[76]

The plot concerns a group of convicts working for the government and living in assigned quarters. The scene is a hut in which Mary, a domestic (soprano) has just given birth to a son, and is later joined by her convict husband John (tenor) who has illegally absconded from a road gang to be with his wife. Other characters include Bridget, another convict servant (contralto); Paddy, her suitor (baritone); Kathy, a young girl of 12 to 14 (soprano); later, an army officer (baritone) and two private soldiers ('red coats') (tenor and bass); and Benelong, an Aborigine (silent role). Following the joyful reunion of Mary and John, the latter is urged to flee before the soldiers arrive to recapture him. They dream of escape and starting a new life together as farmers. The soldiers then arrive to recapture John. Bridget, who, during this episode, has exited the scene, dramatically reappears and says that she has spoken to a man 'close to the Governor' who is about to grant John a pardon. The soldiers, uncertain as to the truth of Bridget's claim, eventually depart, vowing to return shortly. At this point, the two plots diverge. In the earlier version, Governor Phillip arrives with John's pardon and a gift of a small silver cup for the child. The cast form a final tableau around Mary and the child, 'suggesting the Adoration of the Magi' at the birth of Jesus – and singing a carol as the curtain falls. In the cast list on the plot outline for this version, Governor Phillip is included among the characters, but the name has been subsequently crossed out. The cast list for the second 'tragic' version omits Phillip's name and he does not appear in the scores. In the final plot outline and both score versions, after the soldiers

---

[75] This title is an amusing pun on the words 'till he landed on our shore', which is a line taken from the (now discarded) second stanza of the (present) Australian national anthem 'Advance Australia Fair' and refers to Captain Cook's landing at Botany Bay in 1770.

[76] AP, S8b/16. The piano and full scores of the opera make it clear that it is the tragic ending that was finally adopted, while the sketchy correspondence from Flower to Antill held in this file suggests that the earlier 'happier' version may have been abandoned as early as March 1967. No letters have been located covering the decision to change the plot ending. The title of the opera (on a draft of the 'tragic' version of the libretto!) was at one stage given as 'Three Spuds and Half a Cabbage' (the phrase 'Half a Cabbage' appearing also as an alternative title on the title page of the piano score, though not on the full score). The final title 'The First Christmas' is nevertheless also found on the early 'happy ending' version of the libretto.

Example 3.23   *The First Christmas*, bb. 14–21

have departed, Bridget confesses that she did not see the Governor or 'his man' at all, but was buying time for John to escape. Kathy, meanwhile, has mislaid a letter given to her by her father which may foreshadow John's pardon from the Governor. John, in the absence of any concrete evidence of his pardon, makes a break, but is pursued by the returning soldiers and is shot. Too late, Kathy finds the letter promising pardon, and the cast gathers round the cradle in a tragic tableau as Mary collapses in grief.

Antill's musical setting of *The First Christmas* is once again in a continuous 'through-composed' style. Flower's libretto is in prose and largely conversational in character, but also contains ensemble passages where, in Italian operatic style, characters are expressing often conflicting feelings simultaneously. As to Antill's treatment of the text in this opera and his approach to word setting generally, Dean and Carell have commented as follows:

> Antill's work in writing for the voice was never as successful as some of his other endeavours ... He was never bold in encouraging declamation to stress the drama, and to let the music flower into lyricism and melody.[77]

These criticisms are somewhat similar to those of Roger Covell when he stated, in relation to *The Song of Hagar to Abraham the Patriarch* (1957) that 'there are sections where the music seems to be merely "getting through" the task of setting the words'.[78]

These ideas with regard to Antill's approach to word setting will be taken up further in Chapter 5 with reference to *The Song of Hagar* and other vocal works. Meanwhile, with respect to *The First Christmas*, there would seem to be some justification for Dean and Carell's assessment, since the vocal writing rarely departs from a 'conversational' style, while the orchestral accompaniment ranges from sparse interjections separated by rests to continuous, often ostinato, passages over which the voices sing independently in a manner reminiscent of the 'parlante' style found in many passages in Verdi's and – more especially – Puccini's operas. The 'sparse' texture is well illustrated in the opening passage of the opera, where Bridget (after a few bars of orchestral introduction) enters chasing flies by clashing two saucepans together and then settles into the task of cooking the limited Christmas fare (see Example 3.23).

Almost immediately following, a signal is heard offstage to indicate that another escaped convict is being pursued (this subsequently turns out to be John). Bridget notes this apparently frequent occurrence while chopping potatoes, the accompaniment now a dull ostinato, typifying her attitude to her humdrum existence (see Example 3.24 below).

---

[77] Dean and Carell, *Gentle Genius*, pp. 164–5.
[78] Covell, *Australia's Music*, p. 155.

Example 3.24   *The First Christmas*, bb. 24–30

A typically prosaic dialogue passage is illustrated later in the opera (see Example 3.25) where Mary and John discuss John's treatment by the soldiers while in captivity.

Perhaps one of the few occasions where the vocal declamation veers, though only tentatively, towards lyricism occurs shortly after the previous example, in a passage where John expresses his hopes for himself, Mary and the child to begin a new life together (see Example 3.26 below). Here too, the accompaniment moves in broadly spaced chords underpinning the intensity of John's emotions.

Finally, the 'continuous' nature of the opera invites the question as to whether Antill made use of Wagnerian leitmotifs as found to varying extents in late nineteenth- and early twentieth-century operas of a similarly 'continuous' style. As in Antill's previous completed operas, there is little evidence of any systematic use of this technique, although, as in the cases of the youthful *Princess Dorothea* and of *Endymion* (see Chapter 1), Antill does make limited use of recurring themes. In the former operas these are not associated with specific dramatic events or characters but are used as simply unifying themes in a more abstract symphonic manner. In *The First Christmas*, there is one thematic idea which recurs a number of times, but here there is a definite dramatic connection. This is a theme in the orchestra which is of a lullaby character and clearly refers to the newborn child. It is first heard early on where Bridget is soliloquising about her lot and that of Mary

Example 3.25   *The First Christmas*, bb. 326–330(1)

and the child who will be brought up in wretched poverty. Later, Kathy actually sings a lullaby to the baby while Mary and Bridget are conversing, parlante fashion, as Bridget offers Mary some gruel (Example 3.27 below).

This lullaby – clearly the most lyrical passage in the entire opera – is finally heard near the end when Benelong brings a gift for the child. The only other obviously recurrent material (although not in this case involving literal repetition) is the martial music heard at each of the two entrances of the soldiers.

Notwithstanding the predominantly declamatory nature of the vocal writing (or perhaps because of it), *The First Christmas* is a tautly expressed, concise and firmly shaped music drama, which, if somewhat lacking in lyrical warmth, nevertheless effectively portrays this touching story. It is a work that is also highly worthy of revival.

Example 3.26   *The First Christmas*, bb. 369(4)–379

Example 3.27   *The First Christmas*, bb. 233–239(1)

Conclusion

This chapter has attempted to provide an overall perspective of Antill's output of opera and ballet after *Corroboree* and shows the composer's continuing engagement with the theatre, which, as has been seen, began in his earliest years. Viewing his work for these media overall, it may be observed that the neglect of Antill's theatre works, as well as those of other composers of his generation, was first the result of the sudden rise of what may be termed 'high modernist' styles in the music of Australian composers whose careers began in the 1960s and the critical rejection of music of the preceding post-colonial generation of composers. Part of this rejection can be also attributed to the predominantly 'cosmopolitan' preferences of this younger modernist generation and – notwithstanding the persistence of nationalist themes in the music of Peter Sculthorpe among this new generation – a turning away from the depiction of national subjects as well as from the perceived outmoded genres of opera and ballet. Somewhat ironically, however, with the return of a more varied, pluralist, musical language in the postmodern era, as well as a revival of interest in specifically 'Australian' subjects and a renewed interest in theatre works, the rapid efflorescence of such works by an ever larger group of younger composers has inevitably contributed to the continued neglect of the music of Antill's generation.

Chapter 4
After *Corroboree* (2) – Orchestral Works

Overview

> After *Corroboree*, everybody thought of me as a ballet writer. Many stories and commissions came my way. Ballet seemed to be the thing expected of me and it kept pushing the symphonic works into the background. I had been a symphonic man all my life through playing in several orchestras, including the Sydney Symphony.[1]

Thus commented Antill, as reported by Dean and Carell around the time of the composer's 60th birthday (i.e. the mid-1960s). This comment is revealing, and discloses a genuine desire on Antill's part to write substantial concert works for orchestra. As well as his experience as an orchestral player, Antill's work with the ABC also involved him in almost invariably conducting any performances of his own works, including the relatively few major concert pieces that were completed during his years with the broadcaster. That Antill would have composed a greater number of concert works of a more ambitious nature, given the time and opportunity, is clearly implied in the comment recorded above. Furthermore, the comment made in his 'Early history' and quoted in Chapter 1 may be recalled – in which he reminisced on his earliest compositions thus:

> ... my school books always had sketches for future symphonies scribbled on every spare space. Symphonies which did not eventuate ... [2]

The Antill Papers include also a number of sketches and incomplete orchestral scores dating from as early as the 1920s. One can only speculate as to how many more aborted 'symphonies' might have been among a large quantity of manuscripts which Antill is reported to have destroyed following his move from his large harbourside home to a smaller home unit some time after his retirement from the ABC.[3]

As in the case of the theatre works, Antill's orchestral output was also dominated by numerous commissions and undertakings to write relatively minor – and here often brief and 'occasional' – pieces. The energies required to fulfil these commissions undoubtedly contributed to his relatively meagre output of concert

---

[1] Dean and Carell, *Gentle Genius*, p. 165.
[2] AP, S5/2.
[3] Dean and Carell, *Gentle Genius*, pp. 175–6.

works of more substance. The larger works for orchestra will be examined in some detail in the main body of this chapter, while the following introductory survey will attempt a brief documentation of his overall output for this medium. A full list of works will be provided in Appendix 1.

Of Antill's orchestral output, one work stands out as the most significant – namely the three-movement *Symphony on a City* (1959), commissioned by the city of Newcastle (NSW) for celebrations on its centenary. This is undoubtedly Antill's most significant concert work and one of his greatest achievements after *Corroboree*. Other multi-movement orchestral works include *A Sentimental Suite* (referred to in Chapter 3) based on music composed for the abortive ballet which comprises 13 very brief movements totalling approximately 45 minutes; and the Concerto for Harmonica and Orchestra (1961), commissioned by the ABC and intended for the celebrated American harmonica player Larry Adler. This concerto is a relatively short work in three movements with a total duration of some 13 minutes, and was premièred by the Australian harmonica virtuoso Lionel Easton with the Sydney Symphony Orchestra and subsequently released on a commercial LP recording by RCA (now deleted).[4] Antill also provided two movements to a work commissioned to celebrate the centenary (1970) of the birth of his teacher Alfred Hill – *Variations on a Theme of Alfred Hill*. The six movements of this work were contributed by five composers under the general coordination of Antill, who composed the Introduction and Coda. In addition it may be recalled from Chapter 3 that the ballet *The Unknown Land* was written as a suite of four movements which, in its version for strings, has had several concert performances and a recording. Finally, among Antill's 'symphonies which did not eventuate', there is a brief fragment of an uncommissioned work titled *Four Abstract Pieces for Orchestra*, dated 1946 and apparently begun during a visit to London on the occasion of Goossens's UK première of *Corroboree* in the Albert Hall and its subsequent recording by the BBC.

Antill's other concert music for orchestra comprises single-movement works – namely *An Outback Overture* (1954), *Overture for a Momentous Occasion* (1956–1957) and *Paean to the Spirit of Man* (1968). Two of these works were the result of specific commissions: *Overture for a Momentous Occasion* to celebrate the tenth anniversary of the ABC's Youth Concerts; and *Paean to the Spirit of Man*, another ABC commission, for a concert to celebrate the twentieth anniversary of the Universal Declaration of Human Rights. *An Outback Overture* seems not to have been the result of a specific commission, but was composed presumably at the instigation of the ABC and premièred at the Tivoli theatre, Sydney in connection with the royal visit that year. These three works, though 'occasional' in origin and scope, are nevertheless of some musical substance – *Paean* with a length of over ten minutes being both musically and structurally the most substantial. All these

---

[4] Lionel Easton (harmonica) with the Sydney Symphony Orchestra conducted by the composer (RCA LP, SL16372).

works have been recorded on ABC LPs released for educational institutions, while *Overture for a Momentous Occasion* has also been recorded commercially.[5]

Also among Antill's orchestral music are a substantial number of scores for documentary films, of which the Antill Papers list 12 written between 1945 and 1963.[6] Antill's film scores are among a strikingly large quantity of scores for documentary films produced during the same period by such composers as Alfred and Mirrie Hill, Clive Douglas and others as well as Antill. Most of these films were commissioned by the Australian Government for promotional purposes, depicting various aspects of the Australian landscape and people; and most are of less than 30 minutes' duration[7] – some as brief as five minutes – providing opportunities for some descriptive music, especially 'landscape' depictions, but only limited scope for significant musical development. These film scores – all commissions, like those for his ballet scores – also often involved tight deadlines and other constraints. In this respect, Antill has been quoted by Dean and Carell as appealing to film producers to give more thought to the music for films in their early planning, adding that, from his own experience,

> [f]ilm producers don't think of the music until a short time before the film is due to go on screen. I have been phoned to do music for a film, and told that the film must be shown in three weeks. Of course I do it, but I do not go to bed.[8]

As music, Antill's film scores reveal nothing about the range of his compositional style post-*Corroboree* that is not apparent in his theatrical and concert music discussed in this and the previous chapter. A fuller study of his film music, which would involve a more detailed examination of its integration (or otherwise) with the often rather crude cinematic techniques of this time, lies outside the chosen focus of the present study.[9]

As well as film scores, the Antill Papers also list some 12 items of incidental music for television, radio and live theatre productions during this period.

---

[5] NZ Symphony Orchestra conducted by James Judd (Naxos CD 8.570241). An earlier commercial LP recording by Antill conducting the Sydney Symphony Orchestra (Festival Records LP, SFC80019) is now long deleted.

[6] AP, S8e. Dean and Carell (*Gentle Genius*, p. 201) list a further five scores which are unlocated – see Appendix 1.

[7] One film of significant length – c. 50 minutes – with Antill's music – was an ABC commission. The film, titled *The Land that Waited*, concerned the landing of Captain Arthur Philip in 1788 and was produced in 1963 as part of the 175th Anniversary of white settlement discussed in relation to the *Royal Pageant of Nationhood* in Chapter 3 (see Dean and Carell, *Gentle Genius*, p. 159).

[8] Dean and Carell, *Gentle Genius*, p. 163.

[9] Antill's film scores have been discussed by James McCarthy, who was head of the music department of Film Australia from 1964 to 1986. See James McCarthy, 'John Antill and his Film Music for Film Australia', unpublished paper presented at the Symposium of the International Musicological Society, University of Melbourne, July 2004.

However, in a handwritten work list produced by Antill for the ABC and held among the Antill Papers[10] there are several more items of film and television music, bringing the total tally of film and incidental music to well over 30 items. Finally, for orchestra, there are a dozen or so brief fanfares and flourishes composed for various occasions, including *Jubagalee* (A Flourish) written for the royal concert on the occasion of the opening of the Sydney Opera House in 1973.

Major Works for Orchestra

The remainder of this chapter comprises a more detailed examination of Antill's major orchestral works, in order to provide some perspective of the composer's achievements and status as a 'symphonic man'. Of these, the 'recycled' ballet music titled *A Sentimental Suite* will be discussed first, followed by a chronological examination of Antill's purely concert or 'symphonic' works. At this point it should be observed that even here Antill preferred his works to have extramusical dimensions – i.e. descriptive or 'programmatic' features in the case of his concert works. The Harmonica Concerto and his contributions to the Alfred Hill Variations are the only instances of completed post-*Corroboree* orchestral works with no extramusical associations.

A Sentimental Suite (1955)

It will be recalled from Chapter 3 that *A Sentimental Suite* had its origins as a projected ballet score, based on C.J. Dennis's famous poem *The Songs of a Sentimental Bloke*; and that a stage production was prohibited owing to the copyright on all musical versions of Dennis's work being held by the composer Albert Arlen, who wrote a musical play based on the poem, but would not permit a balletic setting to be produced. A perusal of the Antill Papers indicates unmistakeably that Antill's ballet score was essentially complete before the theatrical embargo was known. The manuscript scores (piano and orchestral) are accompanied by extensive production notes and a full scenario.[11] The piano score (but not the orchestral score) also contains detailed stage directions throughout, which coincide with the accompanying scenario and production notes. The piano score is still titled *The Sentimental Bloke*; however the production notes and scenario accompanying it already carry the revised title *A Sentimental Suite*,[12] as does the orchestral score. Both scores are subtitled 'Free Variations on an Original

---

[10] AP, S5/1.
[11] AP, S8/25–29.
[12] The original balletic intention is further indicated here, as the scenario accompanying the piano score carries the note: 'For orchestra. Piano arrangement for rehearsal only. Full orchestra must be used for performance'. It is obvious that a rehearsal score for piano would only be used for a theatrical rather than concert work.

Theme', the original production notes adding 'arranged for ballet ... ' while this reference is missing from the title page of the orchestral score, which merely refers to the Dennis poem as its origin. It seems clear, therefore, that the suite involved no significant rearrangement, but comprises the original ballet score simply retitled. Its organisation as a suite of 13 distinct movements is not inconsistent with Antill's approach to ballet composition elsewhere, as a similar suite-type organisation has already been noted in both the full score of *Corroboree* and *The Unknown Land*. Antill's notes on the suite, presumably written for the concert première by the Sydney Symphony Orchestra under Nicolai Malko in November 1957, still refer to a theatrical dimension, describing the work as 'Free Variations on an original Theme for Orchestra, which can also be presented with interpretative dance'.

The 'original theme' referred to here is a diatonic theme of a distinctly 'sentimental' cast (see Example 4.1 below), which Antill wrote as incidental music on the occasion of the Queen's traditional Christmas Message in 1953, and which was broadcast from Sydney while she was touring Australia and New Zealand. Antill's notes accompanying the scores make it clear as to the origin of the theme and its connection with the genesis of both the original Dennis ballet and the subsequent suite:

> The original Theme chosen was written for the British Broadcasting Corporation's 'Round the World' broadcast on Christmas Day, 1953, for which I was commissioned to compose the music ...
>
> Having a great admiration for the works of C.J. Dennis, I had in mind for many years the adaptation of "The Sentimental Bloke", either as an opera or ballet. Immediately I heard [complimentary comments on the Christmas broadcast theme], the idea of interpretative dance flashed in my mind, based on variations of this theme ...

Antill's full score and piano score both contain all 13 movements, with indications of the eight 'scenes' of the original ballet clearly indicated. The scenario follows the wooing, winning and wedding of the 'bloke', Bill, and his lady love, Doreen. The stages of the story, scene titles and the corresponding suite movements are as follows:

> 1. Theme (Prelude); Fantasie ("Spring Song"): a street scene; Bill's loneliness on a beautiful spring day.
> 2. Sonata ("The Introduction"): Bill's first meeting with Doreen – "love at first sight"; Doreen initially haughty, but agrees to a future date at the beach.
> 3. Rondo and Fugue ("The Stoush o' Day"): Bill attends a boxing match and in a general melée is knocked out; Doreen comforts him.
> 4. Nocturn ("Doreen"): Bill is comforted by Doreen at their beach date.
> 5. Overture and Funeral Music ("The Play"): Bill and Doreen attend a performance of *Romeo and Juliet*.

6. Scherzo ("The Stror 'at Coot" [The Straw Hat Coot]): Bill fights with and injures a former boyfriend of Doreen's – a "flashy type" – and is rejected by Doreen.

7. Chanson Triste ("The Siren"): at Doreen's family home, Doreen and Bill are reunited after Doreen sings a pathetic ballad called "Heart of Stone".

8. Finale – Prelude; Rondo Spiritoso; Processional; Recapitulation; Theme: Bill and Doreen are married and start a family – "life marches on".

For the 1957 concert première – and apparently sole performance – of *A Sentimental Suite*, much of the balletic reference has been dropped and the suite abridged to nine movements. There is no evidence that the original suite of 13 movements has ever been performed. Although, as mentioned earlier, Antill still referred to the possibility of 'interpretative dance', his notes provided for this performance comprise a far more general introduction, while the list of movements omits any reference to their original connection with the scenario:

> The selection played tonight is taken from the full length suite, and each section represents a phase of the well-known classic of Australian humour and sentimentality – a work so widely known that the characters and their sayings are almost household words ... The movements are: Theme; Fantasie; Sonata; Nocturn; Overture; Scherzo; Chanson Triste; Rondo; Recapitulation.

This shorter nine-movement version forms a more concise suite, while the brief movements themselves comprise formally compact miniatures, with only limited scope for thematic expansion or development.

As stated earlier, the musical origin of the work is the 'sentimental theme' which Antill wrote for the Queen's Christmas Broadcast in 1953. As can be seen from Example 4.1, this theme is diatonic and harmonised quite conventionally – as might be expected for music of a popular cast written for such a public occasion.

This theme forms the brief 'Prelude' movement of the suite which precedes the first 'scene' of the ballet score. Antill has described the entire suite as 'free variations' on this theme (hereinafter capitalised as the 'Theme'). Examination of the scores reveals, however, that there is much independent episodic material throughout, but with direct or indirect reminders ('variations') of the Theme appearing in many (but not all) of the movements; while the 'Recapitulation' returns to a diatonic embellished variation followed by a literal repetition of the Theme to close the work. Examples of variations appearing in the 'concise' suite include: a still mainly diatonic, waltz-like version acting as main theme of the 'Fantasie'; some more dissonant variations in the 'Overture', including a passage following the duel in *Romeo and Juliet* (Example 4.2) and two appearances in the 'Scherzo' (Bill's fight with the 'Stror 'at Coot'), the second of these shown in Example 4.3 below.

The relationship between the musical organisation and the scenario events is mostly quite loose and generalised, the structures of the individual movements being quite autonomous – a situation underlined by the choice of abstract generic

Example 4.1 *A Sentimental Suite*, Theme (Prelude), bb. 1–12

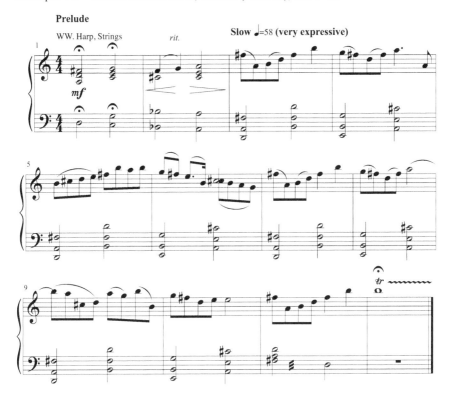

Example 4.2 *A Sentimental Suite*, Scene 5, bb. 605–612

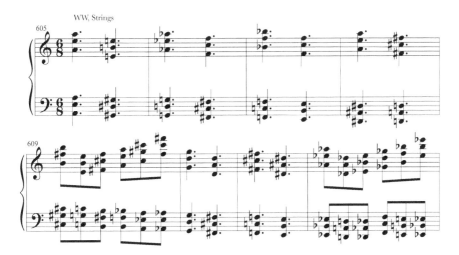

Example 4.3   *A Sentimental Suite*, Scene 6, bb. 838–841

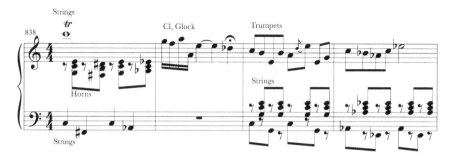

titles for each movement. The most striking instance of a direct musico-dramatic correlation is to be found in the 'Rondo and Fugue' of the original suite, in which the rondo section's main theme (another variation of the Theme) coincides with the beginnings of 'rounds' of the boxing match. This then breaks off as the crowd joins in the ensuing mêlée – effectively represented by the contrapuntal accumulation of 'voices' in a neo-classical-style fugue, the subject of which is yet a further, chromatic variant of the Theme (Example 4.4). The fugue becomes increasingly dissonant as the brawl reaches its climax (Example 4.5).

Example 4.4   *A Sentimental Suite*, Scene 3, bb. 428–433

The forms of the other movements are mostly simple 'closed' structures, the only other movement displaying more formal sophistication, apart from the above-mentioned Rondo and Fugue, being the 'Sonata'. Although brief, there is a vestige of sonata form observable. Following a chromatic introduction for violas over a tambourine roll, a main theme in C major is briefly developed via a chromatic 'bridge passage' leading to its repetition in G major (a kind of 'monothematic'

Example 4.5   *A Sentimental Suite*, Scene 3, bb. 460–465

second subject). The 'development' section comprises new material, following which the movement concludes with a recapitulation of the main theme and finally the introduction, which now acts as a coda.

As can be seen from the above discussion, the musical language of *A Sentimental Suite* betrays a somewhat more 'symphonic' character than that of the ballets examined in Chapter 3, despite the brief scope of the individual movements. The style ranges from the simple diatonicism of the Theme to pages of more astringent dissonance of a neo-classical character, the overall harmonic and tonal idiom being more or less aligned with that of the 'lighter' ballets – *Wakooka* and *G'Day Digger* – discussed in Chapter 3. The lighter, more 'tuneful' elements of the score obviously appealed strongly to the audience at the 1957 première, reviews of the performance all referring to the work's enthusiastic audience reception. Critical comments were somewhat cooler, however, the bland simplicity of the Theme (Example 4.1) and similarly diatonic passages throughout the work evoking negative responses. One reviewer called the piece 'a disappointing pastiche which never seemed to escape the atmosphere of a radio show in which the basic theme was first used',[13] while another reviewer referred to the work as 'a nine-piece set of free variations which offsets the old-fashioned sugariness of its worst moments with the colour, brilliance and variety of the instrumental sport in its best'.[14] Significantly, yet another reviewer opined that Antill's 'tuneful, pleasant, unpretentious music seemed to be illustrating something'; and commented on the composer's programme note that the work could be presented with interpretative dance, suggesting that 'that's probably what it needs to clarify matters'.[15] This comment clearly implies a view that – despite the 'symphonic' qualities mentioned above – the Suite never convincingly transcended its theatrical origins to become a satisfactorily autonomous concert piece. Such is not the case with the following purely concert works, which nevertheless, as commented earlier, are still mostly linked with extramusical associations.

An Outback Overture (1954)

As stated earlier in this chapter, there appears to be no record of this ten-minute overture having been commissioned. However, the title page of the full score held among the Antill Papers[16] records its first performance as taking place at the Tivoli Theatre, Sydney, by the Sydney Symphony Orchestra conducted by Antill. This performance, on 8 February 1954, is described as being part of the 'Royal Command Season' – obviously referring to the occasion of the 1954 royal visit by the Queen and Duke of Edinburgh, for whom the second choreographed version of *Corroboree* was performed at the same venue two days earlier (see Chapter 3). Clearly, therefore, some contractual arrangement with Antill must have existed, presumably with the ABC, for the composition of this work.

Antill's notes accompanying the score say nothing about a commission, but merely give a detailed account of the work's genesis (inspired by recollections of an evening during a bush camping holiday) and 'programme', as follows:

---

[13] *The Sydney Morning Herald*, 14 November 1957.
[14] Sydney *Daily Mirror*, 14 November 1957.
[15] Unidentified newspaper clipping, AP, S16.
[16] AP, S8a/23.

It was a colourful sunset, but we hurried towards our camping place, as we were anxious that darkness should not overtake us. The memory of that enjoyable evening is the subject of this short overture:

The peace and quiet of the Australian Bush.

A running creek.

A woolshed nearby from which the sounds of an antiquated out of repair concertina plays, over and over again, a certain easy phrase.

A conscious atmosphere of preparation and the arrival of guests.

A Woolshed Polka and a Midnight Quadrille, accompanied by much clapping of hands and stamping of feet.

Without a doubt a most enjoyable evening for all concerned.

But that strange phrase of that antiquated out of repair concertina lingers in our memories until this day. It was an obvious, like so many, yet unaccountable tune. We whistled, hummed and even adapted lyrics, beginning with "Land of Sunshine" and ending with "Land of Pride" etc. With us it became of national importance. And it is with this theme the overture is concluded. By this means I hope to be relieved of this constant haunting responsibility and thus free to devote some time to more serious thought.

This 'programme' is clearly reflected in the form of the overture, which is essentially a fairly loosely constructed tone poem. It begins with an extended section of quiet, 'pastoral' music of a modal cast, depicting the bush scene and the running creek. Ruminative, throbbing chords for low woodwind and brass, together with violins and harp arpeggios accompany wisps of melody for celeste and violas (Example 4.6 below).

Following some dissonant shrieks for woodwind and brass, indicating the arrival of guests for the woolshed dance, the extended central section of the overture depicts the dance evening, gradually becoming more and more animated as the foot stamping and clapping gather momentum, represented by ostinato rhythms for low strings, joined intermittently by drums, bells, triangle and cymbals. The main thematic material is a lively dance tune of a distinctly Coplandesque flavour, which is periodically counterpointed with the 'concertina' theme Antill mentions in his 'programme'. At its first appearance, the latter theme is played by muted brass in bitonal combination with the principal dance theme (perhaps reflecting the 'antiquated, out of repair concertina'), and later in a more riotous passage against the dance theme, the whole accompanied by stamping ostinati and chains of dissonant chords in woodwind and brass (Example 4.7 below).

Example 4.6 *An Outback Overture*, bb. 1–6

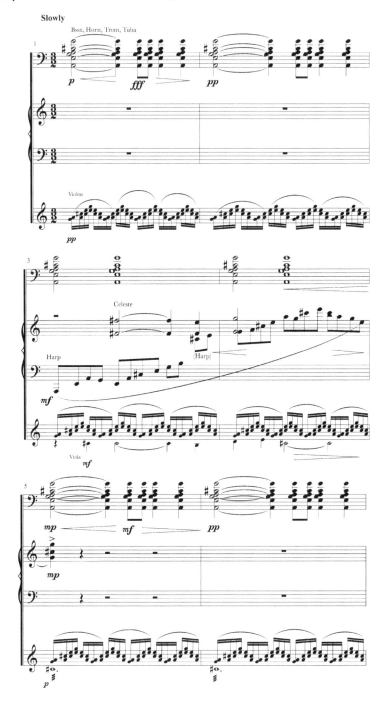

Example 4.7 *An Outback Overture*, bb. 152–159

During this central episode, the 'concertina' theme is barely heard over the dance theme and accompaniment, but finally blazes forth in a broad concluding hymn-like triumphal section in F major, which, following loud dissonant flourishes, brings the work to a rousing close.

An Outback Overture is an attractive, although distinctly lightweight, piece which once more shows Antill in the more relaxed stylistic vein of his 'light' ballets discussed in Chapter 3.

Overture for a Momentous Occasion (1956–1957)

The shorter (approximately six-minute) *Overture for a Momentous Occasion*, in keeping with its celebratory commission, is a more arresting and brilliant score than its concert predecessor, though again (again not surprisingly, given its 'occasional' nature) lacking significantly profound expressive depths. As mentioned earlier in this chapter, the work was commissioned by the ABC to celebrate the tenth anniversary of the broadcaster's Youth Concerts Series, begun by the ABC's Sydney Symphony Orchestra in 1947. The Overture was premièred by this orchestra conducted by Antill at the Sydney Town Hall on 1 April 1957. The piece appears to have grown from an original brief 'Fanfare for an Important Occasion' which may have been the initial scope of the commission, although there is no evidence of this.[17]

As in the case of *An Outback Overture*, Antill has provided a 'programme', in this case of a somewhat whimsical nature, as follows:

a. Dedicated to the Youth Concerts Committee.
b. Could be described as a conversation between Youth and Maturity.
c. A Youthful introduction.
d. Age and Experience give advice (recitative fashion). Interrupted occasionally by a few impatient youthful backbenchers.
e. A little reasoning conversation between both parties, both militant at times, but leading into a –
f. Calming theme on the cello, representing a youthful spokesman. This is seconded by some of the young ladies (oboe and clarinet) with few dissensions and the motion is finally carried.
g. Discussion is then invited and the youthful theme is developed with a few interjections from Maturity.
h. After a heated argument, Youth realises that the inevitable must happen, and that Maturity is gaining ground very fast. So both themes are brought together in harmony. After a silence, each endeavours to have the last word, but it happens to be one of those moments when two people talk at once.[18]

---

[17] The original 'Fanfare' sketch may be found among the Antill Papers (AP, S8a/30).
[18] Quoted in Dean and Carell, *Gentle Genius*, p. 142.

Example 4.8 *Overture for a Momentous Occasion*, bb. 32–36

Antill's 'programme' is realised in a form comprising four broad sections. The main thematic material comprises three ideas: (a) a rapid flourish introduced at the outset on high woodwind and strings, representing 'youth'; (b) the 'voice of maturity' represented by a rhythmic recitative on timpani, this rhythm continued by fanfare-type parallel chords of open fifths and fourths, principally for the brass choir; and (c) the 'calming theme' for the 'cellos, representing the 'youthful spokesman'. These themes are deployed in the four main sections of the overture, loosely perceivable as an exposition (sections 1 and 2), development and recapitulation (the remaining sections). The first section comprises an initial extended dialogue between themes (a) and (b) which coincides with letters C to E of Antill's 'programme'. As the dialogue develops, the two ideas overlap creating bitonal dissonances (Example 4.8 above).

The second section (Antill's letter F) is marked 'trio' in the score and introduces theme (c) for the cellos (Example 4.9) which is gradually developed and, with brief interjections from theme (b), leads to an emphatic statement of (c) for the whole orchestra.

Example 4.9   *Overture for a Momentous Occasion*, bb. 68–75

The third section is led off by theme (a), now extended to a lengthier semiquaver melody, at first in a delicately orchestrated passage for solo violin accompanied by harp, which initiates an extended development section in which all three themes are eventually counterpointed. Antill's 'heated argument' (letter H) refers to the climax of this section, where the semiquavers of theme (a) become the basis of a continuous 'furioso' passage accompanying themes (a) and (c) with the rhythm of theme (b) – i.e. 'maturity' – hammered out by the percussion, and its parallel open fifth and fourth chords subsequently swept up in the continuous semiquaver 'furioso' (Example 4.10).

The final section (fairly brief), marked 'Maestoso', concludes the overture, with themes (b) and (c) combined in a broad fortissimo statement, leading – via a climactic passage of grinding dissonances in the full orchestra and the subsequent dramatic silence mentioned by Antill – to closure on a sustained A♭ major chord accompanied by a final statement of the initial 'youth' theme (a) (Example 4.11 below).

Example 4.10   *Overture for a Momentous Occasion*, bb. 156–159

Example 4.11   *Overture for a Momentous Occasion*, bb. 182–189

The overall language of this overture illustrates the basic sound world of Antill's post-*Corroboree* works. Its origins as a fanfare are perpetuated in the 'maturity' theme – its parallel chord stream of bare fifths and fourths being a stylistic hallmark beloved of Antill since their prominence in *Corroboree*. Here there are also strong stylistic affinities with English composers of the inter-war period such as Walton and Bliss. This general neo-classical 'style area' is also suggested in Antill's subsequent orchestral work – his orchestral magnum opus, *Symphony on a City*, to be examined below.

Symphony on a City (1959)

Antill's *Symphony on a City* may be seen as a further work celebrating a 'momentous occasion' – in this case the centenary in 1959 of the city of Newcastle, New South Wales, the state's second largest city and the centre and port for both a thriving coal mining industry as well as a rich agricultural hinterland. It is also one of Australia's major industrial cities, housing the country's largest iron and steel works together with other heavy industries such as chemical, fertiliser and textile production.

In 1958 the Newcastle City Council began planning celebrations to mark the centenary; and for the occasion, remarkably, decided to commission not only a lavishly illustrated book, but also a major orchestral work. The book was commissioned from Oswald Ziegler[19] and the musical work from Antill. Both the book and the orchestral work were to carry the same title – *Symphony on a City*. Such a musical commission from a large municipal body was at that time unique, and indeed has remained an exceedingly rare – if not still unique – occurrence in Australia's history. Antill was the most obvious choice for the commission, being the most celebrated and publicly recognised Australian composer at this time (largely of course on the basis of *Corroboree*). He accepted the commission after the City Council invited him on a guided tour of the city and surrounding district. His fee was £300, an amount which, ironically, failed – to the tune of another £300 – to cover the composer's costs of producing the score and orchestral parts![20] Despite this, as well as the impossibility of meeting the commission's original deadline of late 1958, Antill expressed considerable enthusiasm for the project, recognising, in particular, the opportunity to realise a long cherished ambition – namely the composition of a major symphonic work (as may be recalled from the composer's remarks quoted at the beginning of this chapter). The extramusical dimension was also an obvious attraction: this aspect will be discussed further later. The symphony was completed on 3 July 1959[21] and the première performance given in the Centenary Theatre, Broadmeadow (a Newcastle suburb) on 13 August, by the

---

[19] Oswald Ziegler, *Symphony on a City* (Sydney: Oswald Ziegler Publications, 1958).
[20] Reported in an unsigned article titled 'Composer's Success Could be a Penalty' in *The Sydney Morning Herald* of 15 November 1960.
[21] Entry in 1959 diary, AP, S4/4.

Sydney Symphony Orchestra conducted by the composer. It was also broadcast over ABC Radio two days later.

Antill's commissioned symphony was widely publicised in the press both in Newcastle and Sydney on and off throughout 1958 and 1959. An article in the *Newcastle Herald* as early as 25 January 1958 titled 'Big Scope for City Symphony' alluded to Antill's great interest in the project as well as his pleasure at being given the opportunity to at last complete his first full scale symphony:

> The Australian composer John Antill sees "great potentialities" in Newcastle and district for a descriptive symphony characteristic of this city. He said ... that the industrial facet of Newcastle would give great scope for his type of musical writing.

Later in the same article, Antill is reported as saying 'that he had several symphonies in the embryo stage, but that the Newcastle symphony would be his first completed'.

Antill originally planned to write a traditional four-movement symphony with a sonata-type first movement, a scherzo, a lyrical slow movement and finale. He envisaged these movements as depicting, respectively, the development of the city from the primeval landscape, the sporting and recreational activities of the citizens, the pastoral regions of the surrounding Hunter River Valley and finally the city's industrial might. As the composition progressed, this plan was modified to a three-movement format, with the scherzo and finale merged into a single movement following the first movement and the slow movement. Antill has provided a detailed description of the piece's intended depiction of the city in an extended note preceding the autograph score:

> The symphony is in three movements, each of which evolves [*sic*] a tone poem representing local development.
>
> The first movement is prefaced by a slow, eerie introduction depicting the formation of our earth into solidity. The movement proper is in accepted sonata form, having first and second subjects with extentions [*sic*], development and recapitulation. This spans a period of time from the wanderings of the Aboriginal to the establishment of the majestic port of today. A coda recalling the opening introduction leads into the second movement.
>
> This movement records the beauty of the Hunter Valley, against a background suggesting the hard toil and struggles of early pioneers. It has majesty and dignity, and is pastoral in concept.
>
> The finale begins scherzando, reflecting the carefree life and sportsmanship on the playing fields. An occasional reminder that here above all exists a great industrial centre. The reminder persists until it eventually takes full control. As

this "Symphony on a City" concludes, we are left in no doubt as to the present importance, and of the imminent greatness, of the City of Newcastle and its environs.[22]

Once again, therefore, Antill is seen linking a concert work for orchestra to an extramusical 'scenario'. However, in his comments upon the relationship of the music to his 'scenario' Antill offers a cautionary statement found among his accompanying notes to the symphony:

> One can hear in the score all the moves and ally them to a particular facet of activity or industry. And this, I hope you do – but in reality, it is fundamentally absolute music not programme music and I would sooner we listened with a musical ear and let the other side be incidental.[23]

Antill's apparent ambivalence between the descriptive and abstract qualities of the symphony also raises a fundamental issue regarding the nature of what is commonly referred to, often too loosely, as 'programme music'. Antill's denial of the symphony as programme music in light of the detailed description of what the music purports to depict, may certainly appear contradictory. However it must be remembered that any effective piece of programme music must possess structural integrity as to its purely musical shape and structure, and this is perhaps what Antill is asking the listener to recognise here. Nevertheless, in relation to *Symphony on a City*, a further question must now be considered – namely, whether it is best categorised as programmatic or more generally descriptive or evocative. Here the fundamental question concerns the manner in which the extramusical elements are not only evoked in the music, but also reflected in its actual shape and structure. In true programme music, as envisaged by Liszt, who first coined the term, there is a close interdependence between the 'programme' – whether generally 'poetic' or more concretely 'narrative' – and the musical structure, affecting the shaping and particular musical sequence of events. In the case of Antill's two concert overtures discussed previously, the form of the music was clearly aligned to a 'programme' or 'scenario' as outlined in the composer's detailed descriptions quoted earlier. In the case of *Symphony on a City*, the descriptions appended to the respective movements are certainly suggested by various qualities in the music; but on the other hand, much of the form and sequence of musical events can be seen as essentially autonomous and linking with the extramusical dimension on a more generalised level. The form and content of the symphony will now be examined in some detail, including a consideration as to what extent the work is a purely descriptive piece according to the

---

[22] AP, S8/31. Antill's text (handwritten) has been slightly edited, omitting some extraneous capital letters and correcting a few punctuation errors or ambiguities.

[23] See 'Notes, script and itinerary, 1958–59', AP, S8/36. It is unclear as to whether this or the preceding programme note was accessible to the public at the time of the Symphony's première.

Example 4.12   *Symphony on a City*, I, bb. 1–7

Example 4.13   *Symphony on a City*, I, bb. 73–78

above criteria, or to what extent it may contain genuinely programmatic elements. The analysis that follows here will also make some reference to a detailed formal analysis that has been provided in a recent monograph by Rhoderick McNeill.[24]

The first movement is, as Antill states, cast in sonata form with a slow introduction, which returns at the end to form a transition to the slow movement. The introduction is principally made up of another of Antill's twisting chromatic melodies (here for bassoons accompanied by a snare drum roll as shown in Example 4.12) of the type already encountered in *The Unknown Land* (see Example 3.1, Chapter 3).

Antill's description of this introduction as 'eerie' and depicting 'the formation of the earth' is, of course, highly evocative. The subsequent Allegro could be seen to evoke a general atmosphere of dynamic activity relating to the evolution of the city from its primeval landscape. However, there is no identification in Antill's 'programme' of themes or sections with specific events or stages of this evolution: the movement is simply an autonomous sonata-allegro of a definitely neo-classical cast, betraying considerable motivic drive and much dissonant harmony. This is well demonstrated in the Allegro's angular main theme, particularly in its statement by full orchestra (Example 4.13).

After a transition, the second subject group enters, its initial, more 'pastoral' theme for violin solo cast in a clear Dorian mode (Example 4.14 below).

A more chromatic theme then leads to a loud tutti passage completing the exposition. The remainder of the movement follows a quite traditional path of development and recapitulation before the return of the slow introduction as mentioned earlier. The introductory theme reappears, initially as a fortissimo climactic statement by woodwind, brass and percussion, before returning to the soft recall of the introduction itself, this time scored mainly for viola solo with percussion accompaniment. This creates a highly effective close as well as a link to the slow movement. Its reappearance at this point, while structurally effective, makes no sense programmatically if the opening movement is to be interpreted – as in Antill's 'programme' – as representing the city's evolution from primeval earth to thriving metropolis, unless the intention is to remind the listener retrospectively of the city's origins (Antill makes no mention of this in his 'programme').

The slow movement is an extended essay in what has been popularly dubbed 'modal harmony' already encountered in various post-*Corroboree* scores. In relation to already noted misconceptions regarding Antill's alleged return to nineteenth-century styles after *Corroboree*, it should be recalled that this idiom, while gentle and consonant, is a thoroughly twentieth-century style and is driven by modal melodic progressions rather than any return to common practice functional tonality. In the case of this symphony's slow movement, McNeill has pointed to it as exhibiting a strong resemblance to the contemplative idiom and character of the

---

[24] Rhoderick McNeill, *The Australian Symphony from Federation to 1960* (Farnham: Ashgate, 2014), pp. 139–47.

Example 4.14   *Symphony on a City*, I, bb. 113–115

Example 4.15   *Symphony on a City*, II, bb. 13–18(2)

slow movement of Vaughan Williams's Fifth Symphony.[25] This is clearly shown in the passage quoted in Example 4.15.

The form of the movement is, as McNeill has shown,[26] an 'arch' shape (ABCBA), of which Example 4.15 quotes the initial appearance of the extended 'B' section. The 'A' sections comprise ruminative solos for oboe and clarinet over quiet ostinati and pedals – typical 'pastoral' scoring. The overall character of the movement is expansively lyrical and the 'pastoral' association effectively evokes the countryside referred to in Antill's 'programme'. Here, there is little to suggest anything beyond a generally 'atmospheric' or descriptive quality, the music otherwise essentially functioning on a purely autonomous structural level – although McNeill has opined that the opening and closing sections, with their plodding ostinati, may be seen as depicting the 'toil ... of the early pioneers'.[27]

The finale returns to the bustling energy, dissonant harmony and angular thematic character found in the first movement. The overall form may be loosely thought of as a rondo, with the opening fanfare-type theme (Example 4.16) recurring a number of times throughout, alternating with no less than five other identifiable themes, of which two are of more significance than the other three.

Example 4.16   *Symphony on a City*, III, bb. 1–8

---

[25] Ibid., p. 144.
[26] Ibid.
[27] Ibid.

The two important 'counter-themes', which also recur a number of times, appear to evoke respectively the 'scherzando' and the 'industrial' elements of the now telescoped scherzo and finale. The former, appearing first immediately following the opening 'fanfare' theme, is in a fast 12/8 metre resembling, as McNeill points out, a gigue rhythm (Example 4.17),[28] while the latter occurs after the first, extended return of the 'fanfare' theme.

Example 4.17   *Symphony on a City*, III, bb. 12–15

This theme (Example 4.18) is dominated by a timpani ostinato which, at the climax of the movement, culminates in a loud crash on a heavy metal plate which Antill asked to be provided at the première as a literal symbol of the city's industrial might. The theme dominates the latter stages of the movement, recalling Antill's 'programme' in which he refers to it as the 'reminder' of Newcastle's industry that finally 'takes full control'. The hypnotically propulsive nature of the timpani ostinato would appear to be a particular passage that may have elicited Roger Covell's rather condescending comment on the symphony – namely that 'Antill does find, even if only momentarily, other ways [i.e. than in *Corroboree*] of presenting energy at high voltage' and for this reason [only?] 'the symphony deserves to be heard again'.[29] The general 'takeover' of the 'industrial' theme from the 'fanfare' and 'scherzando' themes (both of which nevertheless persist until the

---

[28]   Ibid., p. 146.
[29]   Covell, *Australia's Music*, p. 155.

climax) might suggest some sort of programmatic scenario as reflected in Antill's description of this movement – but perhaps still only in a general way. However, the interplay of the various themes essentially operates in an autonomous manner in terms of the finale's structure.

Example 4.18   *Symphony on a City*, III, bb. 65–68

Antill's *Symphony on a City* received an enthusiastic reception at its première and also called forth unanimously positive accolades in the popular press in both Newcastle and Sydney. Subsequent critical appraisal of the symphony has also been positive, ranging from Covell's lukewarm approval already alluded to, to Andrew McCredie's comment (see the Interlude) on the work as 'capturing some of the vivid style of *Corroboree*, but with greater epic sweep and symphonic design'.[30] McNeill is also positive, and in his overall evaluation of Australian symphonic production, he rates *Symphony on a City* and Clive Douglas's 'Namatjira' Symphony (1956) as 'projecting a unique and distinct voice', as 'important sound documents of their time' and as 'containing some of the most memorable Australian music of the period'.[31] Notwithstanding these opinions, James Murdoch was commenting in the early 1970s – more than a decade after the symphony's première – that the symphony is 'a major work which has been

---

[30]   McCredie, *Musical Composition in Australia*, p. 10.
[31]   McNeill, *The Australian Symphony*, p. 147.

performed only once'.[32] Indeed the 1959 première would appear still to have been the symphony's only public performance. Since that time, McNeill reports that the work also received a broadcast performance (presumably the recording which was broadcast at the time of the première) in 1979 on the occasion of the composer's 75th birthday.[33] This recording by the ABC was never released either for educational institutions or commercially. In light of the warm reception accorded to the symphony, it is therefore a pity that it appears to have suffered the same fate as so many other worthy Australian works of the post-colonial period. One can only hope that a greater receptivity to, and interest in, Australia's music before the 1960s may yet address this highly regrettable neglect.

Concerto for Harmonica and Orchestra (1961)

As previously remarked, Antill's Concerto for Harmonica and Orchestra is his only orchestral work of substance that has no extramusical reference. It was written in response to a commission by the ABC and the Australasian Performing Right Association (APRA) and dedicated to the American harmonica virtuoso Larry Adler. The impetus for the commission most likely arose as early as 1957 after Adler had toured Australia as an ABC celebrity and, in November of that year, performed a harmonica concerto by the expatriate Australian composer Arthur Benjamin at a concert with the Sydney Symphony Orchestra conducted by Nicolai Malko – the performance receiving enthusiastic reviews in the press. Dean and Carell report that the then General Manager of the ABC, Sir Charles Moses, 'was a great fan ... of Larry Adler',[34] and the novelty of writing a concerto for such an unusual solo instrument no doubt stimulated Antill.[35] The concerto was written in the hope that Adler would première the work; however, the concerto was not completed till 1961, at which time Adler was not in Australia. The Antill Papers include both a piano score and a full orchestral score of the work,[36] the piano score curiously titled 'Concerto – Sonata for Harmonica and Pianoforte', complete with the APRA registration. Nevertheless, this score also includes, on the title page, full details of the orchestration of the work as a concerto. Interestingly, it must have been a copy of this version that Antill sent to Adler in July 1961 asking Adler for permission to dedicate the work to him.[37] Subsequently, Dean and Carell report that Adler replied to Antill that 'yours is the first sonata written

---

[32] Murdoch, *Australia's Contemporary Composers*, p. 9.
[33] McNeill, *The Australian Symphony*, p. 147.
[34] Dean and Carell, *Gentle Genius*, p. 152.
[35] However, Dean and Carell (Ibid., p. 140) report that Antill had previously composed music for the harmonica – namely incidental music for Douglas Stewart's play *Ned Kelly* (1956). Antill's music was scored for harmonica and timpani and played by Lionel Easton – who was to première the concerto – and timpanist Marie van Hove.
[36] AP, S8a/37.
[37] Letter dated 31 July 1961 – copy included with the piano score, AP. S8a/37.

for the instrument'.[38] Clearly, Adler would not have stated this of the concerto, especially having performed Benjamin's concerto some four years previously. Antill's concerto was premièred in mid-1961 by the Australian harmonica player, Lionel Easton, with the Sydney Symphony Orchestra conducted by Antill; and this performance was broadcast and a commercial recording made by RCA (as noted at the beginning of this chapter). The ABC also included this work in a broadcast of Antill's music on the occasion of his 70th birthday in April 1974. The only performance of the 'sonata' version that the present author has been able to trace was given at a concert in 1974, organised by the Fellowship of Australian Composers, as part of Antill's 70th birthday celebrations.

Antill's concerto is cast in the customary three movements of the traditional solo concerto, the movement tempi being: I: Allegretto; II: Adagio; III: Allegro. The first and second movements are linked by a repeated G for the harmonica alone, the repeated note tied over to the opening of the Adagio. The concerto is notable for the almost uninterrupted playing of the soloist, while the single cadenza is located near the end of the finale rather than in the first movement.

The first movement begins with a heraldic introduction employing dissonant bitonal harmonies (Example 4.19), but tonally centred on A.

Example 4.19   *Concerto for Harmonica and Orchestra*, I, bb. 1–4(1)

The main body of the movement comprises the statement of three themes (a, b and c) which are successively varied and developed. Themes (a) (see Example 4.20) and (c) are played at the basic tempo of crotchet = 88 while theme (b) is marked 'slower'.[39] There is a loose recapitulation of themes (a) and (b) and a coda based on theme (a). The tonality of this movement is mostly quite ambiguous and the harmony predominantly dissonant.

---

[38]   Dean and Carell, *Gentle Genius*, p. 152.
[39]   Curiously the harmonica part is marked crotchet = 100, while the score has this tempo crossed out and crotchet = 88 substituted.

Example 4.20   *Concerto for Harmonica and Orchestra*, I, bb. 19–23

As in *Symphony on a City*, for the concerto's second movement, Antill relaxes the harmonic astringency of the first movement in favour of a broadly modal or 'pastoral' idiom, as can be seen in the opening, principal theme (Example 4.21).

Example 4.21   *Concerto for Harmonica and Orchestra*, II, bb. 1–5(1)

The basic tonality is D, its Aeolian modal flavour infused with some dissonant elements. The form of the movement is ternary, though with two middle sections, the second of these (marked 'delicately') in the contrasting tonality of D♭, but moving gradually, via B♭, back to the D Aeolian of the recapitulated opening section.

As also in *Symphony on a City*, the third movement of the concerto returns to the dissonant harmonic idiom and ambiguous tonality of the first movement. The movement is cast in an arch shape similar to that of the second movement of *Symphony on a City*, but with the work's only cadenza placed between the final two sections, thus: A–B–C–B^1–cadenza–A^1. The principal, fanfare-like theme of section A is led off by the soloist, at first unaccompanied, the orchestra then entering with bitonal harmony (Example 4.22).

Example 4.22   *Concerto for Harmonica and Orchestra*, III, bb. 1–8

The theme of section B is introduced by a rare two-bar passage for orchestra alone, while section C includes a variation and development of the widespread intervals of the opening theme. Overall, then, this concerto is cast in the by now familiar neo-classical vein of the orchestral music covered in this chapter.

Paean to the Spirit of Man (1968)

Paean to the Spirit of Man was, as earlier noted, commissioned by the ABC for performance at a concert to celebrate the twentieth anniversary of the Universal Declaration of Human Rights. This special free concert took place on Sunday, 8

December 1968 in the Sydney Town Hall, with the Sydney Symphony Orchestra conducted by Joseph Post, but with *Paean* conducted by Antill. The programme (appropriately for the occasion) also included Copland's *Fanfare for the Common Man* (although written in 1942, six years before the Universal Declaration). *Paean* has had, perhaps, only one subsequent public airing – in a broadcast of Antill's music (which also included *Overture for a Momentous Occasion* and music from *Corroboree*) by the ABC late in 1974, Antill's 70th birthday year.

In this ten-minute movement[40] – as might be expected from the nature of the commission – Antill reverts once more to the use of an external 'programme' or 'scenario'. The 'programme' itself is, however, of a relatively abstract or philosophical character. Nevertheless, since – as shown below – the 'programme' is directly reflected in the music's structure, the piece may be regarded as genuinely programmatic according to criteria discussed earlier. Antill's 'programme', in its final form as found in a typescript accompanying the score, reads as follows:

> The spirit of man is that immaterial, disembodied soul which mysteriously houses man's intelligent thoughts. It is part of every man, irrespective of colour, race or creed [here Antill has added, in pencil, "or sex"]; an indestructible reservoir of all his values. Being his and his alone, it provides a haven of hope and strength to which he can withdraw when ugliness prevails.
>
> In the opening English Horn improvisation can be traced characteristics representative of the Paean's universal aim. It is based on E, F, F sharp, G, A, B flat, B natural. A strong drum rhythm of life introduces an enquiring chorale-like Paean which culminates in a full brass announcement.
>
> There follows a development section, representing doubts, hopes and frustrations. A restlessness creates mental turbulence and arouses defiance, but has occasional references to the more rational. Even a theme for dancing emerges. Then there is a return to normality with a restatement of a few of the opening bars, in preparation for the chorale-Paean, this time resolute and majestic. Calmness prevails, and – metaphorically – it would appear that the Spirit of Man has at last found a haven of peace and tranquillity.

The music follows the general outline of Antill's 'programme', producing a structure which resembles sonata form, though without the duality of separate subject groups. Instead, the work grows from a single extended melody – the long cor anglais solo (Example 4.23) which Antill labels 'improvisation', heard at the outset and later, in its original unaccompanied form to mark the beginning of the

---

[40] Although Antill's timing on the score is 'about 9½ minutes', the performance, conducted by Antill, as recorded by the ABC, lasts just under 11½ minutes.

work's final recapitulatory section. This melody contains a number of ideas, but the main motivic 'germ' is that heard at the beginning (bars 1–3 of Example 4.23).

Example 4.23 *Paean to the Spirit of Man*, bb. 1–10

Antill's assertion that this 'improvisation' is 'based on' the notes E-F-F♯-G-A-B♭-B is slightly puzzling, since it actually contains all the notes of the chromatic scale except E♭ and D♭; however, it is possible to see these notes as important – especially B♭ which becomes the overall tonal centre of the work. This opening melody has a contemplative character somewhat reminiscent of the 'Faust' theme heard at the outset of Liszt's *Faust Symphony*. Like its 12-note predecessor, Antill's 10-note melody is both unaccompanied and highly chromatic. The symbolism of both Antill's and Liszt's themes would appear to be similar – a soft, isolated 'voice' probing the mysteries of the spiritual realm, also symbolised by the 'cerebral' chromatic atonality of both themes. For Antill, the cor anglais appears to take on a central significance as perhaps typifying the 'spirit of man' since the instrument's part is situated at the place in the score reserved for a concerto soloist, rather than its normal place in the woodwind choir.

Following Antill's 'programme', the violent bass drum strokes interrupt the final bars of the cor anglais melody and punctuate the ensuing transition to the 'enquiring chorale' theme heard in the brass choir (Example 4.24 below).

It can be seen from this example that the chorale develops from the initial motivic shape of the cor anglais melody, with the intervals varied. In the ensuing development section, the pace quickens and the music becomes increasingly dissonant, some passages containing dissonance at least as abrasive as anything in *Corroboree*, although in the context of a more neo-classical muscular thematic drive and 'sweep' than the static ostinato-based harmony of the ballet. Meredith Oakes, in her review of *Paean*'s première,[41] describes this section as the most exciting part of the work and refers to Antill's style as betraying 'a heavy European chromaticism rubbing shoulders with moments of American jauntiness and with

---

[41] Sydney *Daily Telegraph*, 9 December 1968.

Example 4.24   *Paean to the Spirit of Man*, bb. 36–44

purely sonorous experiments'. The overall dissonant character of the section may be seen in the Maestoso passage near the end of the development (Example 4.25) and shortly before the reappearance of the opening cor anglais melody.

Example 4.25 *Paean to the Spirit of Man*, bb. 120–124

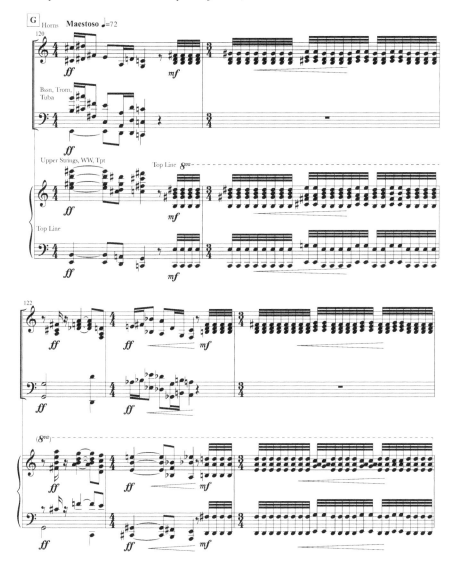

This refers to Antill's characterisation of the development as representing 'doubts, hopes and frustrations … mental turbulence and … defiance'. The 'return to normality' is represented by the recapitulation of the cor anglais melody, while the subsequent 'resolute and majestic' recapitulation of the chorale provides a sense of resolution of conflict. The work closes quietly with the harmony gradually becoming transparently diatonic in B♭ major – Antill's 'haven of peace and tranquility' for the spirit of man. The cor anglais has the 'last word', with its long-held F outlasting the final sustained B♭ triad in the orchestra.

Antill's *Paean* is a significant piece of sustained symphonic writing, and the theme of the 'spirit of man' seems to have touched some deep wellsprings in Antill's sensitive personality. A first-rate recording of the work, as well as further performances – are long overdue!

Conclusion

Paean was Antill's last orchestral work of significant scope and substance. At the time of his retirement from the ABC, however, he was involved in a noteworthy project – namely a collaborative composition to commemorate the centenary of the birth of Alfred Hill and titled *Variations on a Theme of Alfred Hill*. The Department of Music at The University of Western Australia and the ABC commissioned the work from a number of composers who had known Hill, specifically for performance at the Perth Festival in February 1970. Antill was asked to coordinate, as well as contribute to, the project.[42] The planned composition was to be based on a theme from Hill's Symphony No. 7 in E minor (1956) and both the symphony and the Variations were performed at the Festival concert. In its final form, the Variations – and the respective composers – were as follows:

1. Introduction (A major): John Antill
2. Second movement (F major): Raymond Hanson
3. Lento (E minor): Miriam Hyde
4. Andantino (D minor): Dulcie Holland
5. Allegro (C major): Clive Douglas
6. Coda (A major): John Antill

The theme chosen was a rising four-note motif which, in various guises, as Rhoderick McNeill has shown, forms the basis of Hill's entire symphony.[43] The version of the motif for the Variations is that from the slow movement (Adagio) which is in A major; and the theme comprises the ascending notes A-C♯-D-E, with various extensions and developments. Antill's two movements, the Introduction and Coda, are in this key. They are both brief, quiet pieces of respectively 32 and 20 bars in length, each lasting (at Adagio tempo) no more than two and a

---

[42] A copy of the full score (manuscript) of the Hill Variations is housed in the Music Library at the University of Western Australia. Another copy is in the Symphony Australia Collection, housed at the National Library of Australia.

[43] McNeill, *The Australian Symphony*, p. 101.

half minutes (the recording of the Introduction takes slightly longer, but the speed is less than the marked crotchet = 60). The inner movements are also brief, though more substantial. There is, predictably, some discrepancy of styles to be found in the various composers' contributions; however, these styles – ranging from some pastoral associations to more astringent neo-classical crispness – do not clash unduly. In the Perth Festival performance and ABC recording of the work (released on LP for educational institutions), the movements by Hyde and Holland are interchanged and Antill's Coda omitted – the reason for the latter being perhaps that Douglas's Allegro provided a more effective finale, whereas Antill's Coda resumed the quiet Adagio character of his Introduction.

As this chapter has shown, Antill's output of orchestral concert works, of any significant weight or substance, can only be described as numerically meagre. His ambition to create more symphonic works of substance would seem to have faded during the years of his retirement when, theoretically, he would have had more time than ever before to compose substantial works had he so wished. Ironically, his only major project from his retirement period – a planned 'South Pacific Symphony', inspired by a trip to Fiji in 1972 to conduct performances of Mendelssohn's *Elijah* – was abandoned when Antill's home was vandalised and many manuscripts, including sketches of the projected symphony, were destroyed.[44] The completed orchestral works discussed in this chapter nonetheless deserve to be heard again – and more regularly – along with much other neglected repertoire of the post-colonial period. In the following chapter, Antill's again numerically meagre output of major choral and vocal works will be examined; but here too will be found some significant pieces that should take their place as part of Australia's permanent musical heritage.

---

[44] Dean and Carell record this unfortunate incident (see *Gentle Genius*, p. 173).

Chapter 5
After *Corroboree* (3) – Choral and Vocal Works

Introduction

While Antill's output of music with text settings – specifically the genres of choral music and solo song – is numerically extensive in the periods both before and after *Corroboree*, it must be observed that the number of works of any significant scope or substance in either of these two categories is even more meagre than those for the theatre or orchestra. Although his background was strongly steeped in music for church choir, the only choral works of any significant size date from the post-*Corroboree* period. These are the oratorio *The Song of Hagar to Abraham the Patriarch* (1959) and two 'festal' anthem-type pieces: the *Festival Te Deum* (1966) for choir, brass and organ written for St Andrew's Cathedral, Sydney – with whose choir Antill had been associated from his childhood; and *Cantate Domino* (1970), for choir, brass, timpani and organ, composed for the ecumenical welcome service for Pope Paul VI at Sydney Town Hall. Antill's remaining choral works traceable from this period are brief carols, part songs and arrangements written for diverse occasions ranging from public ceremonies to church services and school assemblies. The majority of his output for solo voice (both before and after *Corroboree*) is likewise of a relatively minor nature. The Antill Papers list some 40 songs, many undated, while Dean and Carell claim that Antill produced 'literally hundreds of songs, … song arrangements and settings of psalms',[1] many of which have evidently been lost. The only works of major significance in this genre are three song cycles written in the early 1950s, namely the *Five Australian Lyrics* (1953) for voice and piano and two song cycles on texts from the Psalms – *Five Songs of Happiness* (1953) (for voice, oboe and piano) and *Five Songs of Praise* (1954) for voice and piano. As might be expected, the musical character and idiom of Antill's choral music and solo songs from the post-*Corroboree* period – the focus of this chapter – range from the extreme simplicity of language and form in many of his brief occasional pieces in these genres, to the more complex language of neo-classicism found also in some of these and, of course, in the above listed larger choral and vocal works.

As extensive as possible a documentation of Antill's choral and vocal output will be given in Appendix 1. The remainder of this chapter will follow a similar path to that of the two previous chapters, by examining Antill's major achievements in these genres – first in the field of choral music and finally that of solo song.

---

[1] Dean and Carell, *Gentle Genius*, p. 202.

Choral Works

The Song of Hagar to Abraham the Patriarch (1959)

For a composer and musician steeped in the choral tradition of the church from his youth, the relatively tiny output of major sacred choral works is noteworthy, although hardly surprising given the pressures of extensive commissions for theatre and orchestral works after *Corroboree*. The first work to be examined here is Antill's sole venture into the field of sacred oratorio, a work which – significantly, in light of the composer's lifelong attraction to the theatre – has an added dramatic and scenic dimension (to be discussed later). *The Song of Hagar to Abraham the Patriarch* had its genesis in 1953 when Antill met the Australian writer Ethel Anderson. Her poem of the same title attracted the composer strongly at a time when he was also occupied with the setting of Biblical texts in his song cycles on texts from the Book of Psalms (see later discussion).[2] The fact that Antill was attracted to a subject such as the wanderings of Hagar and Ishmael is also interesting as it resonates strongly with the composer's only prior engagement with a Biblical subject for a large-scale dramatic or narrative composition, namely the incomplete opera *The Lost Child* (discussed in Chapter 1). Both works may be said to deal with Biblical outcasts – the opera based on the story of the repentance and suicide of Judas Iscariot following his betrayal of Jesus. This author can offer no suggestion as to the significance or otherwise of this connection. However, it may be of more immediate significance that Antill's most intense engagement with the composition of *Hagar* seems to have been in the period following the death of his wife in August 1957. It is perhaps worth speculating that the subject of the wanderings of an outcast 'single parent' and her child might well have resonated in the composer's mind with his own situation as a bereaved single parent with the responsibility for an only child – his still dependant teenage daughter. Dean and Carell suggest, furthermore, that at this time Antill 'found solace in his new composition *Song of Hagar*'.[3] Whether or not the above conjecture is valid, it seems that the work held a special place in the composer's affections. It was (unusually at this time) written to no commission or deadline, but rather from simple creative inspiration.

The poem by Ethel Anderson is contemplative throughout and has no narrative structure. In a typescript introduction to the manuscript full score,[4] Antill describes Anderson's text as follows:

> Hagar was the Egyptian handmaid of Sarah, the Patriarch Abraham's wife. She had a son by Abraham called Ishmael, and through Sarah's jealousy they were turned out into the wilderness.

---

[2] Ibid., p. 143.
[3] Ibid., p. 147.
[4] AP, S8c/2.

> This poem is based on the wanderings of Hagar and Ishmael in the desert. It describes their final settlement in the wilderness of Paran where Ishmael takes an Egyptian wife.
>
> It is a song written in the tradition of those archaic marriage-songs sung by prehistoric Semitic tribes; similar songs are said to be assembled in the Song of Solomon. In it the early Gods Elohim and Jahweh are named, and the dethroned God, Azazel, appears. Hagar herself represents the arch-type [sic] of the dispossed [sic] woman still faithful to a great vision. She illustrates the Apocryphal text, "Many waters cannot quench love, nor can the sea drown it".

The narrative background of the story is supplied in Antill's setting by the interpolation of seven passages of spoken narration heard between various of the ten 'numbers' into which the text is divided. The narration – sometimes with orchestral accompaniment and sometimes unaccompanied – is taken directly from the Book of Genesis and traces the story of Abraham's wedding to Sarah; her barrenness and Abraham's taking of her handmaid Hagar who bears him a son, Ishmael; Sarah's jealousy and the banishment of Hagar and Ishmael; their wilderness wanderings; and finally Ishmael's marriage to an Egyptian woman. For this story Antill provided an additional visual scenario for a projected television production that was to comprise mimed action against a series of scenic backdrops which the composer himself created (illustrations of these backdrops may be found with the full manuscript score among the Antill Papers, with the corresponding numbers in the score indicated for each scenic 'panel'). The soloists, choir and orchestra were intended to be hidden, with only the scenery and mimed action visible. The television production never eventuated; and while a choreographed performance was given as part of the 'all-Antill season' during the Captain Cook bicentenary celebrations in 1970 (see Chapter 2), its only other performances have been of the studio broadcast made by ABC radio on 27 April 1959 and subsequently rebroadcast on a few occasions. This performance was given by soloists and members of the Hurlstone Choral Society (Sydney) and the Sydney Symphony Orchestra conducted by Nicolai Malko. The lack of performances in its original television format, which was an essential part of Antill's conception, is disappointing; while the work, as given in concert form, Patricia Brown has dubbed (perhaps unfairly) as 'a rather pale "straight" oratorio'.[5]

The device of the spoken narration obviates the necessity for a traditional recitative/aria/chorus format, and the musical numbers are through-composed in declamatory or arioso fashion. A satisfying sense of formal closure is imparted to the work by the considerable amount of repetition of opening material near the end, echoing similar text reminiscences. The extensive text, however, for a work lasting only 25 minutes, ensures that there is very limited scope for the lyrical expansion of material. This provides some justification for Covell's assertion

---

[5] Brown, 'John Antill', p. 45.

that 'there are sections where the music seems to be merely "getting through" the task of setting the words'.[6] The musical setting is for soprano (Hagar) and tenor (Ishmael) soloists, men's and boys' choir and an unusual orchestra which obviously is intended to evoke the instruments of Biblical times – winds, plucked strings and percussion. That this was Antill's intention is made clear in his statements about the work as quoted by a number of commentators. Following his thorough study of Biblical times for the piece, Antill noted: 'When I was ready to write, I wrote in my own way the idiom I thought would have been used in those far off days'.[7] The instrumentation comprises woodwinds and brass (but no bass instruments), percussion (drums, timpani, glockenspiel and celeste), harp and two double basses. Both soloists and chorus sing in a rhythmically flexible, syllabic and sometimes chant-like manner, while the chorus – apart from some passages of spoken declamation – sings throughout either in unison or sometimes note-against-note polyphony: there is no traditional oratorio-style contrapuntal writing. This, together with the generally unvarying rhythmic structure of the setting, impart a degree of blandness to the overall texture of the work, which has no doubt been responsible for evoking negative or condescending critical comments such as 'pale' (see footnote 5 above), 'docile',[8] 'gentle',[9] 'a mild work of cosy religiosity',[10] or 'part of the lesser English choral tradition'.[11] These comments are significantly misleading, especially when such comments were made in the context of Antill's claimed retreat from the supposedly more individual and 'modern' idiom of *Corroboree*. This can be seen by analysing the melodic and harmonic vocabulary and 'grammar' of the work. Again this ranges from rhythmically flexible, chromatic dissonance in some of the orchestral writing to more block-like textures using triads and open fifths and octaves (often in parallel chains) now familiar from other post-*Corroboree* works already examined. It is true that in *Hagar* Antill undeniably chose a less confronting and pungently dissonant sound world in keeping with the largely contemplative character of the text. However, as in the case of works examined in the previous two chapters, the overall language remains firmly post- (or neo-) tonal, and certainly one no earlier than that which spawned *Corroboree*. Something of the range of Antill's style throughout *Hagar* may be seen in the following selected extracts. Example 5.1 is taken from the work's opening, which comprises a colourful instrumental prelude at once evoking a 'Biblical' or near Eastern atmosphere, with its sinuous writing for piccolo, flutes, cor anglais, celeste, horns, trombones and snare drum.

---

[6] Covell, *Australia's Music*, p. 155.
[7] Dean and Carell, *Gentle Genius*, p. 144.
[8] Covell, *Australia's Music*, p. 155.
[9] Brown, 'John Antill', p. 45.
[10] Murdoch, *Australia's Contemporary Composers*, p. 13.
[11] Covell, *Australia's Music*, p. 154.

Example 5.1 *The Song of Hagar*, Introduction, bb. 1–8

The next extract (Example 5.2) is taken from the first 'number', depicting the marriage of Abraham and Sarah, and illustrates the predominantly unison choral writing, and often stark or spare textures, to be found throughout.

Example 5.2   *The Song of Hagar,* No. 1, bb. 1–8

Note: Bar numbers as they appear in the score = 1st 8 bars of No. 1.

Finally, the declamatory writing for the soprano and tenor soloists is illustrated by a passage (Example 5.3) from near the end (No. 9) for the soprano soloist, when Hagar reminisces on the birth of her son.

Antill's attempt to evoke an appropriately 'near Eastern' character for the music of *Hagar* constituted something of a stylistic deviation from his general post-*Corroboree* manner, although the foundations of his musical language are, as previously discussed, fully in evidence here. In Antill's other two choral works of some substance, his idiom, predictably, takes on a recognisably English association. This is not, as inaccurately claimed for *Hagar*, the nineteenth-century choral tradition, but rather that of the 'post-pastoral' generation of Walton and others.

Example 5.3   *The Song of Hagar*, No. 9, bb. 667–673

Festival Te Deum (1966)

Antill's *Festival Te Deum* and *Cantate Domino* (see below) are two rare extended examples among his output of church choral music, being settings of texts from the Anglican Matins and Evensong services respectively. Both have here been detached from their liturgical contexts, as is common at least for the Te Deum text that has historically been used as a 'festal' piece for public celebratory occasions such as victories in wars. As mentioned elsewhere in this book, Antill's association with the Anglican church, and especially with St Andrew's Cathedral, Sydney, and its music, was a lifelong one. Antill had, it will be recalled from Chapter 1, been writing small sacred settings, including short anthems, during his early years. None of these has survived; while during the years after *Corroboree*, his only choral works apart from the *Festival Te Deum* and *Cantate Domino* comprise a few brief carols and secular settings of an 'occasional' nature. The reasons for the almost complete hiatus in the production of church music during the many intervening years have already been partially canvassed – namely Antill's heavy commitment to fulfilling commissions for theatrical and orchestral music, as well as the heavy demands of his full time employment with the ABC. To these external circumstances may perhaps be added Antill's lifelong attachment to the theatre and also to his perception of himself as a 'symphonic man' (see beginning of

Chapter 4). As has been seen, his most extended essay on a sacred subject – *The Song of Hagar* – also had a 'theatrical' element envisaged as a necessary additional dimension to the music.

Notwithstanding the significance of Antill's two extended anthem-type works in the context of his output of otherwise minor choral pieces, it must be noted that both of these are still relatively short 'occasional' works. The *Festival Te Deum* was written (presumably to a commission) for a special 'ecumenical' concert in St Andrew's Cathedral in April 1966. This concert featured three choirs, respectively representing the Roman Catholic, Russian Orthodox and Anglican churches in performances of works from their respective liturgies. The latter choir was that of the cathedral with Antill conducting the *Festival Te Deum*; while this choir also performed a Magnificat and Nunc Dimitis by the seventeenth-century English composer Thomas Tomkins. The *Festival Te Deum* was given again some two years later at a concert in the cathedral in December 1968 to commemorate its centenary. Antill's work is an approximately ten-minute setting of the Te Deum text as sung (in English) in the Anglican service for Matins. It belongs clearly to the English choral tradition and strongly resembles 'festal' type settings of the text such as Walton's *Coronation Te Deum* of 1953.

Antill's *Festival Te Deum* is scored for choir, trumpets, horns, trombones and organ, although the two performances of the late 1960s appear to have been given by choir and organ only. Its musical language, in keeping with English cathedral music of the 'post-pastoral' years, is somewhat less dissonant than much of that found in his orchestral works discussed in Chapter 4, and its tonal centres are more clearly focussed; however, there is still much freely dissonant writing of a post-tonal, neo-classical style. The work is held together by a number of recurrences of the opening music, which functions somewhat like a ritornello, although set to different parts of the text. The celebratory nature of the Te Deum is captured by the fanfare-like 6/8 metre of this recurring music, which also well illustrates the melodic and harmonic idiom of the work as a whole. Example 5.4 quotes the opening setting of the words 'We praise thee O God: We acknowledge thee to be the Lord'.

The momentum of this brilliant 'festal' music dominates the work. There are only a few quieter episodes, the most striking being the passage setting the words 'The Holy Church throughout the World doth acknowledge Thee, the Father of an infinite majesty'. Here, for the only time, the choir sings unaccompanied, the texture, though still dissonant, being smoother and more lyrical (Example 5.5 below).

Towards the end, the fanfare-like opening music once more dominates, and brings the work to a rousing close with a brilliant chain of dissonant chords for the organ before ending on a triumphal chord of C major – the basic tonality of the work.

Critical reactions to the two performances of the work were varied. Writing of the 1966 première, Romola Costantino (*The Sydney Morning Herald*, 8 April 1966) remarked that 'no special point of note emerged at first hearing from this smooth and workmanlike writing for choir and organ'. Two divergent evaluations arose from the 1968 performance. Meredith Oakes (Sydney *Daily Telegraph*, 9 December 1968) wrote that the choir 'made a good fist of John Antill's dissonant

Example 5.4   *Festival Te Deum*, bb. 1–8(1)

"Te Deum"'; while Roger Covell (*The Sydney Morning Herald*, 9 December 1968) commented: 'the small scale performance of John Antill's brisk and gentlemanly "Te Deum" directed by the composer was reasonably well suited to a work written entirely within the English cathedral tradition and more appropriate for liturgical purposes than for a special festival concert'. Covell's final observation clearly highlights the still relatively modest dimensions of Antill's composition, but perhaps understates the music's effectiveness as a 'festal' work. Antill was

Example 5.5   *Festival Te Deum*, bb. 36(6)–42

to continue this same general idiom in his other extended anthem-type work, the *Cantate Domino*, to be examined below.

Cantate Domino (1970)

The genesis of *Cantate Domino*, a commission from the Australian Council of Churches, once more illustrates graphically Antill's situation during so much of his post-*Corroboree* career. Dean and Carell recount – from papers accompanying the score among the Antill Papers[12] – how the composer was 'called to a meeting' in connection with the planned celebration of the ecumenical visit to Sydney by Pope Paul VI. Antill's account of the meeting is quoted as follows:

> It was just four weeks before the proposed performance. My order was to produce one processional anthem, seven minutes long. I fell for it. Rehearsals had to be arranged. Choirs had to be gathered together. I could use certain brass as room permitted, and the much maligned Town Hall organ. The parts had to be copied and distributed, corrected and learned. All eyes shifted in my direction. Estimated time for producing the score – four days! Each of 24 hours duration, of course! The meeting closed. Result – I was more unapproachable than usual, I believe. But something came off the assembly line.

That Antill could produce an effective 'processional anthem' in such a short time is, of course, consistent with his consummate professionalism in being able to fulfil yet another of his myriad commissions in a timely manner. The planned ecumenical service at which *Cantate Domino* was premièred took place in the Sydney Town Hall on 2 December 1970. Dean and Carell document at least one subsequent performance – at an 'all-Antill' concert at the Sydney Conservatorium of Music on 31 March 1985, along with a number of brief 'celebratory' pieces together with the two overtures discussed in Chapter 4, the *Five Australian Lyrics* (see below) and the *Corroboree* Suite (the particular version not specified).[13]

Cantate Domino is a setting of Psalm 98 (Catholic Bible) or 97 (King James Bible) that forms part of the Anglican Evensong service as well as one of the Catholic canticles for Lauds. The text thus has a suitably 'ecumenical' association, at least with the two Western Episcopal Christian denominations. Perhaps owing to the more 'public' and 'popular' as well as 'festal' occasion, and perhaps also owing to the severely limited rehearsal time, the musical idiom of *Cantate Domino* is less dissonant than that of *Festival Te Deum*, although the largely triadic accompaniment operates in a thoroughly post-tonal idiom of 'non-functional' harmony, with many colourful harmonic juxtapositions and much use of parallel chains of triads which occasionally create bitonal clashes, as may be seen in Example 5.6 which quotes the opening bars.

---

[12] AP, S8i/5; Dean and Carell, *Gentle Genius*, p. 168.
[13] Dean and Carell, *Gentle Genius*, p. 188.

Example 5.6 *Cantate Domino*, bb. 1–8

The scoring is for choir (a large one – numbering 150 at the première), three trumpets, three tenor and one bass trombones, two tubas, timpani and organ. There are only occasional passages where the brass choir accompanies the singers without the organ or has material independent of the organ part. However, the work could easily be performed by choir and organ only, as in the case of *Festival Te Deum*.

The Song Cycles

Antill's three song cycles of the early 1950s are better designated as 'sets' rather than 'cycles' in the stricter sense of nineteenth-century Lieder; as they are unified by neither an implied narrative, as in Schubert's *Die Winterreise* or *Die schöne Müllerin*, nor also by thematic and tonal 'cyclic' integration as in Schumann's *Dichterliebe*. Although Antill's cycles are – as in the case of the above Lieder cycles – settings of texts by a single poet (as in *Five Australian Lyrics*) or at least from one text source – the Book of Psalms as in *Five Songs of Happiness* and *Five Songs of Praise* – they are each integrated only by a general poetic and stylistic unity and a satisfying sequence of tempo and mood. The two cycles of psalm settings display a close similarity as might be expected. The *Five Songs of Praise* exist in manuscript with no title page, while the fourth song, curiously, also carries a full title page labelled *Three Songs of Righteousness* and is designated as No. 2 in this set. However, no other songs from this set have been traced. The examinations below will concentrate on the two song cycles dating from 1953. The first of these, the *Five Songs of Happiness*, was written for the unusual combination of voice, oboe and piano. It is perhaps the most effective of the psalm settings, forms an attractive sequence, and well represents the overall style and structures of Antill's psalm settings for solo voice. The remaining work to be examined in this chapter – the *Five Australian Lyrics* – returns to one of Antill's dominant post-*Corroboree* themes – that of Aboriginal culture – and is arguably his finest excursion into the field of solo song.

Five Songs of Happiness (1953)

This cycle (or set) of songs for high voice, (optional) oboe and piano comprises the setting of the following psalms:

1. Psalm 23: 'The Lord is my Shepherd' (verses 1 and 6);
2. Psalm 24: 'The Earth is the Lord's' (verses 1 and 10);
3. Psalm 27: 'The Lord is my Light' (verses 1 and 13);
4. Psalm 34: 'I Will Bless the Lord' (verses 1, 2 and 22);
5. Psalm 46: 'God is my Refuge' (verses 1 and 11).

Example 5.7 *Five Songs of Happiness*, No. 1, bb. 1–10(2)

As can be seen, only the first one or two verses followed by the last verse of each psalm are set, allowing the composer reasonable scope to achieve an expansive setting of each relatively brief text. The overall character of the set is, in keeping with the theme of 'happiness', one of rejoicing, and there is therefore little dramatic contrast in mood to be found. The tempi of the five songs are given, respectively, as 'Slowly', 'Slowly', 'Moving', 'Moderately' and 'Moving'. These tempi are nevertheless broad rather than sluggish in character, allowing the composer an appropriately expansive means of conveying the constantly positive emotions of the texts. The general texture is strongly 'muscular', involving much spare and disjunct melodic writing as well as dissonant chords in the accompaniment, together with a rhythmic setting for the voice which makes much use of asymmetrical phrases and displaced accents. In addition, Antill frequently employs both shifting and irregular metres such as 5/4 (song 2), 10/8 (song 5) and the alternation of 4/4, 3/4 and 7/4 (song 1). The settings once more display much vitality and energy in an essentially 'cool' and 'neoclassical' idiom. Some idea of Antill's melodic and harmonic language as well as vocal writing in this cycle can be seen in the following examples. In song 1, the opening oboe solo dovetails with the piano, leading into the opening text, 'The Lord is my shepherd, I shall not want' which is irregularly scanned over bars of 7/4 and 3/4 metre (Example 5.7).

Occasionally Antill's rhythmic scanning is perhaps less effective, as may be seen at the end of song 2 (Example 5.8) in the accentuation of the words, 'The Lord of Hosts, He is the King of Glory'.

Example 5.8   *Five Songs of Happiness*, No. 2, bb. 23–26

Song 3, 'The Lord is my Light', involves juxtaposition of bold pandiatonic and bitonal harmonies, the opening bars following the introduction well illustrating the former technique (Example 5.9 below).

Throughout the cycle, the oboe part (which can be played by the pianist if the oboe is not available) varies the ensemble, which at different times may involve all three performers, the voice and piano only, voice and oboe, or the oboe and piano only. The spare, linear piano writing for much of the time blends well with the oboe; and the whole character of the work is of a largely transparent clarity, contrasting at other times with a denser texture where the piano part employs Antill's frequently used dissonant counterpoint of bare or triad-based chords. The style is thus well in keeping with the more astringent tendencies of Antill's post-*Corroboree* musical language.

Example 5.9   *Five Songs of Happiness*, No. 3, bb. 7–11

Five Australian Lyrics (1953)

As mentioned above, in *Five Australian Lyrics* Antill was once more attracted to an Aboriginal theme, but not directly intending, in this case, to evoke the sounds or atmosphere of Aboriginal music. *Five Australian Lyrics* is a cycle of five songs for voice and piano to texts by Harvey Allen that were inspired by Aboriginal legends. The present author has been unable to locate information about Harvey Allen, except for a brief note by Antill that 'Harvey Allen has had a number of songs and lyrics published in England and Australia and has worked closely with John Antill'.[14]

The songs are: 1: 'The Wanderer'; 2: 'Sunset Song'; 3: 'The Stones Cry Out'; 4: 'A Prayer'; and 5: 'Song to the Storm'. Antill has commented on the text and music as follows:

> In these impressions or songs, it would not be possible or desirable to attempt authenticity with regard to music and interpretation. They are intended to convey the fervent expressions of the Australian Aboriginal ... and to indicate the workings of the Aboriginal mind under age-old stresses and emotions.[15]

He also provided a programme note for the work's scheduled première by the baritone Clement Williams, although it is unclear as to whether this performance took place:

> The lyrics are from tribal legends and were written by Harvey Allen, after close study of aboriginal folk-lore and tales handed down by word of mouth through the ages.
>
> No. 1 The Wanderer: This is the story of a young man of the tribe who has lost the bride, pledged to him since childhood, to another warrior, and who wanders through the bush towards the sacred ceremonial ground, and bewildered because everything that he understood as good and promising had come to a sudden end.
>
> No. 2 Sunset Song: This is derived from the ancient tribal belief that the sun stood still and the earth turned its back on the sun and thus was unable to receive any light, except for Memah (the moon) who usurped the place of the sun in a faint way until the world turned around again to see the Sun Goddess shine across the sea.
>
> No. 3 The Stones Cry Out: This depicts the stark barrenness of the earth in times of drought, when the water holes are dried up and skeletons of the bush animals – dingoes [sic], kangaroos and other animals, are seen in the deserted stony wastes, over all of which hangs the unearthly quiet of the Australian open, arid spaces.
>
> No. 4 A Prayer: This is a typical primitive type of appeal to the Unknown, a realisation of a Greater Being, and a supplication for a continuance of the fundamentals of their physical welfare, plus an unswerving faith in the efficacy of prayer.

---

[14] AP, S8j/3.
[15] Dean and Carell, *Gentle Genius*, p. 123.

No. 5 A Song to the Storm: Here is another example of the primitive mind believing the elements are dread and powerful "beings" to whom appeals can be made to propitiate their anger and to aid in personal vengeance.[16]

While the sentiments expressed in Allen's poems sometimes evoke a more Western than Aboriginal sense of the sacred, Murdoch's contention that they 'reflect [...] time-worn Christian cadences of piety and sentiment'[17] represents an unfortunate distortion of the texts' expressive qualities. In terms of the music, Antill's disavowal of 'authenticity' may or may not relate to his earlier-quoted comment (see Chapter 2) regarding the use of a 'contemporary style' when writing about Aborigines. However, as will by now have become clear, there is little observable difference in Antill's basic musical vocabulary from works on non-Aboriginal subjects, notwithstanding the various shifts of stylistic emphasis which have been observed in his post-*Corroboree* output.

The *Five Australian Lyrics* may reflect, as Murdoch has noted, 'squarely English school art song writing',[18] though not, as here indirectly implied by Murdoch, of an early twentieth-century post-Romantic cast. Four of the songs are through-composed but with some opening material returning at or near the end, while the two long stanzas of 'The Stones Cry Out' are set in modified strophic – or rather strophic variation – form. Stylistically, while some of the writing – especially in 'A Prayer' and the middle section of 'Sunset Song' – strongly evokes the songs of Vaughan Williams or John Ireland, the predominant style is 'post' English pastoralism and contains much harmonic astringency of a definitely post-World War 1 character.

The following examples may illustrate the range of Antill's style and expression in this work. The first song, 'The Wanderer', poignantly expresses, in the piano's opening thin-textured, tonally ambiguous figuration, something of the desolation of the rejected bridegroom, revisiting his sacred tribal lands (Example 5.10).

The mood becomes more intense with repeated dissonant chords accompanying the words, 'Speak to me Great Father Spirit, Tell me the path I must take'. The lack of final resolution for the 'wanderer' is underlined by the return of the opening tonally amorphous passage to conclude the song. The middle section of the second song, 'Sunset Song' – an invocation to 'The Great Goddess of Life and Light' – shows a definitely English pastoral idiom already noted in the slow movement of *Symphony on a City* (Example 5.11 below – and cf. Example 4.15 in Chapter 4).

The third song, 'The Stones Cry Out', begins with somewhat similar figuration to the opening of 'The Wanderer', accompanying the words, 'The stones cry out, The earth is still, No moving dust to point the way the wind will come' The latter part of the song reaches a peak of austere intensity at the words, 'Rock moves on rock ... like grinding teeth in rage'. Here the dissonance becomes more abrasive, with the accompaniment ranging from a throbbing ostinato rhythm, through more

---

[16] AP, S8j/3.
[17] Murdoch, *Australia's Contemporary Composers*, p. 13.
[18] Ibid.

Example 5.10   *Five Australian Lyrics*, No. 1, bb. 1–5

linear as well as disjunct chromatic writing, to the stark *Corroboree*-like dissonant counterpoint of chords comprising octaves and fifths only (Example 5.12 below).

The song ends with these stark chords in parallel procession, underpinning the final words, 'Aching, brooding, brooding, aching, Trapped in the great silence of life denied'. Following the once more 'pastoral' setting of the fourth song, 'A Prayer', the last song, 'Song to the Storm' returns to dissonance, with a spare texture redolent of much neo-classical writing. The dance-like character, misleadingly referred to by Murdoch as 'in the measures of a happy English maypole dance',[19] rather imparts an element of energy effectively evoking the robust but stormy nature of the text (Example 5.13 below).

Five Australian Lyrics is a noteworthy example of the English art song genre of the second quarter of the twentieth century and compares worthily with some fine Australian examples of the genre written in the 1940s and 1950s such as Margaret Sutherland's *Four Blake Songs* (1957) and *Six Songs: Settings of Poems by Judith Wright* (1950–1962); and Dorian Le Gallienne's *Four Divine Poems of John Donne* (1947–1951). Indeed, it is not impossible that Antill's sudden production of song cycles at just this time could have been inspired by the

---

[19]   Ibid.

appearance of such cycles by his contemporaries. Like these sets, Antill's cycle has appeared reasonably regularly in recitals of Australian songs and was, as noted in the Interlude, commercially recorded in the late 1960s as part of the two-LP set titled *Australian Music Today*.[20] It is also the only work of Antill, apart from *Corroboree*, which has been taken up by an international commercial publisher (by Boosey and Hawkes, also the publisher of *Corroboree*).

Example 5.11   *Five Australian Lyrics*, No. 2, bb. 17–22(2)

---

[20]   *Australian Music Today*, Vol. 1, LP recording A/601 (Sydney: World Record Club, 1966?).

Example 5.12   *Five Australian Lyrics*, No. 3, bb. 44–55

Example 5.13 *Five Australian Lyrics*, No. 5, bb. 1–10

* glissando black notes;
^ glissando white notes

Conclusion

It is perhaps fitting that this survey of Antill's post-*Corroboree* compositions for voice – and indeed of his music as a whole – has concluded with an examination of what is, perhaps, one of Antill's finest works in any medium in his entire output. One may recall – and perhaps to some extent agree with – Dean and Carell's comments quoted in Chapter 3 on Antill's relative lack of ease when confronted with texts, as distinct from his generally greater compositional felicity in the field of orchestral composition. One may again note, too, Covell's comment quoted earlier in this chapter on Antill's setting of *Hagar*, which referred to 'getting through the task of setting the words'. The occasional infelicity in his Psalm settings in *Five Songs of Happiness* has also been noted. On the other hand, Andrew McCredie's approving comments (see Interlude) should be recalled regarding Antill's 'sensitivity to word and tone and to declamatory possibilities' in *Five Australian Lyrics*, 'which at best invite comparison with Britten' – a truly majestic yardstick for comparison! Indeed, in these songs, Antill seems to have both found a way to convincingly set a text as well as to display an emotional intensity rare in his music, notwithstanding its other fine qualities. In the following brief 'Epilogue' to this book, an attempt will be made to provide an overall evaluation of Antill's work and its place in Australian music of the post-colonial period.

Epilogue
John Antill as a 'One Work Composer'?

This book has attempted to bring to life the artistic achievement of one of Australia's most interesting musical creators, a composer who may rightfully stand alongside some of the most celebrated figures in Australian music and the arts generally of the past century. His highly unusual career path, with its two sharply defined stages – pre- and post-*Corroboree* – has been chronicled, showing in particular how the famous ballet score has cast a gigantic shadow over all of his other achievements. *Corroboree* alone has guaranteed Antill an honourable place in any Australian arts 'hall of fame'; but, as has been seen, its composer has inevitably suffered from this very fame in relation to both the nature of, and critical reaction to, his other works.

In viewing Antill's development as a composer, one fact is clear: that the advent of *Corroboree* signalled Antill's 'arrival' as not only an 'iconic' Australian 'nationalist', but also a composer who was among the relatively few in Australia at this time pursuing a recognisably 'modernist' style – even if, in the case of *Corroboree*, a style that was by then some three decades old. The evidence of his early work, surveyed in Chapter 1, could have but faintly predicted the stylistic breakthrough achieved in *Corroboree* – the predominantly gentle, post-Romantic and pastoral idiom of these pre-*Corroboree* works reflecting trends in the music of many of Australia's more typically conservative composers of the early twentieth century. As also shown in Chapter 1, very few of Antill's major operatic projects were completed during these early years, while his completed works mostly comprised modest vocal and choral pieces, the latter produced as a kind of 'Gebrauchsmusik' for broadcast performances by Antill's radio choirs. Indeed *Endymion*, which did achieve a later performance, is perhaps the only substantial pre-*Corroboree* work worthy of future revivals. Thus, if Antill's musical achievement had not moved, in scope and style, beyond this stage – as it did radically in *Corroboree* and after – it is likely that the name of John Antill would have remained merely a 'footnote' in the history of twentieth-century Australian music. It is therefore to *Corroboree* and the music that followed it that one must look to attempt some evaluation of Antill's achievement and impact on Australian music of the post-colonial period.

As to *Corroboree*, little needs to be added to what has already been discussed at length in this book. The work has achieved almost universal acclaim as not only a major artistic achievement in its own right, but it has also been seen as a major statement of Australia's 'musical nationhood' and 'coming of age'. Despite the changing critical outlook on Australia's music from the perspective of the twenty-first century, this historical status seems unlikely to be seriously challenged at any time in the foreseeable future. The far more problematic issue in evaluating Antill's musical achievement as a whole is the status of the many works that followed; and, in the last three chapters of this book, an attempt has been made to address the two perceptions of Antill's post-*Corroboree* output, as outlined in the Interlude, that have dominated much of the critical commentary on his music during the more than half century following the appearance of the famous ballet score. These perceptions, it will be recalled, are: first, that Antill's post-*Corroboree* works were mostly slighter in musical scope or substance; and second, that the composer adopted, in his later works, an essentially 'milder', 'gentler' or more conservative musical style, seen as a retreat from the more radical style of *Corroboree*.

To take the first of these perceptions: the evidence of Antill's output has made it clear that, following the enormous success of *Corroboree*, the composer found himself besieged by commissions – from both private and public sources – for music of an 'occasional' nature and/or for works (such as film scores or ballets) produced under the most trying circumstances or with the most stringent time restraints or limited musical resources. Antill's professionalism allowed him to fulfil these commissions in a timely and polished manner, but the results may well, in many cases, justify Covell's classification of these as 'the diligent makeweights of an extremely competent musician' (see Interlude). Unfortunately, Covell used this description to cover Antill's total production, which ignores or downplays the composer's achievement in a number of works for which this description seems considerably less than adequate or fair.

However, while it is relatively easy to agree with the general thrust of the above perception of much of Antill's post-*Corroboree* work, and indeed to lament the fact that a greater number of more substantial works did not flow from his pen, it is the second perception – the claim that Antill's post-*Corroboree* output is more conservative (or less 'advanced') in its musical style – that is more contentious. The generally negatively-toned criticisms of Antill's later work from this perspective need to be assessed from two standpoints: that of 'style' or 'character' and that of musical 'language' or idiom. As to the first, the adjectives ' mild', 'docile' or 'gentle' point (albeit rather exaggeratedly) to a basic issue that may be accepted – namely that Antill never wrote another work as 'barbaric' or 'abrasive' in style as *Corroboree*. His later works explore a wider expressive palette in which the 'abrasive' or 'barbaric' elements make only sporadic appearances. Covell comments on this fact approvingly when he notes that Antill, like Stravinsky after *The Rite of Spring,* 'realised ... the folly of repeating himself with diminishing effect'.[1] It is a pity, therefore, that the same writer appears to be prepared to accord a relatively high value to *Symphony on a City* (see Chapter 4) purely in terms of its success in recreating the 'energy at high voltage' found in *Corroboree*. Indeed this points to a theme that runs through most of the criticisms of Antill's later output – namely that it fails to reflect the energy and colour of *Corroboree* – hence the use of the adjectives listed above with their obviously negative connotations.

---

1   Covell, *Australia's Music*, p. 154.

As to the second aspect of Antill's post-*Corroboree* style – that of 'language' or idiom – it is hoped that the discussion of, and musical examples from, representative works in the latter chapters of this book make it clear that Antill's later musical language shows a basic continuity with that of *Corroboree*, and that he made no retreat into what Brown, for example, referred to (see Interlude) as 'the more readily accessible styles of European orchestral writing of the late nineteenth or early twentieth centuries'. Rather, although his later work does encompass the 'gentler' sounds of English pastoralism in sections of some works – and even occasionally encompasses some passages of simple diatonicism – the predominant idiomatic frame of reference is that of post-World War 1 neo-tonality and neo-classicism. In this respect, Antill is clearly writing within a general stylistic range shared by the more progressive Australian composers of the 1940s and 1950s such as Margaret Sutherland, Dorian Le Gallienne, Raymond Hanson and Robert Hughes. Furthermore, this general idiom is one which stems from a mixture of the English post-pastoral styles of Walton, Bliss, Jacob and others; and the neo-classicism and neo-tonality of Bartók, Hindemith and Stravinsky, which was prevalent in Europe and America between the wars and just after. Other composers, to whom Antill's musical style has from time to time been linked, have been identified in previous discussions. It should be recalled that these styles are historically 'later' than that of the early twentieth-century 'primitivism' of *Corroboree* – a fact that should finally put the lie to the claim that Antill's later style constituted any kind of 'retreat' into late Romanticism. Additionally, despite the copious identifications that have been suggested from time to time in this book, between Antill's works and various English, European and American influences, Antill should in no way be regarded as simply an eclectic composer, with no musical personality of his own. His individualism shows clearly in all his best works – an individualism that strongly evokes many of the qualities which are regarded as typically 'Australian' – namely warmth, simplicity, directness and, where appropriate, a quirky sense of humour. Antill has indeed absorbed his stylistic associations rather than been submerged by them.

Finally, then, it might be concluded that the critical reception of Antill's later output has suffered from an overwhelming tendency simply to measure it against the stylistic yardstick of *Corroboree*, rather than evaluating the music on its own terms. *Corroboree*'s place as an Australian musical icon is deservedly assured. But is it the only work by which Antill should be remembered by posterity? Is he indeed merely a 'one work composer'? It is hoped that this book has revealed a composer whose craftsmanship is assured and whose stylistic scope is far wider than the purely 'primitivist' idiom of *Corroboree*. Further, despite the constraints working against Antill's opportunities for untrammelled creative work during the post-*Corroboree* years and the incessant demands to produce 'occasional' works, he was still able to compose a number of works of both substance and quality. These have been identified and examined in the previous chapters of this book. Overall, the best of Antill's works should in future find an honourable place among the achievements of Australia's post-colonial composers.

Appendix 1
List of Original Compositions by John Antill

As stated in the introduction to this book, the vast bulk of John Antill's manuscript scores has been deposited in the Australian Manuscript Collection of the National Library of Australia (NLA) in Canberra. Some further scores have also been deposited in the NLA from the former Symphony Australia (ABC) archives. A perusal of this material and of available work lists provided by The Australian Music Centre, Sydney, the Australasian Performing Right Association (APRA) and by Antill's biographers, Dean and Carell, make it clear that the NLA holdings comprise as comprehensive as possible a collection of Antill's works at present in the public domain. Along with the more substantial works discussed in this book, Antill's numerically vast output includes a multitude of both original compositions and arrangements, a major proportion of which are of exceedingly brief or minor scope, and many of these lost or destroyed. The following list of works, therefore, may claim to be comprehensive, but not exhaustive. The list is also confined to original compositions. Scores and associated materials for all the listed works – apart from those indicated as 'lost' or 'unlocated' – may be found in the collections held in the NLA. With very rare exceptions, Antill's works have remained unpublished (publishers have been indicated where appropriate).

A. Theatre Works

1. Operas

Ouida (?1914–1918) – libretto by composer – lost
Princess Dorothea (1919–1920) – libretto by composer
Heroida (early 1920s?) – lost
The Sleeping Princess (early 1920s?) – lost
Endymion (1929–1930) – libretto by composer (after Keats)
Here's Luck (1931–1932) – libretto by Margery Browne
The Glittering Mask (1931–1932) – libretto by Margery Browne
The Gates of Paradise (1933–1934) – libretto by Margery Browne – incomplete
The Serpent Woman (c. 1938) – libretto by John Wheeler – incomplete
The Lost Child (c. 1940) – libretto by John Wheeler – fragment only
The Scapegoat (c. 1943) – libretto by John Wheeler – fragment only
Body Politic (late 1940s?) – libretto by composer – fragment only
The Music Critic; or, *The Printer's Devil* (1952) – libretto by composer
The First Christmas (1969) – libretto by Pat Flower

2. Ballets

Corroboree (1944) – 1950 scenario and choreography by Rex Reid; 1954 scenario by Victor Carell, choreography by Beth Dean; score published by Boosey & Hawkes (Sydney) – see also under Orchestral Works: *Corroboree* Suites No. 1 (1946) and No. 2 (1950)

The Circus Comes to Town (late 1940s?) – fragment only

Capriccio (subtitled 'from Endymion') – performed Melbourne 1953 – scenario and choreographer unknown

The Sentimental Bloke (1953) – choreography by Beth Dean – incomplete – see also under Orchestral Works: *A Sentimental Suite* (1955)

The Unknown Land (1956) – scenario and choreography by Coralie Hinkley – see also under Orchestral Works (same title)

Wakooka (1957) – scenario and choreography by Valrene Tweedie

G'Day Digger (1958) – scenario by Victor Carell, choreography by Beth Dean

Burragorang Dreamtime (1959) – scenario by Les Jones, choreography by Beth Dean – see also under Choral Works: *Music for a Royal Pageant of Nationhood* (1963)

Black Opal (1961) – scenario and choreography by Dawn Swane

Snowy! (1961) – scenario and choreography by Margaret Barr

Dreaming Time Legends (1964) – rearrangement of *Burragorang Dreamtime* for television

B. Orchestral Works

1. Concert Works

Serenade (early 1920s?)

Nature Studies (1925)

Overture to a Chinese Opera (late 1920s?) – fragment only

Corroboree Suites No. 1 (1946) and No. 2 (1950) – see also under Ballets: *Corroboree* (1944)

Four Abstract Pieces for Orchestra (1946) – fragment only

An Outback Overture (1954)

A Sentimental Suite (1955) – see also under Ballets: *The Sentimental Bloke* (1953)

Nullarbor Dreamtime: Improvisation for Violin and Strings (1956)

The Unknown Land (1956) – see also under Ballets (same title)

Overture for a Momentous Occasion (1956–1957)

Symphony on a City (1959)

Concerto for Harmonica and Orchestra (1961) – see also under Miscellaneous Instrumental Works: Sonata for Harmonica and Piano

Paean to the Spirit of Man (1968)

Variations on a Theme of Alfred Hill (1970) – Introduction and Coda by John Antill

2. Occasional Works

Fanfare on ABC (1950)
Music for the Queen's Christmas Broadcasts (1953 and 1959)
Fanfare for an Important Occasion (1954?) – possibly initial version of *Overture for a Momentous Occasion* (see above)
Australian Themes: Aboriginal, Native, Tribal (1962)
South Pacific Island Themes: New Guinea, Papua, Borneo, all islands south of Equator (1962)
Praised Be Australia (fanfare) (1963)
Centenary Fanfare (1969)
Jubugalee (A Flourish) (1973) – for opening of the Sydney Opera House; see also under Choral Works (same title)
Fughetta: Fanfare for a Festival (1974) – for Musica Viva Australia
Miscellaneous Fanfares (12) – most undated (c. 1974–1985)

3. Film Music

School in the Mailbox (1945) – Film Australia (formerly Commonwealth Film Unit)
Turn the Soil (1948) – Film Australia
Port Jackson (1948?) – Pharos Productions – see also under Incidental Music
The Inlanders (1949) – Kingcroft Productions – score unlocated
The Flying Doctor (1949) – Kingcroft Productions – score unlocated
Our Neighbour Australia (1953 – with Clive Douglas) – Film Australia – score unlocated
This is the ABC (1954) – Film Australia
Australia Now (1957) – Film Australia
This Land Australia (1958) – Film Australia – score unlocated
New Guinea Patrol (1958) – Film Australia
Dark Rain (1958) – Kingcroft Productions
The Sands of Yellow Rock (1959) – Kingcroft Productions
Mantle of Safety (1959) – Kingcroft Productions
The Australian National University (1959) – Film Australia
The Challenge of Water (1961) – Film Australia
The Peoples of Papua and New Guinea (1962 – with Dulcie Holland) – Film Australia – score unlocated
Didjeridoo Difficulties (1962) – ABC – score unlocated
The Land that Waited (1963) – ABC Production

4. Incidental Music for Theatre, Radio and Television Productions

Hassan (Flecker) (1947) – ABC Radio
Port Jackson (1948) – ABC Radio – see also under Film Music

Walkabout (1948) – ABC Radio – score unlocated
Australian Rhapsody (1948) – ABC Radio
Salute to Danger (1948) – ABC Radio
The River (1948) – ABC Radio
The Insect Play (Capek) (1950) – ABC Radio Drama
Singing Dust (tribute to Henry Lawson) (1952) – ABC Radio?
Ned Kelly (Stewart) (1956) – Elizabethan Theatre Trust Production – score titled 'Kelly Koncerto'
The Winds of Amalek (1961) – ABC Radio feature – score unlocated
The Patriots (1962) – theme for ABC Television serial
Wambidgee (1962) – ABC Television puppet show
The Tempest (Shakespeare) (1963) – ABC Radio production
Everyman (morality play) (1964) – ABC Radio
Jonah (1982) – theme for ABC Television drama series

C. Miscellaneous Instrumental Works

Lyric Pieces for piano (late 1920s?)
Sonata for bass clarinet and piano (late 1920s) – lost
Pastoral for Dancing (piano) (1938?) – lost
Sonata for Harmonica and Piano (1961) – see also under Orchestral Works: Concerto for Harmonica and Orchestra (1961)
Elegy for a Headmaster for organ (n.d.)

D. Choral Works

'The Lover's Walk Forsaken' (1936) – words by John Wheeler
'My Sister the Rain' (1936) – words by John Wheeler
'Cradle Song' (1936) – words by John Wheeler
Miscellaneous short choral pieces including songs and arrangements for performance by ABC choral and vocal ensembles conducted by Antill: The Melody Makers Quartet (1933), the Mastersingers Male Quartet (1933–1936) and the Wireless Chorus (1936–1941)
The Song of Hagar to Abraham the Patriarch (1959)
Music for a Royal Pageant of Nationhood (1963) – see also under Ballets: *Burragorang Dreamtime* (1959)
Festival Te Deum (1966)
Cantate Domino (1970)
Jubugalee (A Flourish) (1973) – choral version – see also under Orchestral Works (same title)
Seven original carols composed for St Andrew's Cathedral choir (1965–1974) – words by Dorothy Hulme-Moir

Many short carols, anthems, school songs and arrangements for choir (most lost)

E. Songs (Voice and Piano)

'The Lost Joy' (1926) – words by Harry Lee
'Blue Eyed Mary' (1927) – words by Gene Strett Portec
'My Star' (1928) – words by Robert Browning
'The Garland' (1928) – words by John Dryden
'There is Sweet Music' (1928) – words by Alfred Lord Tennyson
'Four by the Clock' (1928) – words by Henry Longfellow
'A Choice' (1929) – words by M.G. Stewart
'Melbourne Centenary Song' (1934) – words by Margery Browne
'There is Ever a Song Somewhere' (1934) – words by F.W. Riley
'Remembrance' (1935) – words by (?)Castles
'It's Fine to Say Good Morning' (1935) – words anon.
'The Little Things' (1935) – words by William Allingham
'O Ever Ernest Sea' (1935) – words by H. Bona
'If the Heart's Full of Song All Day Long' (1935) – words anon.
'The Heart that Sings Alway' (1935) – words by F.L. Stanton
'What Inspires Me' (1935) – words by composer
'Beauty of Spring' (1941) – words by John Wheeler
'West Bound' (1948) – words by John Wheeler
'Prospector's Song' (1948) – words by John Wheeler
'Black Eyed Susan' (n.d.) – words by Richard Leveridge
'Sweet Scented Sandalwood Bloom' (1951) – words by Ann Lethbridge
'In an Old Homestead Garden' (1952) – words by Ann Lethbridge – published by Allans (Melbourne)
'Barbara's Song' (c. 1953) – words B. Bradshaw
Five Australian Lyrics (1953) – words by Harvey Allen – published by Boosey & Hawkes (Sydney)
Five Songs of Happiness (1953) (with optional oboe) – words Book of Psalms
Five Songs of Praise (1954) – words Book of Psalms (including Psalm 36 marked 'Songs of Righteousness' No. 2)
'Happy Wanderer' (1957) – words by H. Cannon
Miscellaneous songs and arrangements – lost or unlocated

Appendix 2
Corroboree: Antill's Original Choreographic Outline

Characteristic Movements:
Most actions quick and jerky
Grotesque facial expressions
Swift turnings of the head
Always a high knee action
Much hip movement
Quivering of head, hands and body

1. *Welcome Ceremony*: By Witchetty grub men assisted by members of the Emu totem.

Bar 1	Absolute blackout. Gradual brightening to a silhouette to bar 52. The reiterant B/F/E flat representing movements by Medicine man, who is central figure amongst the council of old men.
Bar 30	The Didjeridoo.
Bars 37–53	Smoke signals directed by Medicine man.
Bar 63	Witchetty grub theme.
Bar 73	Tribal jester performs.
Bar 76	Incantation of Council of old men.
to 109	Obvious.
Bar 115	Tribe requests procedure from Council.
Bar 125	Tympani [*sic*] solo:- Medicine man delivers instructions.
Bar 135	Medicine man performs his tricks.

(flint stones etc.) assisted by tribe's jester.

Bar 149	Entrance of the Emu totem – Theme to bar 157.

Witchetty grubs maintain their original rhythm.
Obvious to conclusion.

2. The Thippa Thippa and Bell bird people dance *To the Evening Star*.

3. *A Rain Dance*: By the Frog totem assisted by the Fish men. Characteristic hop and croak. (Grandfather Frog at 73).

Bar 98	Solo.
Bar 102	Fish men enter.
Bar 150	Tremolando – incantations to the clouds.
Bar 174	Frogs a more active part. (Cello, Basses.)
to 286	Obvious.

    Bar 287   Incantations answered – thunderclap and coda.

4. The Snake totem demonstrates the *Spirit of the Wind*.

5. Kangaroo men pay homage *To the Rising Sun*.
    3/8 – Characteristic hop of the Kangaroos.
    After bar 50. Tremolando – Incantations to the east.
    Anticipation of the rising sun.
    Bar 111   Dawn and brighter to conclusion.

6. *Morning Star Dance*: By the Hakea flower totem.

7. *Procession of Totems and Closing Fire Ceremony*:
In which representatives of the Lace Lizard, Cockatoo, Honey ant, Wild cat and Small fly totems participate. Much usage of boomerang, spear and fire stick.
    Bars 1–75   Lace Lizard. 1/8 bars shake of the head.
    Bars 44–75   (Piccolo) Small lizards.
    Bars 76–103   Cockatoo (Soli).
    Bars 103–110   Honey ant.
    Bars 110–180   Wild cat. 182–186 Transition to –
    Bars 186–245   Small fly. Bar 198 onwards suggestions of coming procession.
    Bars 246–249   Uplifting of all totem signs.
    Bar 250   Commencement of procession.
    Bars 256–264   Medicine man gives instructions.
    Bars 265–268   Hakea totem to the fore.
    Bars 269–272   Kangaroo totem prominent.
    Bars 273–274   Snake totem.
    Bars 275–276   Frog and Fish totems.
    Bars 277–278   Bell bird – Thippa Thippa totems.
    Bars 279–280   Witchetty grub and Emu totems to the fore.
    Bars 281–288   All totems raised. Characteristic 'WHA WHA' upraised spears boomerangs etc.
    Bar 289   Waving spears etc. Triplet figure for grotesque comedians plus wild fury of all.
    Bars 313–315   Medicine man again takes charge.
    Bars 315–423   Spear, boomerang and shield tableaux and dance.
    Bar 424   Commencement of fire ceremony. Much smoke and flame. Ignition of large torches and fire sticks. Much movement. Absolute frenzy to bar 600. Concluding bar – prostration.

Appendix 3
Select Bibliography

With the exception of the Antill Papers listed below as the principal source for this book, this select bibliography comprises only books and other published sources referred to in the text and which are devoted to John Antill, or which contain material either directly or indirectly related to Antill's life and work. Miscellaneous sources such as reviews, newspaper reports etc. have been footnoted where appropriate in the text but are not separately listed here. Individual references to Antill's unpublished writings to be found among the Antill Papers have likewise been footnoted but are not separately included here.

Antill, John, *Papers of John Antill (1904–1986)*, MS437, Australian Manuscript Collection, National Library of Australia, Canberra

Brissenden, Alan and Keith Glennon, *Australia Dances: Creating Australian Dance 1945–1965*. Kent Town, South Australia: Wakefield Press, 2010

Brown, Patricia, 'John Antill' in Frank Callaway and David Tunley (eds), *Australian Composition in the Twentieth Century*. Melbourne: Oxford University Press, 1978, pp. 44–51

———, 'Antill, John (Henry)' in Stanley Sadie and John Tyrrell (eds), *The New Grove Dictionary of Music and Musicians*, second edition. London: Macmillan, 2001, Vol. 1, p. 734

Buzacott, Martin, *The Rite of Spring: 75 Years of ABC Music Making*. Sydney: ABC Books, 2007

Covell, Roger, *Australia's Music: Themes of a New Society*. Melbourne: Sun Books, 1967

Crotty, Joel, 'Ballet Australia between 1961 and 1962: A Microcosm of Musical Change', *Brolga: An Australian Journal about Dance*, 1 (December 1994), pp. 41–57

———, 'From Balletic Binge to Cultural Cringe: Choreographic Music in Australia, 1936–1956' in Nicholas Brown, Peter Campbell, Robyn Holmes, Peter Read and Larry Sitsky (eds), *One Hand on the Manuscript: Music in Australian Cultural History 1930–1960*. Canberra: Humanities Research Centre, Australian National University, 1995, pp. 217–28

———, 'Ballet and Dance Music' in Warren Bebbington (ed.), *The Oxford Companion to Australian Music*. Melbourne: Oxford University Press, 1997, pp. 43–5

———, 'Classical Music 1931–60' in John Whiteoak and Aline Scott-Maxwell (eds), *Currency Companion to Music and Dance in Australia*. Sydney: Currency House, 2003, pp. 167–8

Dean, Beth and Victor Carell, *Gentle Genius: A Life of John Antill*. Sydney: Akron Press, 1987

Douglas, Clive, 'Folk-song and the Brown Man – A Means to an Australian Expression in Symphonic Music', *The Canon* 10/3 (1956), pp. 81–5

Hill, Jennifer, 'Clive Douglas and the ABC: Not a Favourite Aunt' in Nicholas Brown, Peter Campbell, Robyn Holmes, Peter Read and Larry Sitsky (eds), *One Hand on the Manuscript: Music in Australian Cultural History 1930–1960*. Canberra: Humanities Research Centre, The Australian National University, 1995, pp. 229–42

Ingamells, Rex, 'Conditional Culture', pamphlet (Adelaide: F.W. Preece, 1938); reprinted in John Barnes (ed.), *The Writer in Australia: A Collection of Literary Documents 1856–1964*. Melbourne: Oxford University Press, 1969, pp. 245–65

McCredie, Andrew, *Musical Composition in Australia*. Canberra: Australian Government Printing Office, 1969

McNeill, Rhoderick, *The Australian Symphony from Federation to 1960*. Farnham: Ashgate, 2014

Moresby, Isabelle, *Australia Makes Music*. Melbourne: Longmans, 1948

Murdoch, James, *Australia's Contemporary Composers*. Melbourne: Sun Books, 1972

Orchard, W. Arundel, *Music in Australia: More than 150 Years of Development*. Melbourne: Georgian Press, 1952

Pask, Edward, *Ballet in Australia: The Second Act 1940–1980*. Melbourne: Oxford University Press, 1982

Petrus, Pauline, 'Antill, John Henry' in Warren Bebbington (ed.), *The Oxford Companion to Australian Music*. Melbourne: Oxford University Press, 1997, pp. 25–6

Plush, Vincent, Huib Schippers and Jocelyn Wolfe (eds), *Encounters: Meetings in Australian Music: Essays, Images, Interviews*. South Brisbane: Queensland Conservatorium Research Centre, 2005

Symons, David, 'Composition in Australia (1): From European Settlement to 1960' in Warren Bebbington (ed.), *The Oxford Companion to Australian Music*. Melbourne: Oxford University Press, 1997, pp. 137–41, 144

———, 'The Jindyworobak Connection in Australian Music c. 1940–1960', *Context: Journal of Music Research*, 23 (Autumn 2002), pp. 33–47

———, 'Words and Music: Clive Douglas and the Jindyworobak Manifesto' in Fiona Richards (ed.), *The Soundscapes of Australia: Music, Place and Spirituality*. Aldershot: Ashgate, 2007, pp. 93–115

———, 'Before Corroboree: Toward a Clearer Perspective of the Early Music of John Antill', *Musicology Australia*, 30 (2008), pp. 29–48

———, 'Corroboree and After: John Antill as a "One-work" Composer?', *Musicology Australia*, 34/1 (2012), pp. 53–80

Tate, Henry, *Australian Musical Possibilities*. Melbourne: Edward A. Vidler, 1924

Wood, Elizabeth, 'Antill, John (Henry)' in Stanley Sadie (ed.), *The New Grove Dictionary of Music and Musicians*. London: Macmillan, 1980, Vol. 1, p. 470

Index

References to footnotes consist of the page number followed by the letter 'n' followed by the number of the footnote, e.g. 104n45 refers to footnote 45 on page 104. References to musical examples are shown in **bold**.

ABC, *see* Australian Broadcasting
    Commission/Corporation (ABC)
The ABC Weekly, Antill interview 112,
    114–15
Aboriginal culture
    Aboriginal legends 10, 45, 180
        Boomerang and Waratah legends
            99–100
    Aboriginal music
        didjeridu 53, 70, 105
        Nathan and Lhotsky arrangements
            of 44
        'song descent' style 53, 105
    and Alfred and Mirrie Hill 46, 53, 81,
        105, 109
    Antill's 'Aboriginal' works 91, 98–9,
        103, 105, 107–9
    and Antill's 'Australian school of
        musical thought' idea 13
    and Antill's *Corroboree* 1, 47–8, 53,
        69, 73–4, 91
    and Antill's *Five Australian Lyrics* 177,
        180–82
    and Antill's *The Unknown Land* 83
    and Australian nationalism 73
    and Australianism 10, 43–4
    and Clive Douglas 53, 105, 109
    Dreamtime 44, 45, 46, 99
    and Jindyworobak movement 30, 45,
        81
    La Perouse Aboriginal settlement 1,
        14, 69
Adler, Larry 128, 154–5
'Advance Australia fair' 31
Agnew, Roy 9, 18
    Dance of the Wild Men 50

Allen, Harvey 180–82
Anderson, Ethel, *The Song of Hagar to
    Abraham the Patriarch* (poem)
    166–7
Antill, John
    assessment of post-*Corroboree* style
        76, 189–91
    and Australian nationalism 2, 10
    and Australianism 10, 18, 46–7, 48
    biographical details, overview 2–3
    biographical details, specific details
        ABC commissions 75, 76, 80, 128,
            131, 136, 140, 154, 157, 162
        ABC Federal Music Editor job 3,
            5, 75, 76, 127
        Aboriginal music, exposure to as a
            boy 1, 14, 48, 69
        Alfred Hill as teacher and mentor
            3, 11, 19, 77
        APRA award 73
        ballet classes, attendance at 36
        church choral music, interest in
            13–14
        death of his wife 166
        Fiji trip 163
        Railways draughtsman
            apprenticeship 2, 13, 15, 17–18
        retirement 75, 117, 162, 163
        Stravinsky's earlier ballets,
            attendance at performances
            of 52
        Sydney Symphony Orchestra,
            association with 127
    biographies and criticism on 3–4
    career, two-stage 5–6, 75
    career after *Corroboree*, overview 75–8

career before *Corroboree*
   beginnings 13–17, **16**
   Conservatorium years (1926–29) 2–3, 5, 18–21, **20**, **21**
   operas 1930-45, chronological perspectives 5, 21–4, **22**, **23**
   Railway years (1920–25) 17–18
   songs and vocal ensemble pieces (1930–45) 35–6, **37**
   stylistic development 1930–45 (*Endymion*) 24–9, **25**, **26**, **27**, **28–9**
   stylistic development 1930–45 (other operas) 30–35, **31**, **32**, **33**
   towards *Corroboree*: ballet compositions 36, 38–41, **39**, **40**, **41**
compositions
   dates of 21, 38
   list of 193–7
sources on
   autobiographical sketch 'Early history' 12–13, 14n20, 15, 17, 36, 127
   diaries (1925-mid-1930s) 13, 21, 22–3, 36, 52
   primary sources 4, 12–13
views and quotes
   Australian Council of Churches meeting and *Cantate Domino* 175
   Australian school of musical thought, need for 13
   being thought of as a ballet writer 127
   C. J. Dennis and *A Sentimental Suite* 131
   Christmas theme for *The First Christmas* 118
   compositional activity, beginning of 13
   'contemporary' style 43, 49, 84, 91, 105, 182
   continuous (or through-composed) operas 115
   Corroboree 43, 46, 49
   Corroboree 1950-51 production 69
   Five Australian Lyrics and the Aboriginal mind 181–2
   St Andrew's Cathedral music, influence of on his musical career 2
   studying music in Australia 18
   symphony sketches in school books 13, 127
   The Unknown Land and 'contemporary style' 49
   The Unknown Land and Coralie Hinkley 83
   writing music for documentary films 129
   writing opera libretti 113
   writing operas before hearing one 15
   writing style for *The Song of Hagar* 168
   see also ballets (John Antill); choral and vocal works (John Antill); *Corroboree* (John Antill); *Endymion* (John Antill); *Gentle Genius: A Life of John Antill* (Dean and Carell); operas (John Antill); orchestral works (John Antill); *separate titles of works*; theatre works (John Antill)
APRA (Australasian Performing Right Association) 3, 73, 154
Arlen, Albert 80, 130
Arts Council Ballet Company 69, 96, 98
Arts Council of Australia 73, 96, 98
Atlanta Ballet 70
atonal music 10, 49, 68
   see also twelve-note music
Australasian Performing Right Association (APRA) 3, 73, 154
Australian Ballet 70
Australian Ballet (Lighfoot and Burlakov) 12, 38
Australian Broadcasting Commission/ Corporation (ABC)
   Antill's commissions from 75, 76, 80, 128, 131, 136, 140, 154, 157, 162
   Antill's *Corroboree* rehearsal at ABC workshop/symposium 1

Antill's Federal Music Editor job 3, 5, 75, 76, 127
Antill's retirement from 75, 117, 162, 163
Antill's works on ABC Radio
　Concerto for Harmonica and Orchestra 155
　Corroboree 158
　The First Christmas 79, 118
　Paean to the Spirit of Man 158
　The Song of Hagar to Abraham the Patriarch 167
　songs and vocal ensemble pieces for ABC radio programmes 35
　Symphony on a City 145–6, 154
Antill's works on ABC Television
　G'Day Digger 96, 98
　Snowy! 110–11
and Australian nationalism 30
and Australianism 44, 47
creation of state symphony orchestras by 11
The Land that Waited (documentary film) 129n7
Variations on a Theme of Alfred Hill, ABC recording of 163
Youth Concerts 128, 140
Australian composers (post-colonial period) 9–12, 50
Australian Council of Churches 175
Australian landscape
　and Australian music 10–11
　and Jindyworobak movement 30, 44, 45, 82
　and promotional films 129
　see also English pastoralism
Australian Manuscript Collection (National Library of Australia, Canberra) 4
Australian Music Centre library (Sydney) 71
Australian Music Today (two-LP set) 78n16, 184
Australian nationalism 2, 10, 30, 73
　see also Australianism
Australian Opera League 11
'Australian' qualities 191
Australianism 10, 18, 43–7, 48, 73

　see also Australian nationalism
Baer, Werner 110
Bainton, Edgar 53
Balanchine, George 90
ballet
　Australian productions and compositions 12, 48–9
　see also ballets (John Antill)
Ballet Australia 80, 103
ballets (John Antill)
　undated works
　　Capriccio 17, 36, 38–9, **39**, 40, **40**, 50, 80
　　The Circus Comes to Town (fragment) 17, 36, 38, 39, 40, **41**, 50, 80, 91
　list of 194
　post-*Corroboree* works
　　Black Opal 79, 80, 91, 98, 103–5, **105**, 106–9, **106–8**
　　Burragorang Dreamtime 79, 80–81, 91, 98–100, **101**, 102–3, **102**, 105
　　Dreaming Time Legends 81
　　G'Day Digger 69, 79, 80, 88n18, 91, 96–8, **97**, 116, 136
　　Music for a Royal Pageant of Nationhood 81, 99
　　Snowy! 79, 80, 109–11
　　The Songs of a Sentimental Bloke (incomplete) 80, 130, 131
　　The Unknown Land 49, 79, 80, 81–4, **85**, 86–8, **86–9**, 91, 95, 128, 131, 149
　　Wakooka 79, 80, 90–95, **92–5**, 116, 136
　see also Corroboree (John Antill)
Ballets Russes 12
　see also de Basil Russian Ballet Company
Barr, Margaret 80, 109–10
Bartók, Béla 2, 10, 39, 49, 50, 84, 191
　Music for Strings, Percussion and Celesta 86
Bax, Arnold 9, 19
　November Woods 10
　Tintagel 10

BBC (British Broadcasting Corporation) 73, 128
Ben Hur (movie) 35
Benjamin, Arthur 9
   The Devil Take Her 24, 113
   harmonica concerto 154
   'Jamaican Rhumba' 76
biographies and criticism, on John Antill 3–4
Black Opal (John Antill) 79, 80, 91, 98, 103–5, **105**, 106–9, **106**, **107**, **108**
Blake, William 183
Bliss, Arthur 145, 191
'Blue Eyed Mary' (song, John Antill) 19, **20**
Bodenwieser, Gertrud 82
Body Politic (John Antill) (fragment) 79n1, 113n70
Boomerang legend 99–100
Boosey and Hawkes (publisher) 29, 71, 184
Boulanger, Nadia 10n1
Brand, Mona, *Coloured Sounds* 110
Bridge, Frank 9, 50
Brissenden, Alan 103, 104
Britten, Benjamin 78, 186
Brown, Patricia 4, 4n16, 75–6, 77, 113, 167, 168n9, 191
Browne, Margery
   Antill's operas based on Browne's texts 21, 22–3, 32
Browning, Robert 19
Burlakov, Mischa 12, 36, 38, 90
Burns, Robert 19
Burragorang Dreamtime (John Antill) 79, 80–81, 91, 98–100, **101**, 102–3, **102**, 105
'bush' subjects 10
Butterley, Nigel 95
   The Tell-Tale Heart 104

Cage, John 49
Cantate Domino (John Antill) 75, 117, 165, 171, 175, **176**, 177
Capriccio (John Antill) 17, 36, 38–9, **39**, 40, **40**, 50, 80
Captain Cook Bicentenary celebrations 69–70, 88n18, 167

Carell, Victor
   and Antill's *The Songs of a Sentimental Bloke* project 80
   scenarios for Antill's works
      Burragorang Dreamtime 98
      Corroboree 1954 production 69, 70
      G'Day Digger 96
   see also Gentle Genius: A Life of John Antill (Dean and Carell)
Centenary Theatre (Broadmeadow) 145
choral and vocal works (John Antill)
   list of 196–7
   post-*Corroboree* works, overview 165
   post-*Corroboree* works by title
      Cantate Domino 75, 117, 165, 171, 175, **176**, 177
      Festival Te Deum 165, 171–3, **173**, **174**, 175, 177
      Five Australian Lyrics 77–8, 165, 175, 177, 180–84, **183**, **184–6**, 186–7
      Five Songs of Happiness 165, 177, **178**, 179–80, **179**, **180**, 186
      Five Songs of Praise 165, 177
      The Song of Hagar to Abraham the Patriarch 69–70, 88n18, 121, 165, 166–8, **169**, 170, **170**, **171**, 172, 186
      Three Songs of Righteousness (incomplete) 177
   songs for voice and piano (1930–45) 35–6, 39
      'To the Heart that Sings Alway' 35
      'If the Heart's Full of Song All Day Long' 35
      'The Lover's Walk Forsaken' 35–6, 39, 49
      'Melbourne Centenary Song' 35
      'My Sister the Rain' 35–6, **37**, 39, 49
   songs for voice and piano (Conservatorium years) 19, 24
      'Blue Eyed Mary' 19, **20**
      'The Garland' 19
      'The Lost Joy' 19, **21**, 24
      'My Star' 19
church choral music
   and Antill 13–14

Index

see also choral and vocal works (John Antill)
The Circus Comes to Town (John Antill) (fragment) 17, 36, 38, 39, 40, **41**, 50, 80, 91
'Click go the Shears' (country tune) 94
Collitts' Inn (music by Varney Monk) 48
composers
    Australian composers (post-colonial period) 9–12
    'Jindyworobak composers' 47
    'one work composers' 76, 191
Concerto for Harmonica and Orchestra (John Antill) 128, 130, 154–7, **155**, **156**, **157**
Conservatorium, *see* New South Wales Conservatorium of Music
Constable, William 68
constructivism 86
'contemporary' style
    as identified with 1950s–60s avant-garde 77–8
    as understood by Antill 43, 49, 84, 91, 105, 182
continuous (or through-composed) operas 15, 34, 96, 100, 114–15, 121, 122
Copland, Aaron 137
    Appalachian Spring 94
    Fanfare for the Common Man 158
corroboree, use of term and musical form 48
Corroboree (John Antill)
    ABC Radio broadcast 158
    and Aboriginal culture 1, 47–8, 53, 69, 73–4, 91
    analysis
        Antill's choreographic outline 51, 53, 56–7, 61, 63, 67, 199–200
        Dance to the Evening Star 51, 56, **56**, 67–8
        Homage to the Rising Sun 51, 59–60, **60**, 61
        The Morning Star Dance 51, 61, **62**
        overview 50–53, 67–8
        Procession of Totems and Closing Fire Ceremony 51, 54, 61–2, 63–4, **63**, **64–6**, 66–7, 68
        A Rain Dance 51, 56–7, **57**
        Spirit of the Wind 51, 58–9, **58**, **59**
        Welcome Ceremony 51, 53–4, **54**, **55**, 61–2, 63–4, 67, 68
    and Antill's two-stage career 5–6
    and 'Australian contemporary style breakthrough' claim 49–50, 189
    and Australian nationalism 10
    comparisons with
        Burragorang Dreamtime 98, 100
        Capriccio 38, 39
        The Circus Comes to Town 38, 39
        Snowy! 111
        The Unknown Land 81–2, 84
    composition date 12, 21
    and continuity with Antill's later work 191
    and cultural appropriation 51n24
    dissonant style 12, 35, 39, 40–41, 50, 52, 67–8, 159
    and Eugene Goossens
        first performances 1, 5, 35, 52n25
        first suite 50n21, 70–71
        second suite 50n21, 70–71
        UK première 72–3, 128
    genesis of 47–9
    impact and aftermath 72–4
    impact and iconic status 2, 74
    and Jindyworobak philosophy 47
    primitivist style 2, 35, 40–41, 49–50, 52, 67, 77, 105, 191
    production of 1950–51 (conducted by Antill) 50, 68–9, 72n48, 73
    production of 1954 (conducted by Antill) 3, 50, 68, 69, 70, 73
    production of 1970 (Captain Cook Bicentenary celebrations) 68, 69–70
    recordings 72, 73
    suites from
        Corroboree as ballet and concert suite 68–72
        first concert suite 50n21, 68, 70–71, 175
        second concert suite 50n21, 68, 70, 71–2, 73, 175
        suite-type organisation 131
    views on from

Andrew McCredie 78
Eugene Goossens 1
John Antill 43, 46, 49
Peter Sculthorpe 74
Vincent Plush 74
Costantino, Romola 172
Covell, Roger
   on Antill as 'composer-laureate for state occasions' 5
   on Antill's post-*Corroboree* work 5, 75–6, 77, 190
   on Antill's specific works
      Black Opal 104–5, 104n47, 107
      Festival Te Deum 173
      Music for a Royal Pageant of Nationhood (*Burragorang Dreamtime*) 81, 99
      Snowy! 111
      The Song of Hagar to Abraham the Patriarch 121, 167–8, 168n8, 168n11, 186
      Symphony on a City 152, 153, 190
   on 'Jindyworobak composers' 47
   writings on Antill 4
criticism and biographies, on John Antill 3–4
Crotty, Joel 12, 90–91, 104n45, 107–8
cultural appropriation
   and *Corroboree* illustrated manuscript score 51n24
   and Jindyworobak philosophy 45, 73
Cummins, Constance 95
Cunningham, Merce 82

Dana Navytis Creative Dance Group 38
de Basil Russian Ballet Company 12, 52
Dean, Beth
   and Antill's *The Songs of a Sentimental Bloke* project 80
   choreography for Antill's works
      Burragorang Dreamtime 98
      Corroboree 1954 production 69, 70, 74
      G'Day Digger 96
      Music for a Royal Pageant of Nationhood 81
   see also *Gentle Genius: A Life of John Antill* (Dean and Carell)

Deane, Daphne 36
Debussy, Claude 34, 49, 50
   Jeux 52
Delius, Frederick 9, 19
Dennis, C. J., *The Songs of a Sentimental Bloke* 80, 130, 131
Devaney, James, *The Vanished Tribes* 45
Diaghilev, Sergei 12
diaries 1925–mid-1930s (John Antill) 13, 21, 22–3, 36, 52
didjeridu 53, 70, 105
Disraeli, Benjamin 24
documentary film music 129, 195
Donizetti, Gaetano, *Lucia di Lammermoor* 117
Donne, John 183
Douglas, Clive
   Antill's contemporary 9
   on Australian musical idiom 46
   documentary film music 129
   and Jindyworobak movement 47, 53, 81
   use of Aboriginal melodies 53, 105
   use of Aboriginal themes 109
   works
      A Bush Legend 30, 47
      Carwoola 10, 47
      Corroboree 47, 48, 50
      'Namatjira' Symphony 10, 153
      Variations on a Theme of Alfred Hill (collaborative work) 162, 163
      Wongadilla 10
Dreaming Time Legends (John Antill) 81
Dreamtime 44, 45, 46, 99
Dreyfus, George 95
Dryden, John 19
Dukas, *La Péri* 52

'Early history' (Antill's autobiographical sketch) 12–13, 14n20, 15, 17, 36, 127
Easton, Lionel 128, 154n35, 155
Elizabethan Opera Ballet Company 90
Elizabethan Theatre (Sydney) 103
Empire Theatre (Sydney) 68
Endymion (John Antill)
   analysis 24–9, **25**, **26**, **27**, **28**–**9**
   assessment of for future revivals 189
   comparisons with

'The Lover's Walk Forsaken' 36
The Serpent Woman 34
  connections with
    Capriccio 38–9
    Corroboree 49
  date of composition 6, 17–18, 21, 22–4
  libretto 113
  plot 24, 30
  première 18
  Sydney and Melbourne performances (1953) 5, 24, 29, 34, 38
  use of recurrent theme 16, 25, 122
English art song genre 183
English choral tradition 77, 172, 173
English 'national school' 100
English pastoralism
  and Alfred Hill 19
  and Antill 12, 19, 46, 47, 49
  and Antill's post-*Corroboree* works 78, 191
  and Antill's pre-*Corroboree* works 189
  and Antill's specific works
    Black Opal 105, 106
    Burragorang Dreamtime 100
    Endymion 24, 29, 38
    Five Australian Lyrics 182
    Nature Studies 20
    The Song of Hagar to Abraham the Patriarch 170
    songs (1930–45) 35, 36
    Symphony on a City 156
    The Unknown Land 86
  and Australian post-colonial composers 9–10, 50
  and Clive Douglas 46
  and *Variations on a Theme of Alfred Hill* (collaborative work) 163
English poeticisms 45

Farnsworth-Hall, John 1, 5
Fellowship of Australian Composers 155
Festival Te Deum (John Antill) 165, 171–3, **173**, **174**, 175, 177
Fiji, Antill's trip to 163
film music 129, 195
The First Christmas (John Antill) 79, 91, 113, 117–19, **120**, 121–3, **122**, **123**, **124–5**

Five Australian Lyrics (John Antill) 77–8, 165, 175, 177, 180–84, **183**, **184–6**, 186–7
Five Songs of Happiness (John Antill) 165, 177, **178**, 179–80, **179**, **180**, 186
Five Songs of Praise (John Antill) 165, 177
Flower, Pat 118–19, 121
  Tilley Landed on Our Shores 119
Fokine, Mikhail 90
Four Abstract Pieces for Orchestra (John Antill) (fragment) 128
French impressionism 19

'The Garland' (song, John Antill) 19
Garraway, H. E. 80n3
The Gates of Paradise (John Antill) (incomplete) 17, 21, 22, 32–3, 34
G'Day Digger (John Antill) 69, 79, 80, 88n18, 91, 96–8, **97**, 116, 136
Gebrauchsmusik 189
Gentle Genius: A Life of John Antill (Dean and Carell)
  about the biography
    background 3–4
    inaccuracies 6, 12
  Antill
    ballet classes, attendance at 36
    Black Opal 104, 105
    church choral music, interest in 13–14
    Corroboree 51, 68, 69, 70, 72, 72n48, 73
    dates of his compositions 21, 38
    G'Day Digger 98
    harmonica works 154n35
    his wife's death and *Song of Hagar* 166
    lack of ease with texts 121, 186
    post-*Corroboree* output 75
    Railway years 17
    Snowy! 110, 111
    sonata during Conservatorium years 19
    song writing 165
    The Unknown Land and Coralie Hinkley 82, 83

Antill on
    Australian Council of Churches meeting and *Cantate Domino* 175
    being thought of as a ballet writer 127
    Corroboree 43
    writing music for documentary films 129
    Boomerang and Waratah legends 99
    Larry Adler 154–5
Gilbert and Sullivan, *The Pirates of Penzance* 31
Gillen, F. J. 44
Glanville-Hicks, Peggy 9, 10n1, 18
Glennon, Keith 103, 104
The Glittering Mask (John Antill) 17, 21, 22–3, 30, 31–2, **33**, 38, 39–40, 48, 49, 91, 114
Goldberg, Austin 3
Goossens, Eugene
    on Antill's *Corroboree* 1
    Antill's *Corroboree* first performances 1, 5, 35, 52n25
    Antill's *Corroboree* first suite 50n21, 70–71
    Antill's *Corroboree* second suite 50n21, 70–71
    Antill's *Corroboree* UK première 72–3, 128
    Sydney Symphony Orchestra appointment as chief conductor 1, 72–3
Graham, Martha 82, 109
Grainger, Percy 9, 44
    'Country Gardens' 76
Grieg, Edvard 19

Hanson, Raymond 9, 162, 191
harmonica, *see* Concerto for Harmonica and Orchestra (John Antill)
Hart, Fritz 9, 10n1, 11
    The Bush 10, 44
Hart-Smith, William 44
Hembrowe, Bruce, *Mexico!* 109n54, 110
Here's Luck (John Antill) 17, 21, 22–3, 30–31, **31**, **32**, 91, 114
Heroida (John Antill) (lost) 17

Hill, Alfred
    and Aboriginal culture 46, 53, 81, 105, 109
    Antill's teacher and mentor 3, 11, 19, 77
    documentary film music work 129
    first generation of post-colonial composers 9
    musical influences 19
    opera work 11
    works
        'Australia' Symphony 10
        Lady Dolly 21
        Symphony No. 7 in E minor 162
    see also Variations on a Theme of Alfred Hill (collaborative work)
Hill, Mirrie
    and Aboriginal culture 46, 53, 81, 105, 109
    'Arnhem Land' Symphony 10
    documentary film music work 129
    second generation of post-colonial composers 9
Hindemith, Paul 10, 191
Hinkley, Coralie 80, 81, 82–3, 90, 109
Holland, Dulcie 162, 163
Holst, Gustav 9, 19
    Egdon Heath 10
    The Planets 52
Honegger, Arthur 84, 87
Hort, Harold 76
Hove, Marie van 154n35
Hudson, Flexmore 44
Hughes, Robert 9, 191
Hurlstone Choral Society (Sydney) 167
Hyde, Miriam 9, 18, 162, 163

'If the Heart's Full of Song All Day Long' (song, John Antill) 35
impressionism 19, 47, 49
Ingamells, Rex 30, 44–5, 46, 53, 81–2, 83
    'Conditional Culture' 45
Ireland, John 9, 19, 182
    The Forgotten Rite 10
    Mai-Dun 10
Italia Prize, 1962 entry 80, 110, 111

Jacob, Gordon 191

Jacobs, Harry 48
J.C. Williamson Opera Company 3, 11, 12
Jindyworobak movement 30, 44–7, 53, 73, 81–2
   Jindyworobak Anthology 45
Jubagalee (A Flourish, John Antill) 130
Judd, James 72

Keats, John 5, 21, 24, 34n39

La Perouse Aboriginal settlement 1, 14, 69
Lambert, Constant 49
Lanchbery, John 72
The Land that Waited (documentary film) 129n7
landscape, *see* Australian landscape; English pastoralism
Le Gallienne, Dorian 9, 191
   Four Divine Poems of John Donne 183
Lhotsky, John 44
Lightfoot, Louise 12, 36, 38, 90
Liszt, Franz 147
   Faust Symphony 159
London Symphony Orchestra 71
Long, Martin 18
The Lost Child (John Antill) (fragment) 21, 33, 34–5, 40, 113, 166
'The Lost Joy' (song, John Antill) 19, **21**, 24
Lovejoy, Robin 68
'The Lover's Walk Forsaken' (song, John Antill) 35–6
Lyly, John 24
Lyric Pieces (John Antill) 19–20
Lyster Company 11, 12

McCarthy, James 129n9
McCredie, Andrew 4, 78, 153, 186
McNeill, Rhoderick 149, 151, 152, 153, 154, 162
Mahler, Gustav 80, 110
Malko, Nicolai 131, 154, 167
Marsh, Stephen Hale, *The Gentleman in Black* 11
Marshall-Hall, G. W. L. 9, 11
Martinů, Bohuslav 84, 87
Massine, Léonide 90
Mastersingers Male Quartet 35

Meale, Richard 95
'Melbourne Centenary Song' (John Antill) 35
Melody Makers Quartet 35
Mendelssohn, Felix, *Elijah* 163
Mewton, Fred 2, 18, 19
modal harmony 149, 156
modern dance movement 82, 109
modernism 77, 78, 95, 126, 189
Monk, Varney, *Collitts' Inn* 48
Moses, Charles 154
Moses, John 29, 112–13
Mozart, Wolfgang Amadeus, *The Magic Flute* 34
Mudie, Ian 44
Murdoch, James
   on Antill's post-*Corroboree* work 75–6, 77–8
   on Antill's specific works
      Corroboree 2n4
      Five Australian Lyrics 182, 183
      The Song of Hagar to Abraham the Patriarch 168n10
      Symphony on a City 153–4
   writings on Antill 4
The Music Critic (John Antill) 79, 91, 112–17, **115**, **116**, **117**
Music for a Royal Pageant of Nationhood (John Antill) 81, 99
musique concrète 80, 96, 98
Mussorgsky, Modest 77
'My Sister the Rain' (song, John Antill) 35–6, **37**
'My Star' (song, John Antill) 19

Nathan, Isaac 44
   Don John of Austria 11
National Ballet 68
National Institute of Dramatic Art (NIDA), University of New South Wales 109
National Library of Australia (Canberra), Australian Manuscript Collection 4
nationalism, *see* Australian nationalism
Nature Studies (John Antill) 19, 20, **22**, **23**, 24
neo-classicism
   and Antill's works
      choral and vocal works 165

Concerto for Harmonica and
    Orchestra 157
Festival Te Deum 172
Five Songs of Happiness 179
The Music Critic 116
*Overture for a Momentous
    Occasion* 145
Paean to the Spirit of Man 159
post-*Corroboree* work 191
A Sentimental Suite 136
Symphony on a City 149
The Unknown Land 86
*Variations on a Theme of Alfred
    Hill* (collaborative work) 163
Wakooka 91
between-the-wars neo-classicism 50, 78
neo-tonality 78, 91, 191
    see also neo-classicism
*The New Grove Dictionary of Music and
    Musicians* 4
New South Wales Conservatorium of Music
    Antill's Conservatorium years
        (1925–29) 2–3, 5, 18–21, **20, 21**
    Arundel Orchard's performance of
        Holst's *The Planets* 52
    Edgar Bainton's performance of
        Vaughan Williams's *Job* 52–3
New South Wales National Opera 24, 112,
    113, 117
New South Wales (NSW) Government
    Railways 2, 13, 15, 17–18
New Zealand Symphony Orchestra 72
Newcastle (NSW), centenary 128, 145–6
NIDA (National Institute of Dramatic Art),
    University of New South Wales 109
'number' operas 15, 30, 114

Oakes, Meredith 159, 161, 172–3
O'Dowd, Bernard, *The Bush* 44, 45
'one work composers' 76, 191
opera
    Australian opera 11
    Italian vs Wagnerian opera 115
    'number' operas 15, 30, 114
    through-composed (or continuous)
        operas 15, 34, 96, 100, 114–15,
        121, 122
    see also operas (John Antill)

opera buffa 115–16
operas (John Antill)
    early projects 5, 11
        Heroida (lost) 17
        Ouida (lost) 14, 15, 30, 113
        Princess Dorothea 14–16, **16**, 17,
            20, 23–4, 30, 113, 122
        The Sleeping Princess (lost) 17
    list of 193
    operas (1930–45)
        chronological perspectives 5, 21–4,
            22, 23
        Endymion, see Endymion (John
            Antill)
        The Gates of Paradise (incomplete)
            17, 21, 22, 32–3, 34
        The Glittering Mask 17, 21, 22–3,
            30, 31–2, **33**, 38, 39–40, 48, 49,
            91, 114
        Here's Luck 17, 21, 22–3, 30–31,
            31, 32, 91, 114
        The Lost Child (fragment) 21, 33,
            34–5, 40, 113, 166
        The Scapegoat (fragment) 21, 33,
            40, 113
        The Serpent Woman (incomplete)
            21, 33, 34, 40, 113
    post-*Corroboree* operas
        Body Politic (fragment) 79n1,
            113n70
        The First Christmas 79, 91, 113,
            117–19, **120**, 121–3, **122, 123,
            124–5**
        The Music Critic 79, 91, 112–17,
            115, 116, 117
Opportune Club (Sydney), opera/musical
    comedy competition 23, 30, 114
Orchard, William Arundel 3, 52
orchestral works (John Antill)
    concert works, list of 194
    documentary film music 129, 195
    incidental music 129–30, 195–6
    list of (all types) 194–6
    overview 127–30, 163
    recordings 128–9, 155
    by title (early and Conservatorium
        years)
        Lyric Pieces 19–20

Nature Studies 19, 20, **22**, **23**, 24
Overture to a Chinese Opera
    (fragment) 19–20
'Serenade' 16–17, 19–20
by title (post-*Corroboree*)
    Concerto for Harmonica and
        Orchestra 128, 130, 154–7,
        155, **156**, **157**
    Four Abstract Pieces for Orchestra
        (fragment) 128
    Jubagalee (A Flourish) 130
    An Outback Overture 128, 136–7,
        138–9, 140
    Overture for a Momentous
        Occasion 128, 129, 140–42,
        141, **142**, **143–4**, 145, 158
    Paean to the Spirit of Man 128,
        157–9, **159**, **160**, 161–2, **161**
    A Sentimental Suite 80, 128,
        130–32, **133–4**, 134–6, **135**
    'South Pacific Symphony'
        (abandoned) 163
    Symphony on a City 78, 128,
        145–7, **148**, 149, **150**, 151–4,
        151–3, 156–7, 182, 190
    The Unknown Land (concert
        performances of ballet) 128
    Variations on a Theme of Alfred
        Hill (collaborative work) 118,
        128, 130, 162–3
Ouida (lost) 14, 15, 30, 113
An Outback Overture (John Antill) 128,
    136–7, **138–9**, 140
Overture for a Momentous Occasion (John
    Antill) 128, 129, 140–42, **141**, **142**,
    143–4, 145, 158
Overture to a Chinese Opera (John Antill)
    (fragment) 19–20
The Oxford Companion to Australian
    Music 4

Paean to the Spirit of Man (John Antill)
    128, 157–9, **159**, **160**, 161–2, **161**
pandiatonicism 91, 94
Pask, Edward 12, 90, 96
pastoral idiom, *see* English pastoralism
Penberthy, James 46, 81, 109
Perth Festival (1970) 162, 163

Petrus, Pauline 4n17, 76, 77
Plush, Vincent 74
poeticisms (English) 45
Post, Joseph 158
post-impressionism 105
Prerauer, Curt 95
primary sources, on John Antill 4, 12–13
primitivism
    and Antill's 'Aboriginal' works 91,
        105
    and Antill's *Black Opal* 107
    and Antill's *Corroboree* 2, 35, 40–41,
        49–50, 52, 67, 77, 105, 191
    and Antill's *The Glittering Mask* 32
    and Jindyworobak movement 47
Princess Dorothea (John Antill) 14–16,
    16, 17, 20, 23–4, 30, 113, 122
programme music 147, 149, 152–3, 158–9
Prokofiev, Sergei 39, 49, 77
Puccini, Giacomo 121
    Madama Butterfly 14

Quo Vadis (movie) 35

Rachmaninov, Sergei 19
Railways, *see* New South Wales (NSW)
    Government Railways
Ravel, Maurice 19
    Daphnis and Chloe 52
Reid, Rex 68, 69, 74
Robinson, Roland 44, 95
Romanticism
    and Australian nationalism 30
    late/post-Romanticism
        and Antill 12, 38, 46
        and Antill's *Nature Studies* 20
        and Antill's post-*Corroboree* work
            191
        and Antill's pre-*Corroboree* works
            189
        and Antill's *Princess Dorothea* 16
        and Antill's *The Gates of Paradise*
            33
        and Australian post-colonial
            composers 10, 50
    romantic plots 30
Rossini, Gioachino 117
Russian school 19

sacred music
   and Antill 13–14
   see also choral and vocal works (John Antill)
St Andrew's Cathedral Choir School, Sydney 2, 13
St Andrew's Cathedral, Sydney 165, 171, 172
The Scapegoat (John Antill) (fragment) 21, 33, 40, 113
Schoenberg School 10
   see also atonal music; twelve-note music
Schubert, Franz
   Die schöne Müllerin 177
   Die Winterreise 177
Schumann, Robert, *Dichterliebe* 177
Science Theatre, University of New South Wales 110
Scott, Cyril 50
Scriabin, Alexander 19, 50
Sculthorpe, Peter 11, 74, 126
   Sun Music I 2
A Sentimental Suite (John Antill) 80, 128, 130–32, **133–4**, 134–6, **135**
'Serenade' (John Antill) 16–17, 19–20
The Serpent Woman (John Antill) (incomplete) 21, 33, 34, 40, 113
Sibelius, Jean 19
Simpson, Colin 68
Sitsky, Larry 95
The Sleeping Princess (John Antill) (lost) 17
Snowy! (John Antill) 79, 80, 109–11
Snowy Mountains Hydro-Electric Scheme 80, 109
'song descent' style 53, 105
The Song of Hagar to Abraham the Patriarch (John Antill) 69–70, 88n18, 121, 165, 166–8, **169**, 170, **170**, **171**, 172, 186
songs, *see* choral and vocal works (John Antill)
The Songs of a Sentimental Bloke (John Antill) (incomplete) 80, 130, 131
'South Pacific Symphony' (John Antill) (abandoned) 163
Spencer, Baldwin 44
Stewart, Douglas, *Ned Kelly* 154n35

Strauss, Richard 9
Stravinsky, Igor 2, 10, 10n1, 39, 47, 91, 191
   The Firebird 52
   Petrushka 52
   The Rite of Spring 49, 52, 67, 190
Sullivan, Chris 48
Sutherland, Margaret 9, 18, 50, 191
   Four Blake Songs 183
   Six Songs: Settings of Poems by Judith Wright 183
Swane, Dawn 103, 108
Sydney Conservatorium of Music 175
Sydney Dance-Drama Group 80, 109, 110
Sydney Opera House 79, 118, 130
Sydney Showground 81
Sydney Symphony Orchestra
   and Antill 127
   and Antill's *Snowy!* 111
   Antill's works performed by
      Concerto for Harmonica and Orchestra 128, 155
      Corroboree 1, 70, 71, 72
      An Outback Overture 136
      Overture for a Momentous Occasion 140
      Paean to the Spirit of Man 157–8
      A Sentimental Suite 131
      The Song of Hagar to Abraham the Patriarch 167
      Symphony on a City 145–6
   Goossens' appointment as chief conductor 1, 72–3
   harmonica concerto (Arthur Benjamin) 154
Sydney Town Hall 1, 75, 140, 158, 165, 175
Symphony on a City (John Antill) 78, 128, 145–7, **148**, 149, **150**, 151–4, **151–3**, 156–7, 182, 190
symphony orchestras, creation of by Australian Broadcasting Commission/Corporation (ABC) 11

Tate, Henry 44
   Dawn: A Bush Rhapsody 44n4
Tchaikovsky, Pyotr 19
theatre works (John Antill)

introductory perspectives 79–81, 126
list of 193–4
see also ballets (John Antill); operas (John Antill)
Three Songs of Righteousness (John Antill) (incomplete) 177
through-composed (or continuous) operas 15, 34, 96, 100, 114–15, 121, 122
Tivoli Theatre (Sydney) 69, 128, 136
'To the Heart that Sings Alway' (song, John Antill) 35
Tomkins, Thomas, 'Magnificat' and 'Nunc Dimitis' 172
'The Trumpet Sounds Australia's Fame' (song) 43
Tweedie, Valrene 90, 96, 103
twelve-note music 10, 49, 86
see also atonal music

University of New South Wales
National Institute of Dramatic Art (NIDA) 109
Science Theatre 110
University of Western Australia 162
University of Wollongong 3
The Unknown Land (John Antill) 49, 79, 80, 81–4, **85**, 86–8, **86–9**, 91, 95, 128, 131, 149

Varèse, Edgard 49
Variations on a Theme of Alfred Hill (collaborative work) 118, 128, 130, 162–3
Vaughan Williams, Ralph 9, 10n1, 19, 100, 182
Fifth Symphony 151
Job 52–3
Norfolk Rhapsodies 10
Verdi, Giuseppe 117, 121

Viennese School 49, 86
see also atonal music; twelve-note music
vocal works, *see* choral and vocal works (John Antill)

Wagner, Richard 9, 115
Wagnerian leitmotifs 122
Walenn, Gerald 3
Walton, William 145, 170, 191
Coronation Te Deum 172
Waratah Legend 99–100
Waters, Thorold 47
Welch, Stanton 70
Wellesz, Egon 10n1
Wheeler, John
Antill's works based on Wheeler's texts
The Lost Child (opera fragment) 21, 33, 34, 40, 113
'The Lover's Walk Forsaken' (song) 35–6, 39, 49
'My Sister the Rain' (song) 35–6, **37**, 39, 49
The Scapegoat (opera fragment) 21, 33, 40, 113
The Serpent Woman (incomplete opera) 21, 33, 34, 40, 113
Williams, Clement 181
Williamson, J. C., Opera Company 3, 11, 12
Wireless Chorus 35
Wood, Elizabeth 4n16
Wright, Judith 183

Youth Concerts (ABC) 128, 140

Ziegler, Oswald, *Symphony on a City* (book) 145

CPSIA information can be obtained
at www.ICGtesting.com
Printed in the USA
JSHW021510221219
3113JS00001BA/82